Annie and Margrit

RECIPES AND STORIES
FROM THE ROBERT MONDAVI KITCHEN

Annie and Margrit

Annie Roberts, Margrit Biever Mondavi, and Victoria Wise

PHOTOGRAPHY BY Laurie Smith

TEN SPEED PRESS

Berkeley | Toronto

For Our Mothers

A Kirsty Melville Book

🔟

Ten Speed Press
PO Box 7123
Berkeley, California 94707
www.tenspeed.com

Distributed in Australia by Simon and Schuster Australia, in Canada by Ten Speed Press Canada, in New Zealand by Southern Publishers Group, in South Africa by Real Books, in Southeast Asia by Berkeley Books, and in the United Kingdom and Europe by Airlift Book Company.

Jacket and text design by Nancy Austin
Food styling by Annie Roberts, Victoria Wise, and Nancy Austin

Library of Congress Cataloging-in-Publication Data

Roberts, Annie.

Annie and Margrit : recipes and stories from the Robert Mondavi kitchen / Annie Roberts, Margrit Biever Mondavi, and Victoria Wise.

p. cm.

Includes index.

ISBN 1-58008-437-0 (hardcover)

1. Cookery. 2. Wine and wine making—California—Napa Valley. 3. Robert Mondavi Winery.
I. Biever, Margrit. II. Wise, Victoria. III. Title.

TX714 .R58 2003

641.5—dc21
2002015169

First printing, 2003
Printed in China

1 2 3 4 5 6 7 8 9 10 – 07 06 05 04 03

Thursday October 10, 2002

LUNCHEON

Dungeness Crab Salad
Citrus Fruits and Avocado
Robert Mondavi Winery Stags Leap District Sauvignon Blanc

*

Seared All-Natural Beef Tenderloin
Roasted Fingerling Potatoes
Mâche and Sweet 100 Tomatoes
Robert Mondavi Winery Napa Valley Cabernet Sauvignon Reserve

*

Apple and Huckleberry Crisp
Vanilla Bean Ice Cream
Robert Mondavi Winery Napa Valley Moscato d'Oro

Chef: Annie Roberts

CONTENTS

═══

ACKNOWLEDGMENTS

FOR HELPING TO MAKE THIS BOOK, the authors would like to thank Harvey Posert, former Public Relations Director, Robert Mondavi Winery, supposedly retired but constantly working, for keeping everyone on track; Clay Gregory, Vice President, General Manager, Oakville, Robert Mondavi Winery, for smoothing out the contractual arrangements; Julie Prince, Cultural Events Manager and Margrit's assistant for twenty years, who knows how to schedule the densest agenda in the world and remain calm, cool, and collected, then go home and make a twenty-five-egg pasta for her own party. We also thank the astute people at Ten Speed Press: Kirsty Melville, head honcho, who recognizes a good set of stories when she sees one; Holly Taines White, who did a keen edit on the manuscript; and Nancy Austin, art director. Also, Carolyn Miller, our copyeditor, and the photographer, Laurie Smith. Thanks as well to Martha Casselman, our agent extraordinaire, who not only takes care of the business part between authors and publisher, but also tirelessly lends her considerable editing expertise to smooth out first-draft prose. Carole Bidnick, co-agent, gets special applause for helping to direct the marketing aspects of the book.

Annie also thanks her intrepid and skilled kitchen crew, especially Amy Troutner, and the dining room crew in the Vineyard Room, who helped make lunch an event to look forward to as the authors met over the details of this book; and her husband, Keith, who sweetly relinquished his weekend mornings alone with Annie so she could spend endless time on the phone going through details of the instructions and headnotes for the recipes. Margrit, as always, thanks Bob for his abiding love and enthusiasm over her proclivity to expand culture and the arts at the winery and beyond. Victoria offers special thanks to her husband, Rick, and son, Jenan, who, when the recipes were done, tested, and tasted, said they were sad they wouldn't be eating Annie's and Margrit's dishes every night ("They're so good"), but glad that there were so many fabulous new recipes in the family's repertoire.

ANNIE'S PREFACE

I FELL IN LOVE WITH FOOD as a child eating my mother's good cooking. I remember pork chops with homemade applesauce and fluffy mashed potatoes, juicy roasted chicken, salads with sharp vinaigrettes, delicious homemade soups and breads. (I actually had to hide my funny-looking sandwiches in my school lunch, because we never had Wonder Bread.) And there were always pies and tarts made with seasonal fruit. In addition to the wonderful food at home, I was exposed to many different foods and tastes during my childhood. Because my father was in the service, we moved every three years. I lived in Japan and Germany, and spent occasional summers and my sophomore year in high school in Switzerland.

I met my husband, Keith, when he was hitchhiking to college in Napa one day (we were both attending Napa Valley College) and I stopped to give him a ride. It was love at first sight, and we decided we wanted to see the world together. We hitchhiked through France, Switzerland, and Italy tasting wonderful street food. The *crocques monsieurs* and sugared crêpes in France were heavenly. In Switzerland, it was French fries served in a paper cone with mayonnaise, and *heise maroni* (hot roasted chestnuts) to fill our pockets while walking through the Niederdorf in Zurich in the middle of December. For three months we rented a flat just outside Zurich, where I had an aunt and uncle who helped us find jobs in a factory that made rubber parts so we could replenish our coffers and travel some more.

Buying and cooking food there was such a joy; because of the high-quality ingredients, everything tasted so good.

After returning to California, we married and planted a garden and I cooked, trying out new dishes that I saw Julia Child make on television. Our two sons, Quinn and Nathan, were born, fourteen months apart. Keith was working at the Robert Mondavi Winery as a cooper's apprentice. As he had always had a love of carpentry, he took an immediate interest in the craft of making wine barrels. He then traveled to France and learned the almost lost art of making oak wine barrels. Shortly thereafter, he started his own cooperage business in California, a trade he still practices today.

It was the early 1970s, and I began helping my mother with some of the small lunches she prepared for invited friends at the winery. One day she turned to me and asked if I would like to do this myself. I said yes.

As I started to sink my teeth into my work, I realized that what I was doing was more than just cooking meals. I was also matching food with wine, and I knew that one of the best ways to do that would be to have more than a main course and a dessert. We needed a first course. This would not only provide a way to show another wine, it would also help me out in the kitchen so I would have time to prepare the hot entrée. With three courses, we could serve a Fumé Blanc, Sauvignon Blanc, or Chardonnay with the first course, a Pinot Noir, Cabernet Sauvignon, Merlot, or Zinfandel with the main course, and a Moscato d'Oro with dessert. I thought of foods that are light, like seafood salads with vinaigrettes, for first courses; heartier, meatier dishes like roasted chicken and grilled meats for the main course; and fruit tarts for dessert. I wonder where I came up with those ideas? It was from my mother's and grandmother's cooking and my childhood memories of those wonderful meals, along with my exposure to different foods from my travels around the world.

The Robert Mondavi Winery sent me to France in 1980 to cook with the chef at Mouton Rothschild. She used the finest ingredients and prepared them elegantly by letting their clean, natural flavors come through. That's when I grasped what Bob Mondavi meant when he said food should be simple but elegant.

On returning to California, I craved the quality of ingredients that I had tasted in France. Could we plant a garden at the winery? We expanded the already growing herb garden and put in tomatoes, peppers, and lettuces. This was still a time when I had to go to the plant nursery for basil. I would buy the basil in small pots, cut off the tops to use for cooking, plant what was left to grow in the herb in garden, and wait for a second crop.

When our sons were children, we always tried to make sure the family was together for dinner meals. They loved watching and helping me as I cooked at home, and as teenagers, they worked with Keith in the summer, learning their father's trade until they went away to college (both have become coopers). When we get together, they still love watching and helping me cook at home, doing what I love.

MARGRIT'S PREFACE

IT ISN'T BY CHANCE that my daughter Annie has the instinct to choose and prepare the best food. We come from a family of *mangioni*, people who love to eat. At lunch my mother and father would talk about dinner. I grew up in a garden of delicious fruits and vegetables in an ambience of celebrating and sharing good food and good wine with family and friends. The kitchen was the heart of the house, where friends and family gathered to shell peas, debate, try the new vintages. We would set the table under the old magnolia tree overlooking Lago Maggiore and bring out the rabbit and polenta on the *planca,* while mother was still sticking roasted almonds into the most delicious dessert, called "the porcupine."

Annie was there too, at an early age and later as a teenager, poking her pretty nose into the pots and pans. Right away she had a talent for cooking. She also has a great sense of humor and a great memory for weird jokes, and she has always brought this joie de vivre into her cooking, even when she burned the chocolate in home ec class because she forgot to add water.

Of course, at home, we cooked family-style together, whether it was fondue, chestnut *vacherin,* or the best potato salad. Later on, Annie helped me at the winery. Whenever I roasted the chicken quarters for a fast lunch, she had a way of arranging the food that made it evident this kid was going to be a chef. She has more patience than I do, and more knowledge. How great it is when our children surpass us.

In retrospect, it was one of the greatest times in my life when my children were at home. And a great part of our good times were spent in the kitchen, Annie and Phoebe buzzing around helping me to get dinner on the table while my creative son, Babo, was checking on his pear wine or his homemade beer under the sink. When the brix was right, the beer had to be bottled at that very instant, be it noon or be it midnight. What a mess, and how much we laughed when we were all young and everything was funny. We may be more serious about food and wine today, but we still get together in the kitchen, where so much that matters happens.

INTRODUCTION

ANNIE ROBERTS, EXECUTIVE CHEF, and Margrit Biever Mondavi, Vice President, Art and Culture, join talents at one of the renowned wineries in the world, the Robert Mondavi Winery in the Napa Valley. They happen also to be mother and daughter. Their extraordinary relationship flourishes against the background of demanding schedules, and though each is a steady burning flame in her own right, they manage to work together with fluid grace professionally and to enjoy each other's companionship on family occasions. The recipes and stories in this book tell the tale of their collaboration over the years, and how Margrit has passed along her cooking wisdom and recipes to Annie and learns from her daughter as Annie creates dishes for the winery's kitchen and family celebrations.

The history began with Margrit's mother, Greta, whom Margrit describes as a born cook. "Even during the war, Mother bartered for butter. We had the best from our garden, and I remember my sweet mama whacking off the head of a chicken. This allowed her to prepare a feast every day." Annie also fondly remembers her maternal grandmother, and the time, dedication, and love she had for food and mealtime. "Eating was a delicious event and always fun. Meals would end with crazy card games and Swiss chocolate rewards for the winner." That was in the lush Ticino canton around Lake Maggiore in the Italian part of Switzerland, where the family had moved from Appenzell in northern Switzerland.

Later, when Margrit married an American army officer, traveling became a way of life as they moved frequently from base to base according to the dictates of the military. Through all those years, though the home venue changed, food and cooking remained central to their family life. Depending on where they were, sometimes the provender was exotic and culturally challenging, as in Japan. Sometimes it was just plain challenging, as in South Dakota in the postwar 1940s. But home cooking remained the tradition that Margrit passed on to her three children, Babo, Annie, and Phoebe.

In 1962, the family moved to the Napa Valley, and Margrit began working at the Robert Mondavi Winery in the marketing division. She recounts, "Bob would call and ask me to get some salami sandwiches for a lunch meeting. After a few times, I said, 'Let's just do some nice lunches. It's so easy to make a nice lunch.'" Then, she thought, why not have some music also and have a picnic on the grass? The winery agreed, as long as there wasn't any overhead. Margrit invited a local band and some friends for the occasion. It was so successful that the next year she continued the event, cooking the lunch herself and charging a little money to cover the cost of hiring musicians but still borrowing folding chairs from a local church. It turned out the folding chairs weren't necessary because the attendees were more than happy to sit on the grass, enjoying the music and balancing plates on their laps. Since there was no cost to the winery, Margrit tucked away the receipts with the dream of continuing. Within three or four years, she had created enough of a bank account to hire name performers like Ella Fitzgerald. By that time, the party had grown so large that she couldn't do all of the cooking.

Meanwhile, Annie had met and married Keith Roberts, and they took off to hitchhike through Europe and see the world. When they returned and settled in Calistoga to raise a family, Margrit asked Annie to help with the lunches. Annie's understanding of how to run a kitchen perfectly matched Margrit's own ideas. In fact, they were a dream team. As Margrit explains, "All my children cooked, but it was clear from the start that Annie had a special talent. She was about one and a half years old when one day I came into the kitchen to find her on the floor tearing up newspaper and shifting the pieces from pot to pan. She told me she was making dinner for Snoopy, our dog. I knew then that I had a chef on my hands." Annie's own history of her cooking career begins a little later in her life. Though she always loved preparing food and being in the kitchen with Margrit, she says, "My interest in cooking started after I left home, when I realized that if I wanted to continue to eat well, I had better learn to cook."

Eventually, as Margrit puts it, "I married the boss," and, under her direction, the Robert Mondavi Winery cultural events widened to include a diverse number of activities most of the year, not just summer concerts. Margrit is now a driving force in the establishment of music and art centers throughout northern California. Annie became the first Executive Winery Chef in the Napa Valley, and under her hand, the Robert Mondavi kitchen has become acclaimed. Famous chefs from all over the world travel there to teach master classes at the winery, and the invitation-only Vineyard Room that showcases Annie's cuisine is constantly busy.

Away from the winery, Margrit maintains a kitchen garden at her Napa Valley home, which is named Wappo Hill after the Native Americans who were the original inhabitants of the area. It's a place she describes as "a bit of paradise that should be shared." And she does share it, from using her garden produce for intimate home-meal entertaining to hosting expansive fundraising gatherings for the arts.

Unlike Margrit, who seems to thrive on nonstop social interaction and adores having throngs of people in her home, Annie considers her home in Santa Rosa, California, a refuge from the demands and nonstop intensity of being a successful chef. Her children are grown, so providing a large daily meal is not essential, though she still cooks for her husband and sometimes close friends every day. She relaxes by swimming in her pool and walking her dogs in the surrounding hills.

. . .

Annie and Margrit is the serendipitous outcome of a conversation between Margrit and Martha Casselman, mutually our agent from previous separate projects, who were casually conversing one day about food, wine, and cooking. Martha said, "Let's do a cookbook of the stories and recipes that come out of your and Annie's cooking and working together for so many years. And I know just the person to write the book: Victoria Wise." Martha went on to explain that I have written many cookbooks, and that she thought I'd share Margrit and Annie's sensibility and style. And so it came to be.

In *Annie and Margrit,* I have the pleasure of drawing back the curtain to present a bit of the daily lives of this remarkable mother and daughter as they cook and entertain together and separately, formally and informally. In more than 130 recipes with anecdotes, professional tips, and wine suggestions, you will get to know Annie and Margrit as I have. Some of the recipes are Annie's, some are Margrit's, and some are a collaboration of ideas and cooking experiences they have shared since Annie was old enough to stir the chocolate milk. There's a wealth of treasured family recipes and also a plenitude of dishes inspired by the extraordinary comestibles from the Napa Valley. Best of all, whether you live nearby or not, you can share in Annie and Margrit's élan and their warm hospitality that welcomes people to the table as they cook.

—Victoria Wise

THE PANTRY

Following is a list of staples to have on hand for Annie's and Margrit's recipes, from oils, vinegars, and pantry vegetables to seasonings, dairy, and cheeses they use regularly. See also the Basics section for those vegetables and sundries, such as roasted peppers and stocks, that need cooking before using or storing.

BREAD CRUMBS
There's no substitute for homemade bread crumbs, and any dish that calls for them will be enhanced in a way that cannot be duplicated by store-bought crumbs. See page xix for homemade bread crumbs.

DAIRY
Butter: unsalted butter, the best quality available.

Cheeses: Parmesan, preferably Parmigiano-Reggiano, freshly grated for the dish; and feta, preferably French feta, which Annie prefers for its low salinity and creamy texture.

Cream: heavy cream, not ultra-pasteurized, for smoothing and thickening sauces and for topping sweets; also, crème fraîche, which is called for in several of the recipes and very easy to make (page xx).

OLIVES
To add salt, tart, and vegetable flavors all at once to sauces and salsas.

OILS
Extra virgin olive oil, for everything from marinades to sauces.

Peanut or grapeseed oil especially for frying, because they heat to a high temperature without burning or smoking.

SEASONINGS
Herbs: fresh flat-leaf parsley, thyme, rosemary, oregano, cilantro, chervil, tarragon, and basil; dried bay leaves.

Pepper: black and white peppercorns, used freshly ground.

Salt: kosher salt.

VEGETABLES
Chiles: jalapeños or serranos, almost always seeded, and poblanos (often called pasillas in California), usually roasted (page xx).

Lemons: freshly squeezed lemon juice, of Eureka or Meyer lemons, enhances many sauces, broths, and marinades; and lemon zest as garnish is a signature of both Annie and Margrit.

Onion family: yellow, white, and red; shallots; leeks; and garlic.

Red bell peppers: raw or roasted (page xx), to julienne, finely chop, or purée for garnishes, salads, salsas, and sauces.

Other vegetables: avocados, mushrooms, fennel, celery root, English (hothouse) cucumbers, tomatoes, and green beans are produce staples; fennel bulb and celery root are often used as aromatics, not just as vegetables.

VINEGARS
Balsamic, white wine, red wine, sherry wine, plus Margrit's homemade vinegar (page 53), for the vinaigrettes that are a signature of Annie's cooking.

WINES
Both Annie and Margrit use wine to liven the flavor of stocks, sauces, soups, and braises. Fumé Blanc or Sauvignon adds a crisp, dry flavor. Chardonnay adds a more fruity note. Pinot Noir and Merlot impart red richness without overpowering, and they are often called for in wine-reduction sauces. For a deep, more complex flavor, earthy Zinfandel or ethereal Cabernet Sauvignon are used.

BEEF STOCK

Makes about 4 quarts

6 pounds meaty beef bones, such as shanks

4 carrots, peeled and cut into chunks

4 yellow onions, quartered

4 cloves garlic

1/2 cup chopped tomatoes

1 cup Cabernet Sauvignon

1 bay leaf

2 teaspoons freshly ground black pepper

5 quarts water

Preheat the oven to 375°F. Place the beef bones in a roasting pan and roast for 1 hour, turning every 30 minutes. Add the carrots, onions, garlic, and tomatoes and continue to roast for 15 minutes. Transfer the bones and vegetables to a large stockpot and set aside.

Place the roasting pan over medium-high heat and add the wine. Cook to reduce the wine to about 1/2 cup. Add the wine reduction to the bones and vegetables, along with the bay leaf, pepper, and water. Bring to a boil over high heat, then decrease the heat to medium-low. Simmer, partially covered, for 4 hours, skimming from time to time. Remove from the heat, allow to cool slightly, then strain through a fine mesh sieve, discarding the solids. Allow to cool to room temperature, then skim off the fat before using. Or, better yet, refrigerate overnight to allow the flavors to mellow and blend together. Lift off the layer of congealed fat before using. Refrigerate for up to 7 days, or freeze for up to 3 months.

CHICKEN STOCK

Makes 9 to 10 cups

1 (31/2- to 4-pound) chicken, cut up, giblets removed

1 carrot, peeled and cut into chunks

1 leek, including light green parts, cut into 1-inch pieces

1 yellow onion, quartered

2 sprigs thyme

2 sprigs flat-leaf parsley

1 bay leaf

1/2 teaspoon freshly ground black pepper

Put the chicken in a large pot and add water to cover by 1 1/2 inches. Bring to a boil over high heat and skim off the foam. Add all the remaining ingredients and return to a boil. Decrease the heat to medium-low, partially cover, and simmer for 3 hours. Remove from the heat and allow to cool. Strain through a fine mesh sieve, discarding the solids. Set aside for 30 minutes to allow the fat to rise to the top. Skim the fat off the top and use right away. Or, without skimming off the fat, refrigerate for up to 5 days or freeze for up to 3 months and skim before using.

BREAD CRUMBS

Makes 1 1/2 cups fine crumbs or 1 3/4 cups coarse crumbs

Cut 1 day-old baguette into 1-inch chunks. Spread the chunks on a baking sheet and toast in a preheated 350°F oven for 10 minutes, or until golden and crisp but not toasted hard all the way through. Remove from the oven and set aside to cool to room temperature. In batches, swirl the toasted bread pieces in a food processor until as fine as you'd like, anywhere from somewhat coarse to almost sandy, depending on the recipe. Use right away or store in an airtight container for up to 3 months.

(continued)

If you don't happen to have day-old bread, you can cut fresh bread into 1-inch pieces, place the pieces on a baking sheet, and set the baking sheet on top of the stove for 20 minutes or so while the oven heats.

CRÈME FRAÎCHE

In a small bowl, mix 1 cup heavy cream with 1 tablespoon buttermilk. Cover with cheesecloth and let sit at room temperature for 18 to 24 hours, until thickened like sour cream. Use right away, or cover and refrigerate for up to 1 week.

ROASTING AND PEELING BELL PEPPERS AND LARGE CHILES

Place the peppers (or chiles) on the rack in a preheated 475°F oven. Set a baking sheet or length of aluminum foil on the rack below to catch spills. Cook, turning once or twice, until the peppers are charred all around and have collapsed, about 25 minutes. Using tongs, transfer them to a plate, cover with a towel, and allow to cool to the touch, at least 15 minutes or up to 1 hour.

Or, roast the peppers on a gas burner or a grill: Set the peppers on the burner or grill rack and char all over, turning several times, until blackened and soft, 15 to 20 minutes. Proceed as above.

Or, place the peppers in a preheated broiler and cook, turning once, until charred all over, about 15 minutes. Proceed as above.

Peel away the skins and pull off the stems. Open out the peppers and scrape away the seeds. Use right away, or refrigerate for up to 1 week.

PITTING OLIVES

Spread the olives on a counter and, with a mallet or hammer, tap each one hard enough to break it open but not so hard as to crack the pit. Pull out the pits with your fingers. The olive meat will be coarsely broken up, just the right size for salad without any chopping. Or, if the recipe calls for halves, cut them in half with a paring knife.

PEELING AND SEEDING TOMATOES

Plunge the tomatoes into boiling water for 10 seconds. Drain and plunge into cold water. When cool enough to handle, slip off the skins with your fingers. Cut the tomatoes in half crosswise and gently squeeze out the seeds. Store in the refrigerator for up to 5 days, or freeze for up to 6 weeks.

ROASTING TOMATOES

Place the tomatoes on a baking sheet in a preheated 425°F oven and cook, turning twice, until the skins char and pull away, about 15 minutes. Allow to cool. Pull off the skins. Cut the tomatoes in half crosswise and gently squeeze out the seeds. Store in the refrigerator for up to 5 days, or freeze for up to 6 weeks.

Appetizers and
Starters

WHEN ANNIE AND MARGRIT ENTERTAIN, they always offer a taste treat to welcome the guests. Sometimes everyone is invited to gather in the kitchen, warming themselves as they chat and perhaps help roll out the dough or prepare the toppings for a pizza starter. At other times, guests are served tidbits off a tray as they gather in the dining room to become acquainted as they sip wine. Or the opener may be presented at the table: a warming bowl of soup, a delicate slice of quiche, a bite or two of grilled fish garnished with a fresh salsa that's just enough to pique the appetite.

At home, Margrit is partial to serving guacamole or a cup of soup by her kitchen fireside—unless she's made pasta in *brodo* to present when the guests are seated at the table. Annie shares the aesthetic of simple-to-begin, and at home might fire up the grill to toast flat bread pizza for the guests to nibble on—or, for the Vineyard Room, create a small plate to begin a fancier meal. Up or down, stand or sit, the idea is the same: openers are an opportunity for people to come together and get to know each other even if they haven't met before, so that the meal is convivial and never stiff.

FROM THE BAKERY

Whole-Wheat Country Loaf   4

Babo's Artisan Bread   6

Appenzell Cheese Tart   7

Goat Cheese and Heirloom Tomato Galette   8

California Express Pizza with Chicken, Peppers, Mushrooms, and Cilantro   9

Fresh Tomato Pizza with Three Cheeses, Basil, and Ham Strips   10

Grilled Flat Bread Pizza with Roasted Red Onions, Tomatoes, and Mushrooms   12

Pizzette Crostini   14

Crostini with Spicy Crab Salad   15

Swiss Quiche with Gruyère, Emmental, and Bacon   17

Goat Cheese and Zucchini Torta Squares with Tomato Concassé   18

SOUPS

Gazpacho   19

Rock Shrimp Gazpacho   20

Bread, Sage, and Tomato Harvest Soup   21

Pasta in Brodo   22

French Green Lentil and Mushroom Soup with White Truffle Oil   24

Yellow Split Pea Soup with Pancetta and Garlic Croutons   25

Asparagus Soup with Dungeness Crab and Red Bell Pepper Cream   26

Parslied Crêpe Ribbons in Beef Broth   28

Fennel and Celery Root Soup   29

Dungeness Crab, Roasted Pepper, and Fresh Corn Soup   30

SMALL PLATES

Portobello Mushrooms with Bulgur, Couscous, and Orzo Salad   31

Corn Cakes with Smoked Salmon, Chive Oil, and Crème Fraîche   32

Chiles Rellenos with Roasted Tomato Salsa   34

Grilled Halibut with Cucumber, Tomato, and Ginger Salsa   35

Seared Tuna with Cabbage Slaw and Lemon Mayonnaise   36

Seared Tuna with Fennel and Red Pepper Slaw   37

Margrit's Fish Terrine with Beurre Blanc–Type Sauce   39

Chilled Udon Noodles with Shrimp and Shiitake Mushrooms   41

Shrimp and Flageolet Beans with Baby Arugula and Red Bell Pepper Aioli   42

Lobster Tartlets with Leek and Fennel Confit, Haricots Verts, and Lobster Sauce   44

Annie's Crab Cakes with Tartar Sauce   47

Jumbo Shrimp with Celery, Roma Tomatoes, and Watercress   48

Breaded Scallops with Rémoulade Sauce and Micro-Greens   49

WHOLE-WHEAT COUNTRY LOAF

Makes one 3-pound loaf

When Annie was living the communal life in Calistoga, California, in the late 1960s, she spent a lot of time learning to make bread. She wanted to know what makes bread rise and where all those great flavors come from. The oven was wood burning, so before anything could be cooked, firewood had to be chopped. At first, the breads came out as hard as rocks, not suitable for eating but just fine for using to make mobiles. Undeterred, she pressed on until she mastered the *technique* and could turn her energy to the *art* of bread making. From that experience came her favorite table bread. It's a toothsome whole-wheat loaf with a crisp crust and a medium crumb that suits any savory course.

STARTER

1/2 cup warm (105° to 115°F) water

1/4 teaspoon active dry yeast

1/2 cup all-purpose or bread flour

BREAD

1 teaspoon active dry yeast

2 cups warm (105° to 115°F) water

3 1/2 cups bread flour, plus extra for kneading

1 cup whole-wheat flour

2 teaspoons kosher salt

ANNIE'S TIPS

Bread flour, which is higher in gluten than all-purpose flour, is necessary to achieve the chewy texture of this country-style bread.

For the starter, either all-purpose or bread flour will do, but not whole-wheat flour because its low gluten content won't make a starter spongy enough for a chewy-textured loaf.

Unlike pizza dough starter, the starter for this bread is proofed at room temperature to achieve a slightly tangy flavor.

To make the starter, combine 1/4 cup of the water with the yeast in a small bowl. Let stand for 10 minutes. Add the remaining 1/4 cup water and the flour and mix well. Cover with plastic wrap and set aside at room temperature for 24 to 72 hours.

To make the bread, combine the yeast and water in a large bowl. Stir to dissolve. Add the starter and stir to break it up. Add the bread flour, whole-wheat flour, and salt and stir until the mixture gathers into a ball. Transfer to a floured work surface and knead the dough for 10 minutes, or until smooth and elastic, reflouring the surface when it gets sticky (this will take up to 1 1/2 cups extra bread flour). Lightly coat a large bowl with olive oil. Put the dough in the bowl and turn to coat all over. Cover with plastic wrap and set aside in a warm place to rise for 3 hours, or until tripled in volume.

Deflate the dough and place it on a baking sheet. Shape into an 8-inch round loaf. Let rise, uncovered, for 1 hour, or until doubled in volume.

To bake the bread, preheat the oven to 450°F. Place the loaf in the oven and bake for 10 minutes. Decrease the heat to 400°F and bake for 45 minutes, or until the crust is hard and well browned and a knife inserted in the center comes out clean. Transfer to a wire rack to cool. Serve right away or store in a plastic bag for up to 4 days.

BABO'S ARTISAN BREAD

Makes one 1-pound loaf

Bread making runs in the family, and Annie loves to recount the story of how Babo's bread came to be. "One summer on our yearly family vacation in Lake Tahoe, my brother, whom I nicknamed Babo, and who has always been a great inventor, announced that he was going to make some *real* bread. The kind with a real crust, and chewy inside. We were just leaving the house to make our daily trek to the local supermarket. 'Don't buy any of that overpriced bread,' he grumbled. We brought home a bag of flour and some yeast and he began digging around in the kitchen for a large roasting pan with a lid. After a lot of clatter and banging of pots and pans, we heard a relieved sigh. Success. The technique is nothing short of brilliant: it creates an oven within an oven that acts like a professional baker's oven."

1 package (about 1 tablespoon) active dry yeast

¼ cup warm (105° to 115°F) water

1 cup water, at room temperature

3 cups all-purpose flour mixed with 1 tablespoon kosher salt, plus extra flour for kneading

---

ANNIE'S TIPS

A Dutch oven is essentially a large cast-iron stew pot with a lid. A large roasting pan will also do, but it has to have a tight-fitting lid; aluminum foil won't do the job.

This bread must rise twice in order to fully activate the yeast and ensure that the bread isn't heavy.

Placing the bread in a cold oven allows it to rise a third time, during which air holes form in the dough, making the loaf light.

In a large bowl, combine the yeast and warm water and set aside until bubbly, about 15 minutes. Pour in the room-temperature water and gradually stir in the flour mixture. Gather the dough into a ball and transfer to a floured work surface. Knead the dough for 5 minutes, or until smooth and elastic, adding extra flour as needed to prevent the dough from sticking. Cover with a kitchen towel and set aside until doubled in volume, about 3 hours.

Lightly oil an 8-quart Dutch oven or a large roasting pan with a tight-fitting lid. Punch down the dough and knead again for 5 minutes. Shape into a round, transfer to the Dutch oven, cover with a towel, and set aside in a warm place. Let rise again for 2 hours, or until doubled in volume.

To bake the bread, half fill a heatproof 8-ounce cup, such as a custard cup, with water and place alongside the bread in the pan. Cover the pan with its fitted lid and place in a cold oven, taking care not to spill the water. Turn the oven on to 400°F and bake for 1½ hours, or until golden on top. Transfer the loaf to a wire rack to cool. Slice and serve.

APPENZELL CHEESE TART

Makes one 11 by 14-inch tart; serves 8 to 10

From her kitchen overlooking the evergreen lush hills outlining the Napa Valley, Margrit describes this as a "rich winter dish for the snow-covered time, a rather hearty tart we must serve with a good wine." Lack of snow aside, in January and February it does get cold enough to light a winter fire and prompt a tart of Appenzeller cheese, a prized product of the Ticino canton of Switzerland where Margrit grew up. It's spunky as soft melting cheeses go, yet supple and yielding. It may be difficult to find if you don't live near a specialty cheese shop, but Swiss Gruyère, Emmentaler, or vacherin make good substitutes. Like its Provençal cousin *pissaladière,* only more custardy, this tart is baked on a baking sheet.

Serve with a CHARDONNAY

1 recipe savory crust dough (page 17)

FILLING

1 tablespoon unsalted butter

3 tablespoons finely chopped yellow onion

2 large eggs

2 tablespoons all-purpose flour

1/2 cup heavy cream

3/4 cup milk

Pinch of ground coriander

2 1/2 cups (10 ounces) shredded Appenzeller cheese

On a floured work surface, roll the dough out to a 12 by 15-inch rectangle. Line an 11 by 14-inch baking sheet with the dough, leaving a 1/2-inch overhang. Pinch the overhang into rim around the crust. Cover with plastic wrap and refrigerate for at least 15 minutes.

Preheat the oven to 400°F. To prepare the filling, melt the butter in a small sauté pan over medium-high heat. Add the onion and cook for about 2 minutes, until translucent. Set aside to cool.

In a bowl, whisk together the eggs, flour, cream, milk, and coriander. Spread the cooled onions over the pastry dough. Sprinkle the cheese over the onions. Pour in the egg mixture and tilt the pan to distribute it evenly. Bake until puffed and golden, 35 to 40 minutes. Allow to cool slightly, then slice and serve warm or at room temperature.

GOAT CHEESE AND HEIRLOOM TOMATO GALETTE

Makes one 12-inch galette; serves 8

A galette is a free-form tart with a somewhat thick pielike crust and folded-over edges, cooked on a baking sheet. Galettes—sweet and savory—are one of Annie's signature dishes. Heirloom tomatoes, readily available in Napa Valley markets from the beginning of July almost to mid-November, can be substituted with any fully ripe, juicy tomatoes in their high season.

Serve with a FUMÉ BLANC

GALETTE DOUGH

1¹/₂ cups all-purpose flour

Pinch of kosher salt

¹/₄ cup cold unsalted butter

¹/₂ cup cold water

TOPPING

2 tablespoons unsalted butter

4 small leeks, including light green parts, thinly sliced (about 2 cups)

¹/₂ teaspoon kosher salt

¹/₄ teaspoon freshly ground black pepper

2 tablespoons water

¹/₂ cup (about 3 ounces) soft goat cheese

3 large tomatoes, thinly sliced

1 egg yolk beaten with 1 tablespoon water

To make the galette dough, combine the flour and salt in a food processor. Add the butter and pulse until the mixture resembles coarse meal. Add the water and pulse to mix. Gather the dough into a ball, wrap in plastic wrap, and press to smooth into a flat disk. Refrigerate for at least 1 hour or up to 3 days.

On a floured work surface, roll the dough out into a 14-inch round. Place on a baking sheet and refrigerate for 30 minutes.

Preheat the oven to 400°F. To make the topping, melt the butter in a sauté pan over high heat. Add the leeks, salt, and pepper and stir to mix. Add the water, decrease the heat to medium-low, and simmer until the leeks are soft and the liquid is mostly evaporated, about 5 minutes.

Spread the leeks over the chilled dough, leaving a 1-inch border. Crumble on the goat cheese. Arrange the tomato slices over the cheese in a circular pattern. Fold over the border to make a crust edging. Brush the crust with the egg mixture. Bake for 45 minutes, or until the crust is golden and flaky. Serve right away.

CALIFORNIA EXPRESS PIZZA
with Chicken, Peppers, Mushrooms, and Cilantro

Makes one 12-inch pizza; serves 8

Goat cheese and Jack cheese, poblano chile and red bell pepper, chicken seasoned with cilantro, and mushrooms come together on a crispy crust Annie calls California Express Pizza. Its combination of ingredients conjures a kind of Agatha Christie journey, not on a train through the Orient, but up and down the coast of California. Not a shy dish, it deserves an equally forthright wine.

Serve with a COASTAL ZINFANDEL

1/2 recipe flat bread pizza dough (page 12)

TOPPINGS

1 tablespoon extra virgin olive oil, plus extra
    for drizzling

1 small boneless, skinless chicken breast, cut into
    1/4-inch strips

1/2 poblano chile, seeded and julienned

1/2 red bell pepper, julienned

1/4 pound cremini mushrooms, thinly sliced

1/2 cup thinly sliced red onion

1/2 teaspoon kosher salt

2 tablespoons cilantro leaves

3/4 cup (3 ounces) shredded Monterey Jack cheese

Crushed red pepper flakes

1/2 cup (2 ounces) soft goat cheese

Preheat the oven to 400°F. On a floured work surface, roll the pizza dough out into a 12-inch round. Place on a baking sheet.

To prepare the toppings, heat the oil in a large sauté pan over medium-high heat. Add the chicken, poblano, bell pepper, mushrooms, onion, and salt and sauté until the vegetables wilt and the chicken is still partially pink, about 3 minutes. Stir in the cilantro.

Spread the Jack cheese over the pizza dough. Drizzle with olive oil and sprinkle with pepper flakes. Spread the chicken mixture over the Jack cheese and dot with the goat cheese. Bake for 20 minutes, or until the crust is golden and the cheese is bubbling. Serve right away.

FRESH TOMATO PIZZA
with Three Cheeses, Basil, and Ham Strips
Makes two 8- to 10-inch pizzas; serves 4 to 6 each

Annie attributes her repertoire of pizzas to her bread-making days in the commune. She begins with a simple homemade starter to ensure a full-bodied, chewy crust. The tomato, cheese, and basil toppings are classic, but Annie takes them beyond prosaic with the added ham strips. Also, though it's a bit unusual, she points out that red wine rather than white is her preference to serve with pizza appetizers.

Serve with a CABERNET SAUVIGNON

STARTER

1/4 teaspoon active dry yeast

1 cup all-purpose flour

1/2 cup warm (105° to 115°F) water

PIZZA DOUGH

1/2 cup warm (105° to 115°F) water

1/4 teaspoon active dry yeast

2 cups all-purpose flour

Cornmeal, for sprinkling

1 tablespoon extra virgin olive oil, for brushing

1 cup shredded mozzarella cheese

1 cup shredded Monterey Jack cheese

1/4 cup freshly grated Parmesan cheese

3 tomatoes, thinly sliced

2 tablespoons chopped fresh basil

2 ounces thinly sliced ham, cut into 1/8-inch strips

To make the starter, combine the yeast, flour, and water in a small bowl and stir until smooth. Cover and refrigerate overnight or up to 2 days. Remove from the refrigerator 1 hour before using.

To make the dough, pour the water into a large bowl. Sprinkle the yeast over the top and set aside for 10 minutes, until foamy. Add the starter and flour and mix with an electric mixer on low speed until the dough is smooth and elastic, about 10 minutes. The dough will be sticky.

Coat a large bowl with olive oil and put the dough in the bowl, turning it to coat all over. Cover with a towel and let rise in a warm place for 2 to 3 hours, until 2 1/2 times its original size. The dough may be used right away or wrapped in plastic wrap and refrigerated for up to 3 days.

To make the pizzas, preheat the oven to 500°F. Divide the dough in half. On a lightly floured work surface, roll each half out into an 8- to 10-inch round. Place 2 baking sheets in the oven and, when hot, sprinkle with cornmeal. Place 1 dough round on each baking sheet and bake for 5 minutes. Remove from the oven and brush each round with oil. Layer the rounds first with half of each cheese, then the tomatoes and basil, then the remaining cheese. Top with the ham strips. Bake until the crust is golden and the cheese is melted, 10 to 12 minutes. Serve right away.

TOMATO-PESTO PIZZA

Once the pizza dough is rolled out, Annie has lots of variations for topping her fresh tomato pizza. A favorite is one she likes to make in summer when the basil in her home garden is resplendent, practically asking to be turned into pesto.

To make the pesto: In a small sauté pan over low heat, toast $^1/_2$ cup pine nuts, shaking the pan every few seconds, until the nuts are golden. Transfer them to a food processor and add 1 cup tightly packed fresh basil leaves and 1 tablespoon chopped garlic. Process until finely chopped. With the machine running, add $^1/_2$ cup olive oil in a slow, steady stream and process until the mixture forms a well-blended paste. Stir in 3 tablespoons freshly grated Parmesan cheese and season with salt. Use right away, or transfer to a bowl and cover with plastic wrap, pressing the wrap directly onto the surface of the pesto to prevent discoloration. Refrigerate for up to 3 days.

To make the pizza, follow the instructions for fresh tomato pizza, eliminating the fresh basil and ham strips. After baking, spread a thin glaze of the pesto over each pizza and serve.

Annie in the Robert Mondavi Winery herb garden.

GRILLED FLAT BREAD PIZZA
with Roasted Red Onions, Tomatoes, and Mushrooms
Makes two 12-inch or four 8-inch pizzas; serves 16

Grilling may not be the first way you think of cooking pizza. Under Annie's deft hand, the pizza goes on the grill, receives the same subtle smoky flavor as in a wood-fired pizza oven, and comes out crisp underneath and meltingly moist on top. (The same dough for grilled pizza can be used for oven baking.)

Serve with a PINOT NOIR

FLAT BREAD PIZZA DOUGH

1 package (about 1 tablespoon) active dry yeast

3/4 cup warm (105° to 115°F) water

1 tablespoon extra virgin olive oil

1 teaspoon kosher salt

2 cups all-purpose flour, plus more for kneading
   and rolling

1 1/2 red onions, cut into 1/2-inch wedges

1 tablespoon balsamic vinegar

1/4 cup plus 1 tablespoon extra virgin olive oil, plus extra
   for brushing and drizzling

1/4 pound fresh cremini mushrooms, thinly sliced

1/4 teaspoon kosher salt

1 1/2 cups (6 ounces) shredded fontina or Monterey Jack
   cheese

2 tomatoes, thinly sliced

Kosher salt and freshly ground black pepper

To prepare the dough, sprinkle the yeast over the water in a bowl. Let stand for 5 minutes, or until foamy. Stir in the oil, salt, and flour. Gather into a ball and knead on a floured work surface, adding more flour as necessary to make an elastic and smooth dough, 2 to 3 minutes. Lightly oil the dough and return it to the bowl. Cover with plastic wrap and set aside in a warm place until doubled in volume, about 40 minutes. Punch down the dough. Use right away, or let sit at room temperature for up to 1 hour, or wrap in plastic wrap and refrigerate overnight. Bring to room temperature again before rolling out.

Preheat the oven to 400°F. In a baking dish, combine the onions, vinegar, and the 1/4 cup oil. Toss to coat and separate the onion wedges into layers. Cover with aluminum foil and roast until soft, 15 to 20 minutes. Set aside.

Heat the 1 tablespoon oil in a sauté pan over medium-high heat. Add the mushrooms and salt and sauté until wilted, 2 to 3 minutes. Set aside.

Prepare a medium-hot fire in a charcoal grill or preheat a gas grill to medium-high. On a lightly floured work surface, divide the dough into 2 or 4 sections, depending on what size pizza you are making. Roll each out into a 12- or 8-inch round. Brush the rounds with oil on both sides and place on the grill. When the surface bubbles up, 30 seconds to 1 minute, turn and grill on the other side until the bottom is nicely browned, about 1 minute. Arrange the onions, mushrooms, cheese, and tomatoes on top of the pizzas. Drizzle oil over the tomatoes and sprinkle with salt and pepper. Cover the grill or place aluminum foil over the pizzas, and cook until the cheese is melted and the crust is browned, 6 to 7 minutes. Serve right away.

PIZZETTE CROSTINI

Makes 24 pieces; serves 8

Two of the world's favorite finger foods, pizza and crostini, are combined in these easy-to-manage canapés. Annie and Margrit often serve them in the Vineyard Room for cocktail-hour fare.

Serve with a FUMÉ BLANC

CROSTINI

1/4 cup extra virgin olive oil

2 large cloves garlic, minced or pressed

24 (1/2-inch-thick) diagonal baguette slices

24 thin slices tomato, about the size of the bread slices

1 tablespoon chopped fresh flat-leaf parsley

1 tablespoon chopped fresh basil

24 slices fontina or Gruyère cheese, slightly larger than the bread slices

To make the crostini, preheat the oven to 450°F. In a small bowl, mix together the oil and garlic. Brush one side of each bread slice with the mixture, placing them, brushed side up, on a baking sheet. Place in the oven and toast until they begin to turn golden, about 3 minutes. Remove from the oven and set aside until cool to the touch.

Increase the oven temperature to 500°F. Place a tomato slice on top of each toast. Sprinkle some parsley and basil over the tomato. Top with a cheese slice. Return to the oven and cook until the cheese is melted, 3 to 4 minutes. Serve right away.

Margrit often illustrates and hand-letters menus for special meals.

CROSTINI *with Spicy Crab Salad*

Makes 24 pieces; serves 8 to 12

There's no doubt about it. Crab-topped crostini are for a posh affair, like a winter holiday party. For such an occasion, both Annie and Margrit are "hands-on," and their collaboration is well honed: Annie prepares the crostini while Margrit mingles with the guests.

Serve with a SAUVIGNON BLANC

SPICY CRAB SALAD

2 tablespoons white sesame seeds

1 pound fresh Dungeness crabmeat, picked over for shell

1/2 teaspoon minced garlic

1 tablespoon finely chopped fresh ginger

1/4 cup finely diced red bell pepper

1/4 cup finely diced yellow bell pepper

1 jalapeño chile, seeded and finely chopped

2 tablespoons finely chopped cilantro

1/4 cup freshly squeezed lemon juice

1/4 cup freshly squeezed lime juice

1 tablespoon rice wine vinegar

1/4 cup peanut oil

1 teaspoon low-sodium soy sauce

24 crostini (page 14), made without garlic

Place the sesame seeds in a dry sauté pan over medium-high heat and toast for 5 minutes, or until they begin to pop. (The seeds can also be toasted in a microwave oven on high for 5 minutes, stirring once.)

In a bowl, combine all the salad ingredients, including the sesame seeds, and toss to mix. Place a generous dollop of the crab salad on top of each toast. Serve right away, before the crostini become soggy.

VARIATIONS

Crostini can transport an almost endless number of taste tidbits from hand to mouth. Don't pile the toasts too high, though—a little dab will do. Following are some of the variations Annie has created:

- Field mushrooms sautéed in butter and tarragon
- Grilled portobello mushrooms (page 31), thinly sliced, topped with red bell pepper aioli (page 42)
- Guacamole (page 130) topped with finely chopped kalamata olives
- Goat cheese topped with sun-dried tomatoes and shredded basil
- Tapenade of green olives topped with lemon zest
- Roasted red bell peppers (page xx), thinly sliced and topped with capers
- Grilled radicchio tossed with balsamic vinegar
- Duck confit, shredded and topped with cracked green peppercorns
- Smoked trout spread
- Roasted red onions (page 12), slivered and topped with parsley
- Sun-dried tomato vinaigrette (page 153), topped with micro-greens
- Fennel ratatouille (page 100)
- Grilled asparagus (page 135), finely chopped and topped with Meyer lemon aioli (page 135)

SWISS QUICHE
with Gruyère, Emmental, and Bacon
Makes one 9- to 10-inch quiche; serves 6 to 8

Margrit's rendition of a classic quiche Lorraine includes scallions and parsley for a spark of color and tilts the balance in the filling more toward the cheese than the egg-cream custard of the French version. The tender crust translates easily to any savory pie.

Serve with a PINOT NOIR

SAVORY CRUST DOUGH

1 cup all-purpose flour

1/2 teaspoon kosher salt

6 tablespoons cold unsalted butter

2 tablespoons vegetable shortening or extra virgin olive oil

1/4 cup ice water

FILLING

3 strips thick bacon

2 large eggs

3/4 cup heavy cream

3 scallions, including light green parts, finely chopped

1 tablespoon chopped fresh flat-leaf parsley

1/2 teaspoon kosher salt

1/4 teaspoon freshly ground black pepper

Pinch of ground nutmeg (optional)

1 cup shredded Gruyère cheese

1 cup shredded Emmental cheese

To make the dough, combine the flour, salt, and butter in a food processor and pulse until the mixture resembles coarse meal. Add the shortening, pulse briefly to incorporate, add the water, and pulse briefly again. Gather the mixture into a ball and wrap in plastic wrap. Press into a thick disk and refrigerate for at least 30 minutes or up to overnight. Remove from the refrigerator 30 minutes before rolling out.

On a floured work surface, roll the dough out into a 10- to 11-inch round and line a pie plate or removable-bottom tart pan with it. Fold under the edges and pinch all around. Refrigerate for 15 to 30 minutes.

Preheat the oven to 400°F.

To prepare the filling, heat a skillet over medium-high heat. Add the bacon and cook, turning once, until lightly crisp, about 5 minutes on each side. Transfer to paper towels to drain, then cut into 1/2-inch pieces. In a bowl, whisk together the eggs, cream, scallions, parsley, salt, pepper, and nutmeg. Sprinkle the cheeses, then the bacon pieces in the pie crust. Pour in the egg mixture and tilt the pan to distribute it evenly. Bake for 20 minutes. Decrease the heat to 375°F and continue baking until a knife inserted in the center comes out clean, about 10 minutes more. Serve warm or at room temperature.

GOAT CHEESE AND ZUCCHINI TORTA SQUARES
with Tomato Concassé

Serves 18 as a passed appetizer

Annie devised this torta for a food and wine pairing event that featured Pinot Grigio. Here, she tops the squares with tomato concassé and serves them with a Sauvignon Blanc for its hint of sweetness that counterbalances the mild acid of the topping. The torta, which is similar to a frittata or a baked omelette, can also make a light meal. In any case, be sure to serve it within an hour or two of cooking, because after that it starts to weep and loses its fresh loveliness.

Serve with a SAUVIGNON BLANC

TOMATO CONCASSÉ

6 Roma tomatoes, peeled, seeded, and cut into
   1/4-inch dice (page xx)
2 tablespoons extra virgin olive oil
Kosher salt and freshly ground black pepper

TORTA

3 large eggs
1 pound zucchini, grated
1/4 cup chopped scallions, including green parts
1 teaspoon chopped garlic
1 teaspoon chopped fresh thyme
1 teaspoon chopped fresh flat-leaf parsley
3/4 cup heavy cream
3/4 pound soft goat cheese
3/4 teaspoon kosher salt
1/4 teaspoon freshly ground black pepper

To make the concassé, combine the tomatoes, oil, and salt and pepper to taste in a bowl and mix well. Set aside.

To make the torta, preheat the oven to 350°F. Butter a 9 by 12-inch baking dish. In a large bowl, beat the eggs lightly. Add the zucchini, scallions, garlic, thyme, parsley, cream, cheese, salt, and pepper. Stir to mix, breaking up the cheese to blend it in. Pour into the prepared dish and bake until a knife inserted in the center comes out clean, about 40 minutes. Remove from the oven and allow to cool to room temperature.

To serve, cut the torta into eighteen 2-inch squares. Place them on a serving platter and top each with a spoonful of the tomato concassé.

GAZPACHO

Serves 8

Vibrant with fall color, intense with summer flavor, Annie's gazpacho celebrates the changing seasons. It's a refined version of gazpacho, smooth rather than chunky, in a South-of-France style inspired by Roger Vergé.

Serve with a FUMÉ BLANC

3 cloves garlic

1 English cucumber, peeled, seeded, and cut into 1-inch pieces

1 red bell pepper, cut into 1-inch pieces

1 celery stalk, peeled and cut into 1-inch pieces

3 pounds ripe tomatoes, quartered

1/2 jalapeño chile, seeded

1/2 cup extra virgin olive oil

1/4 cup red wine vinegar

Dash of Tabasco sauce

Kosher salt and freshly ground black pepper

GARNISHES

1/2 baguette, crust removed, cut into 1/2-inch cubes

2 tablespoons extra virgin olive oil

Kosher salt and freshly ground black pepper

1/2 cup finely diced red bell pepper

1/2 cup finely diced white onion

1/2 cup peeled, seeded, and finely diced English cucumber

1/2 cup chopped cilantro

1 avocado, coarsely chopped

1/2 cup crumbled soft goat cheese

8 sprigs cilantro

In batches, purée the garlic, cucumber, bell pepper, celery, tomatoes, and jalapeño together in a food processor or blender. Pass the mixture through the medium plate of a food mill set over a large bowl. Stir in the oil, vinegar, and Tabasco and season with salt and pepper. Cover and refrigerate until thoroughly chilled, at least 4 hours or up to overnight.

Just before serving, preheat the oven to 375°F. Toss the bread cubes with the oil and sprinkle with salt and pepper. Spread on a baking sheet and bake for 10 minutes, until toasted. Remove from the oven and allow to cool on the baking sheet.

To serve, ladle the chilled soup into 8 bowls. Place a bit of the bell pepper, onion, cucumber, chopped cilantro, and avocado in separate piles in each bowl. Top with toasted bread cubes, a sprinkle of goat cheese, and a sprig of cilantro. Serve right away.

ROCK SHRIMP GAZPACHO

Serves 6 to 8

With lots of ingredients, like a minestrone or garbure but not so dense, Annie's rock shrimp gazpacho is a soup that reminds of the Andalusian plain, home to all gazpachos. Rock shrimp have a special taste of the sea that works well here; they also have the advantage of coming shelled and ready to cook. If you can't find them, substitute small uncooked shrimp of another sort.

Serve with a SAUVIGNON BLANC

4 large cloves garlic, unpeeled

1 teaspoon plus 1 tablespoon extra virgin olive oil

3/4 pound rock shrimp

SOUP

1 cup cubed French bread without crusts

1/4 cup red wine vinegar

1/4 cup extra virgin olive oil

2 cups tomato juice or V-8

2 cups chicken stock (page xix)

3 pounds tomatoes, peeled, seeded, and finely diced (page xx)

2/3 cup finely chopped red onion

1 cup peeled, seeded, and finely chopped English cucumber

1/2 cup finely chopped red bell pepper

1/2 cup finely chopped celery

1 teaspoon seeded and finely chopped serrano or jalapeño chile

2 tablespoons finely chopped fresh basil

1/4 cup finely chopped cilantro

2 teaspoons finely chopped fresh mint

2 tablespoons freshly squeezed lemon juice

1 teaspoon kosher salt

GARNISHES

1 Hass avocado, finely diced

8 cilantro sprigs

6 to 8 garlic croutons (page 25)

Preheat the oven to 400°F. In a baking dish, toss the garlic with the 1 teaspoon oil and bake until soft, about 8 minutes. Remove from the oven, allow to cool, and peel.

Heat the 1 tablespoon oil in a sauté pan over medium-high heat. Add the shrimp and sauté until they begin to firm and turn pink around the edges, 1 1/2 to 2 minutes. Transfer to a plate and set aside to cool.

To make the soup, combine the roasted garlic, bread, vinegar, and olive oil in a food processor and process until smooth. Transfer to a large bowl. Stir in the shrimp, tomato juice, stock, tomatoes, onion, cucumber, bell pepper, celery, chile, basil, cilantro, mint, lemon juice, and salt. Add water if a thinner consistency is desired. Cover and refrigerate until completely chilled, at least 4 hours or up to overnight.

To serve, ladle the soup into bowls. Garnish each bowl with some avocado, a cilantro sprig, and a crouton. Serve right away.

BREAD, SAGE, AND TOMATO HARVEST SOUP

Serves 4

Annie calls her rendition of classic Mediterranean bread and tomato soup a harvest soup because she typically makes it for September meals when Napa Valley tomatoes are at their tastiest prime, just as the grapes are being harvested. She gently "braises" the bread in olive oil until golden so it absorbs the unctuous liquid that becomes part of the dish. Don't be tempted to rush this dish with a quicker sauté, or the garlic and sage will burn and taste bitter.

Serve with a CHARDONNAY

1 tablespoon plus 1 cup extra virgin olive oil

1 yellow onion, thinly sliced

6 tomatoes (1½ pounds), peeled, seeded, and chopped (page xx), about 4 cups

1½ cups Chardonnay

4 cups beef stock (page xix)

1 teaspoon kosher salt

Freshly ground black pepper

1 tablespoon minced garlic

½ cup finely chopped fresh sage, plus 4 fresh sage leaves, thinly sliced

4 (¾-inch-thick) slices French or Italian bread, or 12 (¾-inch-thick) slices baguette

⅓ cup freshly grated Parmesan cheese

In a large saucepan, heat the 1 tablespoon oil over medium-high heat. Add the onion and sauté until wilted, about 2 minutes. Add the tomatoes and cook until softened and juicy, 3 to 5 minutes, depending on the ripeness of the tomatoes. Stir in the wine and stock and bring to a boil. Add the salt and pepper to taste, decrease the heat to low, cover, and simmer for 45 minutes.

While the soup simmers, prepare the bread. In a large sauté pan, heat the 1 cup oil over medium heat. Add the garlic and chopped sage and cook for 1 minute, taking care not to let the garlic brown. Add the bread and cook until golden on the bottom, 3 minutes. Turn the slices over and cook until golden on the other side, about 2 minutes more. Set aside in the sauté pan.

To serve, divide the bread among 4 bowls. Ladle the soup over the bread, sprinkle the cheese and sliced sage over the top, and serve.

PASTA IN BRODO

Serves 6

Margrit's pasta in *brodo* is always made with homemade pasta and homemade stock. Though beef stock is also traditional for pasta in *brodo,* she typically uses her own chicken stock, a rich, deep essence of chicken flavor.

Serve with a SAUVIGNON BLANC *or* CHARDONNAY

8 cups chicken stock (page xix)

1 teaspoon kosher salt

1 recipe Margrit's Homemade Pasta (page 71), cut into angel hair strands

Zest of 1 small lemon, cut into long, very thin strands

2 teaspoons chopped fresh flat-leaf parsley

Wedge of Parmesan cheese, for serving

In a large pot, combine the stock and salt. Bring to a boil over high heat. Cut the pasta into 3-inch-long pieces and add to the pot. Cook until al dente, about 2 minutes.

Divide the zest among 6 soup bowls. Ladle in the pasta and broth and sprinkle the parsley over the top. Serve right away, accompanied with the Parmesan cheese and a cheese grater on the side.

Annie and Margrit

A Fiftieth Birthday Dinner

Annie and Margrit cooked up this menu for the taping of a Swiss television lifestyle program. They chose a selection of photogenic recipes for the show. As it turned out, it was Annie's fiftieth birthday, so she was filmed celebrating *en famille* with her husband, Keith; their sons Nathan and Quinn and Quinn's wife, Molly; Annie's sister, Phoebe, and her husband, Hal; and Margrit and Bob. A good time was had by all and Annie chuckles still over how she spent that landmark birthday, sipping reserve wines, surrounded by her loved ones, under the eye of a film crew.

Pasta in Brodo (page 22)
1997 Robert Mondavi Chardonnay Reserve

Quail Marinated in Verjus and Honey (page 136)
Fennel Ratatouille (page 100)
1997 Robert Mondavi Stags Leap District Pinot Noir

Fresh Plum Galette (page 176)
1998 Robert Mondavi Moscato d'Oro

FRENCH GREEN LENTIL AND MUSHROOM SOUP
with White Truffle Oil

Serves 4 to 6

During the fall rains, a surfeit of mushrooms spring up in Napa Valley markets. Dried lentils are in the cupboard, and white truffles, though not part of the produce of the region, add an earthy exuberance in an oil infusion readily available in gourmet markets. Put together in Annie's recipe, they make a soup that's a little bit extravagant and a lot warming.

Serve with a CHARDONNAY

1/4 cup unsalted butter

2 cloves garlic, chopped

1 small yellow or white onion, chopped

3/4 pound cremini mushrooms, coarsely chopped

1 teaspoon kosher salt

6 cups chicken stock (page xix)

1 cup French green lentils, rinsed

GARNISHES

1 tablespoon chopped fresh chives

1 tablespoon white truffle oil

Sour cream

In a large pot, melt the butter over medium heat. Add the garlic and onion, stir to mix, and cook, stirring occasionally, until they just begin to turn golden, about 7 minutes. Stir in the mushrooms and salt, increase the heat to medium-high, and cook until well wilted, about 5 minutes.

Add the stock and lentils, stir to mix, and bring to a boil. Decrease the heat to medium and cook until the lentils are very tender, about 30 minutes. Remove from the heat and set aside until cool enough to handle.

In a blender or food processor, process the mixture in batches until well puréed. (This will take a little longer in a food processor, about 5 minutes per batch.)

To serve, reheat briefly and ladle into soup bowls. Garnish each serving with chives, a generous swirl of truffle oil, and a dollop of sour cream.

YELLOW SPLIT PEA SOUP
with Pancetta and Garlic Croutons

Serves 6 to 8

For a homey beginning to a fall meal, Annie serves yellow split pea soup with a forthright, full-bodied Chardonnay. Together they create a warm glow around the table.

Serve with a CHARDONNAY

2 tablespoons extra virgin olive oil

1 small yellow onion, chopped

1 large clove garlic, chopped

$1/2$ carrot, peeled and chopped

1 celery stalk, chopped

1 teaspoon chopped fresh thyme

2 cups yellow split peas

8 cups chicken stock (page xix)

1 teaspoon kosher salt

GARLIC CROUTONS

12 to 16 ($1/2$-inch-thick) slices baguette

Extra virgin olive oil

1 clove garlic, halved

4 ounces pancetta, chopped

ANNIE'S TIP

When cooked, split peas come out more or less dense according to their age, Annie advises having a cup or two of extra stock handy to thin the soup if it's too thick.

In a large soup pot, heat the oil over medium-high heat. Stir in the onion and garlic and cook until softened but not browned, about 1 minute. Decrease the heat to medium-low. Stir in the carrot, celery, and thyme, and cook until they begin to brown, 4 to 5 minutes. Increase the heat to high and add the split peas, stock, and salt. Stir to mix, and bring to a boil. Decrease the heat, cover, and simmer for $1^1/2$ hours. Check the pot from time to time to make sure it's not bubbling too fast. Remove from the heat and set aside until cool enough to handle. In a food processor or blender, purée the soup in batches until smooth (this will take 2 minutes or so). Transfer to a clean pot as you go and return to the stove top to reheat gently.

To make the croutons, preheat the oven to 375°F. Place the bread slices on a baking sheet and lightly brush or spray the tops with oil. Toast in the oven until barely golden around the edges, 3 to 5 minutes. Remove from the oven and allow to cool to the touch. Rub each slice on both sides with a cut side of the garlic. These will keep in an airtight container for up to 3 days.

Place a sauté pan over medium heat. Add the pancetta and cook, stirring occasionally, until slightly crisp but not hard, about 8 minutes. Using a slotted spoon, transfer to paper towels to drain.

If the soup is too thick, thin with some extra stock. Ladle into soup bowls. Garnish each bowl with 2 croutons, sprinkle pancetta over the top, and serve.

ASPARAGUS SOUP
with Dungeness Crab and Red Bell Pepper Cream

Serves 6

Though Annie finds peeling asparagus a contemplative pleasure when preparing the spears for salads, she never peels them for soup because "the green is in the peel." To make the soup velvety without peeling the spears, she uses a fine mesh sieve to extract the strings after the stalks are cooked. With a swirl of red bell pepper cream, the soup is delicious and picture-perfect. A scoop of Dungeness crab on top turns it extraordinary.

Serve with a SAUVIGNON BLANC *or* FUMÉ BLANC

RED BELL PEPPER CREAM

1 (12-ounce) red bell pepper, roasted and peeled (page xx)

1 tablespoon crème fraîche (page xx) or sour cream

Kosher salt and freshly ground black pepper

SOUP

2 tablespoons unsalted butter

2 yellow onions, thinly sliced

1 (8-ounce) russet potato, peeled and cut into 1/2-inch chunks

6 cups chicken stock (page xix)

1 teaspoon kosher salt

3 pounds asparagus, trimmed and cut into 2-inch lengths

1 cup (6 ounces) fresh crabmeat, preferably freshly cooked (see Annie's Tip, page 30), picked over for shell

2 tablespoons chopped fresh chives

ANNIE'S TIP

Chilling the soup after puréeing preserves the bright color and fresh, green taste.

To prepare the bell pepper cream, purée the pepper in a food processor. Stir in the crème fraîche and season with salt and pepper. Use right away or cover and refrigerate for up to 5 days.

To make the soup, melt the butter in a large soup pot over medium heat. Add the onions and cook until completely wilted, about 5 minutes. Add the potato, stock, and salt and bring to a boil over high heat. Decrease the heat to medium, cover, and simmer until the potato is soft, about 15 minutes. Add the asparagus and simmer, uncovered, until pierceable with a fork, about 5 minutes, depending on the size of the asparagus. Remove from the heat and allow to cool slightly. In batches, purée the soup in a blender or food processor, then pass through the fine plate of a food mill or a fine mesh sieve. Transfer to a stainless steel bowl set in a larger bowl of ice water to chill the soup as you go (see Annie's Tip).

To serve, return the soup to the pot and gently reheat just until warm. Ladle into 6 soup bowls. Mound about 2 tablespoons crabmeat in the center of each bowl. Swirl red pepper cream around the crab and over the soup. Sprinkle chives over the top and serve.

PARSLIED CRÊPE RIBBONS IN BEEF BROTH

Serves 6 to 8

From Margrit's mother to Margrit to Annie, a dish of parslied crêpe ribbons floating in a rich beef broth has been a pass-along treasure of the family. Annie especially wanted it included in this cookbook for those sentimental reasons, and also because it's quite delicious. The crêpe batter can be varied in many savory ways and even be made sweet, as in Annie's Walnut Crêpes with Caramelized Apple Filling (page 188).

Serve with a PINOT NOIR

CRÊPES

3 large eggs

1/4 cup packed chopped fresh flat-leaf parsley

3/4 cup all-purpose flour

3/4 cup milk

Kosher salt and freshly ground black pepper

2 tablespoons unsalted butter

SOUP

6 cups beef stock (page xix)

2 small carrots, peeled and thinly sliced into rounds

1/4 cup freshly grated Parmesan cheese

To make the crêpes, break the eggs into a bowl and whisk until foamy. Mix in the parsley and flour. Slowly whisk in the milk to make a smooth batter. Season with salt and pepper.

Melt 1 teaspoon of the butter in a 10-inch nonstick sauté pan over medium-low heat. Add a scant 1/4 cup of the batter and tilt the pan around to spread the batter evenly over the bottom. When the batter has set and the bottom is lightly golden, about 2 minutes, turn over the crêpe. Cook for 1 minute longer and transfer to a platter. Repeat with the remaining butter and batter, remixing the batter each time.

When the crêpes are cool, roll them up loosely and cut them crosswise into ribbons 1/4 inch wide. Put the ribbons in a soup tureen and set aside in a warm place.

To prepare the soup, bring the stock to a boil in a saucepan over medium-high heat. Add the carrot slices and cook until barely tender, about 5 minutes.

To serve, pour the stock and carrots over the crêpe ribbons in the tureen. Sprinkle with the Parmesan cheese and serve right away.

FENNEL AND CELERY ROOT SOUP

Serves 6

Annie acquired a taste for underground vegetables like celery root and leeks from Margrit. Without the expected potato but with fennel instead, she combines those old favorites in a silken and sublime soup that's like a California vichyssoise, only warm.

Serve with a CHARDONNAY

2 tablespoons unsalted butter

1/2 cup water

3 leeks, including light green parts, thinly sliced

1 (1-pound) fennel bulb, quartered and thinly sliced

1 (1-pound) celery root, peeled, quartered, and thinly sliced

1/2 teaspoon kosher salt

6 cups chicken stock (page xix)

1/4 cup chopped fennel fronds, watercress leaves, or arugula, for garnish

In a large soup pot, melt the butter with the water over medium-high heat. Add the leeks, fennel, celery root, and salt. Stir, decrease the heat to low, cover, and cook until the vegetables are translucent, about 20 minutes. Check once during the cooking to make sure there is ample moisture in the pot, and add a little water if necessary.

Pour the stock into the pot, increase the heat to high, and bring to a boil. Decrease the heat to medium-low, cover, and simmer for 15 minutes, or until the vegetables are mashable. Remove from the heat and set aside to cool slightly.

In a food processor, purée the soup in batches, blending each batch for a full 1 to 2 minutes to make it smooth. Transfer to a clean pot as you go and return to the stove top to reheat gently. Ladle into 6 soup bowls, garnish with the fennel fronds, and serve hot.

DUNGENESS CRAB, ROASTED PEPPER, AND FRESH CORN SOUP

Serves 6 to 8

Dungeness crab is native to coastal waters from Alaska south almost to Santa Barbara. It is a major catch of the fishing industry along that pathway and is especially prominent in San Francisco cuisine. A few hours north of San Francisco, the crabs arrive live and kicking in the Napa Valley, just out of the water and ready for the soup pot. Here, Annie pairs their ocean-fresh meat with the terrestrial flavors of corn and roasted pepper, and adds a spicy tang with cumin, cilantro, and lime.

Serve with a FUMÉ BLANC *or* SAUVIGNON BLANC

2 ears fresh corn

2 tablespoons unsalted butter

1 red onion, finely chopped

1 red bell pepper, roasted, peeled, and cut into thin strips (page xx)

1 yellow bell pepper, roasted, peeled, and cut into thin strips (page xx)

1 poblano chile, roasted, peeled, and cut into thin strips (page xx)

1 tablespoon ground cumin

8 cups chicken stock (page xix)

2 tablespoons chopped cilantro

2 tablespoons freshly squeezed lime juice

Kosher salt and freshly ground black pepper

1¹/₂ cups (8 ounces) fresh Dungeness crabmeat, picked over for shell (see Annie's Tip)

Cut the kernels off the corn cobs and blanch in boiling salted water for 1 minute. Drain and set aside.

In a soup pot, melt the butter over medium heat. Add the onion and cook until softened, about 5 minutes. Stir in the bell pepper and poblano strips and turn off the heat.

Put the cumin in a small nonstick sauté pan and stir over medium heat until lightly toasted, about 3 minutes. Add to the onion and peppers and return the heat to high. Add the stock and corn and bring just to a boil. Stir in the cilantro, lime juice, and salt and pepper to taste. Ladle into soup bowls and garnish each with a mound of crabmeat in the center of the bowl. Serve right away.

ANNIE'S TIP

Annie prefers to cook the crab live and remove the crabmeat herself to retain both the fresh sea flavor and to have some large pieces of meat for the soup. You can use fresh crabmeat bought in bulk; it's a good product though not as sea fresh as that you've cooked yourself. Be sure to pick through it for any remnants of shell. What is not a particularly good option is whole crab already cooked. Though this saves the time and mess of cooking and cleaning the crab, unless you know the crab was cooked that day, you might as well go with already picked-over flash-frozen crabmeat and save yourself all the trouble.

PORTOBELLO MUSHROOMS
with Bulgur, Couscous, and Orzo Salad

Serves 4

Annie invented this multigrain salad topped with meaty portobello mushrooms for a cooking demonstration at the *Sunset Magazine* offices in Menlo Park. It features a Merlot dressing to go with a Robert Mondavi Merlot wine. Be sure to make the vinaigrette first so it can mellow.

Serve with a MERLOT

MERLOT VINAIGRETTE

1 shallot, finely chopped

1/4 cup balsamic vinegar

2 tablespoons Merlot

1/2 cup extra virgin olive oil

Kosher salt and freshly ground black pepper

BULGUR, COUSCOUS, AND ORZO SALAD

1/2 cup bulgur wheat

1/2 cup couscous

1 cup boiling water

1 tablespoon extra virgin olive oil

1/2 cup orzo pasta

2 cups cold water

2 slices pancetta, coarsely chopped

1/2 head radicchio, thinly sliced

1 cup arugula, thinly sliced

2 scallions, including green parts, thinly sliced

1/4 cup finely chopped fresh flat-leaf parsley

4 (4-ounce) portobello mushrooms, stems and gills removed

1/2 cup cherry tomato halves, for garnish

To prepare the vinaigrette, combine all the ingredients in a small bowl and whisk to mix. Set aside at room temperature for at least 30 minutes or up to 2 hours.

To prepare the salad, combine the bulgur and couscous in a large bowl. Stir in the boiling water and let stand until the water is absorbed and the grains are tender, at least 30 minutes or up to 1 hour.

In a small saucepan, heat the oil over medium-high heat. Add the orzo and stir until lightly toasted, about 2 minutes. Add the cold water and bring to a boil. Decrease the heat to medium and cook until al dente, 8 to 10 minutes. Drain and add to the bowl with the bulgur and couscous.

In a small sauté pan, sauté the pancetta over medium-high heat until barely crisp, about 5 minutes. Using a slotted spoon, transfer to a paper towel to drain briefly, then add to the grains. Add the radicchio, arugula, scallions, parsley, and half of the vinaigrette to the bowl. Gently toss to mix and set aside.

To cook the mushrooms, heat a grill pan or cast-iron skillet over medium-high heat. Brush both sides of the mushrooms with some of the remaining vinaigrette and cook until they begin to turn golden and limp but are still firm in the center, about 2 minutes on each side.

To serve, mound the grain salad on a platter or 4 plates. Slice the mushrooms about 1/2 inch thick and arrange over the top of the grains. Garnish with the cherry tomato halves and serve.

CORN CAKES
with Smoked Salmon, Chive Oil, and Crème Fraîche
Serves 8

"Creamy, fruity, and rich" is how Annie describes Chardonnay wine. In a perfect pairing of wine and food, she combines corn, smoked salmon, and crème fraîche to reflect the Chardonnay. The chive oil and fennel garnish provide just the right foil for the nuance of sweetness in wine and food.

Serve with a CHARDONNAY

CHIVE OIL

1/2 cup packed coarsely chopped fresh chives, about
 1 large bunch

1/2 cup extra virgin olive oil

1/2 teaspoon kosher salt

CORN CAKES

1 tablespoon active dry yeast

1/4 cup warm water

6 ears fresh white corn, kernels cut from the cobs

1/2 cup milk

13/4 cups all-purpose flour

2 large eggs, beaten

2 tablespoons unsalted butter, melted

1/2 teaspoon kosher salt

Freshly ground black pepper

2 tablespoons unsalted butter, for frying

1 fennel bulb, thinly sliced

1 tablespoon freshly squeezed lemon juice

2 tablespoons extra virgin olive oil

Kosher salt and freshly ground black pepper

1/2 cup crème fraîche (page xx) or sour cream

2 tablespoons milk

1/2 pound thinly sliced smoked salmon

2 tablespoons chopped fresh chives, for garnish

1/4 cup micro-greens, for garnish

To make the chive oil, drop the chives into a pot of boiling water, drain right away, and rinse under cool water. Transfer to a paper towel and squeeze dry. In a food processor or blender, combine the chives with the oil and salt and purée for 1 minute. Transfer to a plastic squeeze bottle.

To make the corn cakes, combine the yeast and water in a bowl and set aside until bubbly, about 10 minutes. Purée half of the corn kernels in a food processor or blender until creamy. Add to the yeast mixture, along with the milk, flour, eggs, melted butter, salt, and remaining corn kernels. Whisk to mix and season with black pepper.

To cook the corn cakes, melt 1 tablespoon of the butter in a large sauté pan over medium-high heat. Drop 1/4-cup amounts of the batter into the pan, without crowding. Fry, turning once, until nicely browned, about 2 minutes per side. Transfer to paper towels and repeat to cook the remaining batter. You should have about 16 corn cakes.

In a bowl, toss together the fennel, lemon juice, and oil and season with salt and pepper.

In a small bowl, whisk together the crème fraîche and milk until smooth. Transfer to a plastic squeeze bottle.

To serve, place 2 corn cakes in the middle of each plate. Drape a slice of smoked salmon over the corn cakes. Place a small amount of the fennel on top of the salmon. Squirt the crème fraîche mixture around the corn cakes. Squirt the chive oil on the crème fraîche. Sprinkle on the chopped chives, top with a pinch of micro-greens, and serve.

CHILES RELLENOS
with Roasted Tomato Salsa

Serves 6

Learned from the Mexican immigrants who make up the main workforce tending the vineyards, chiles rellenos have become part of the Napa Valley's culinary heritage. For the Blessing of the Grapes ceremony at Robert Mondavi Winery each fall (see page 193), Annie serves them alongside achiote-marinated young chicken, and accompanies them with a rich Pinot Noir wine. On other occasions, she might serve the chiles rellenos and salsa as a small appetizer on their own, accompanied with a glass of well-chilled Fumé Blanc.

Serve with a PINOT NOIR *or* FUMÉ BLANC

ROASTED TOMATO SALSA

2 large cloves garlic, unpeeled

2 jalapeño chiles

4 large, ripe red tomatoes

2/3 cup finely chopped yellow onion

1/2 cup chopped cilantro

1/2 teaspoon kosher salt

CHILES RELLENOS

6 poblano chiles, roasted (page xx)

1 cup (4 ounces) shredded Monterey Jack cheese

Peanut or grapeseed oil, for frying

3 large eggs, separated

1 tablespoon all-purpose flour, plus additional for coating

To prepare the salsa, heat a large nonstick sauté pan or cast-iron skillet over medium-high heat. Add the garlic cloves, jalapeños, and tomatoes, and roast, turning frequently, until blackened all around. This will take about 5 minutes for the garlic, 7 to 8 minutes for the jalapeños, and 10 to 12 minutes for the tomatoes. Transfer each vegetable to a plate as it's done and allow to cool.

Holding the tomatoes over a bowl to catch the juices, peel them, discarding the peel, and break up the flesh with your hands, dropping it into the bowl. Peel the jalapeños and garlic and put them in a food processor.

Chop as finely as possible, scraping down the sides of the bowl a couple of times during the process. Add the tomatoes and their juices and pulse until the tomatoes are coarsely chopped. Transfer to a bowl and stir in the onion, cilantro, and salt. Use right away, or cover and refrigerate up to overnight.

To cook the chiles rellenos, peel the chiles, taking care to keep them whole. Make a small slit in the side of each and pull out the seeds. Stuff each chile with one-sixth of the cheese.

Pour the oil into a large sauté pan to a depth of 1 inch. Heat over high heat. While the oil is heating, beat the egg whites until they hold stiff peaks. Mix in the 1 tablespoon flour, then the egg yolks, one at a time, beating until each is fully incorporated before adding the next. Spread about 1/4 cup flour on a plate. Line a baking sheet with paper towels.

When the oil is hot, hold a chile by the stem, dredge it in the flour on the plate, and gently shake off the excess. Working quickly, dip the chile into the egg batter and place in the hot oil. Fry 3 chiles at a time, until golden on the bottom, 3 to 4 minutes. Turn over and fry until golden on the bottom again, another 3 to 4 minutes. With a slotted spoon, transfer the chiles to the prepared baking sheet and keep warm in a 200°F oven while cooking the second batch (no need to preheat the oven).

Top each stuffed chile with a dollop of the salsa and serve as an appetizer or a side dish.

GRILLED HALIBUT
with Cucumber, Tomato, and Ginger Salsa

Serves 4

From March to November, halibut are fished off the shores of the Pacific Ocean from the Bering Sea all the way south to Baja. Here, Annie takes advantage of that catch of the day by quickly grilling halibut fillets and dressing them with a very-California fusion salsa.

Serve with a SAUVIGNON BLANC

CUCUMBER, TOMATO, AND GINGER SALSA

1/2 English cucumber, peeled, seeded, and cut into
   1/4-inch dice

1/2 cup seeded and diced ripe red tomato

1/4 cup seeded and diced yellow tomato

1 tablespoon finely chopped fresh ginger

2 tablespoons finely chopped white onion

2 tablespoons champagne vinegar or white wine vinegar

3 tablespoons extra virgin olive oil

Pinch of kosher salt

HALIBUT

1 1/2 pounds halibut fillets, at least 3/4 inch thick,
   cut into 4 equal pieces

Extra virgin olive oil, for brushing the fillets

Kosher salt and freshly ground black pepper

Prepare a medium-hot fire in a charcoal grill or pre-heat a gas grill to medium-high.

To prepare the salsa, combine all the ingredients in a small bowl and stir to mix. Set aside for the flavors to blend for 30 minutes or so while the fire heats.

To cook the halibut, brush the fillets with olive oil and sprinkle lightly with salt and pepper on both sides. Grill the fillets until flaky on the outside but still a little moist on the inside, about 3 minutes on each side. Transfer to a plate and let rest for 5 minutes to allow the juices to settle.

To serve, arrange the fillets on a serving platter or 4 plates. Spoon some of the salsa over the top of each fillet and serve with the remaining salsa on the side.

SEARED TUNA
with Cabbage Slaw and Lemon Mayonnaise

Serves 4

From the time she lived in Japan as a child, the simply presented, clean, bright flavors of that cuisine have remained a part of Annie's aesthetic. In this composition, she pairs sturdy, almost beefy tuna with gossamer strands of multicolored cabbage and peppers and brings them together with a sauce of lemony mayonnaise. The mayonnaise should be thin; if it isn't thin enough to pour in a thick stream, blend in a tablespoon or so of water.

Serve with a CHARDONNAY

CABBAGE SLAW

1/2 head red cabbage, cored

1/2 head green cabbage, cored

1 (6-ounce) yellow bell pepper

1 (4-ounce) poblano chile

4 scallions, including green parts, very thinly sliced

3 tablespoons chopped cilantro

1/4 cup champagne vinegar or white wine vinegar

1/2 teaspoon Dijon mustard

1/2 teaspoon minced garlic

1/2 teaspoon kosher salt

Pinch of freshly ground black pepper

1/3 cup extra virgin olive oil

4 (4- to 6-ounce) tuna steaks, 1/2 to 3/4 inch thick
   (see Annie's Tip, page 37)

Extra virgin olive oil, for coating

Kosher salt and freshly ground black pepper

LEMON MAYONNAISE

1 large egg

2 tablespoons freshly squeezed lemon juice

1/2 teaspoon kosher salt

Pinch of freshly ground white pepper

1 cup extra virgin olive oil

To make the slaw, slice the red and green cabbages 1/8 inch thick using a mandoline or the slicing blade of a food processor. Place in a large bowl. Slice the bell pepper and poblano chile 1/8 inch thick, starting at the bottom and cutting crosswise toward the top until you get to the seeds. Add to the bowl with the cabbage. Add the scallions and cilantro and toss to mix. Combine the vinegar, mustard, garlic, salt, and pepper in a small bowl. Whisk in the oil. Pour into the bowl with the vegetables and toss to mix. Set aside at room temperature for 1 hour, or refrigerate for up to 4 hours.

Coat the tuna steaks with oil and sprinkle both sides with a little salt and a generous amount of pepper. Cover and refrigerate for 30 minutes or up to 4 hours. Bring to room temperature before cooking.

To make the mayonnaise, blend together the egg, lemon juice, salt, and pepper in a food processor. With the machine running, gradually add the oil in a thin stream until emulsified. Cover and set aside in the refrigerator until chilled, or up to overnight.

To cook the tuna, heat a cast-iron or heavy nonstick pan over high heat. Sear the tuna steaks until browned on both sides and rare in the center, 2 to 3 minutes on each side. Transfer to a platter and let rest for 10 minutes.

To serve, divide the slaw among 4 plates. Slice the tuna about 1/2 inch thick and arrange the slices over the slaw. Drizzle a tablespoon or so of the mayonnaise over the tuna and serve with the remaining mayonnaise on the side.

SEARED TUNA
with Fennel and Red Pepper Slaw

Serves 4

Fish and fennel is a time-honored pairing. French cooks like to grill mackerel over dried fennel branches. In California, barbecue chefs might cook salmon on a bed of fresh fennel stalks to add a unique flavor to the fish. Here, Annie reserves the fennel for a sprightly fresh salad with crunchy red bell pepper strips to set alongside the tuna.

Serve with a CHARDONNAY

¼ cup finely chopped shallots

¼ cup champagne vinegar

2 tablespoons freshly squeezed lemon juice

2 tablespoons freshly squeezed orange juice

½ cup extra virgin olive oil

½ teaspoon kosher salt

¼ teaspoon freshly ground white pepper

2 fennel bulbs with tops, bulbs very thinly sliced, tops reserved for garnish

½ large red bell pepper, very thinly sliced

2 tablespoons chopped fresh chives

1 pound fresh tuna steaks, ½ to ¾ inch thick (see Annie's Tip)

2 tablespoons peanut oil

In a small bowl, combine the shallots, vinegar, lemon juice, orange juice, oil, salt, and pepper. Whisk to mix.

In a bowl, combine the fennel slices, red bell pepper, and chives. Add half of the vinaigrette and toss to mix. Set aside.

Sprinkle the tuna steaks with salt and pepper on both sides. In a heavy sauté pan, heat the peanut oil over high heat. Add the tuna steaks and sear on both sides just until the outside is cooked and the inside is rare, 2 to 3 minutes on each side. Transfer to a platter and let rest for 10 minutes.

Divide the fennel and red pepper salad among 4 plates. Slice the tuna about ½ inch thick and arrange the slices over the salad. Drizzle with the remaining vinaigrette, garnish the plates with the fennel fronds, and serve.

ANNIE'S TIP

Either ahi or albacore tuna will do for light small plates such as this one and the seared tuna with cabbage slaw on page 36. With both varieties, the trick is to sear the tuna over a very hot fire, then allow it to set up for 10 minutes before slicing. That way, the outside ¼ inch of the tuna is cooked to a creamy beige while the center is rosy, the flesh slices neatly without flaking, and the inside is firm, not flabby.

MARGRIT'S FISH TERRINE
with Beurre Blanc–Type Sauce
Serves 8 to 10

A terrine is always special. It requires a bit of forethought and a few extra steps on the part of the cook. Margrit and Bob love to serve this one in their home on Wappo Hill for dinner parties that are intimate but still a bit formal. Blanching the romaine leaves has the surprising effect of turning them a bright green that doesn't fade during the oven cooking. To garnish the plates, Margrit adds a final wide stroke of red, the tomato wedges, which also add a soft-sour note that blends beautifully with the other flavors.

Margrit's variation on traditional beurre blanc is the addition of fish stock. Sometimes, though, in a time crunch, she foregoes the stock and increases the vinegar and wine by a tablespoon or so each. With or without the stock, her method of making beurre blanc is quite different from Annie's (page 158), demonstrating how things change even while they remain the same.

Serve with a FUMÉ BLANC

1¹/₂ pounds firm white fish fillets, such as red snapper or petrale sole, cut into 1-inch chunks

8 to 10 large, unblemished romaine lettuce leaves

3 egg whites

2 tablespoons dry white wine, such as Fumé Blanc

1 teaspoon brandy

¹/₂ teaspoon finely chopped lemon zest

¹/₂ teaspoon finely chopped orange zest

1 tablespoon freshly squeezed lemon juice

¹/₄ teaspoon finely chopped fresh ginger

1 tablespoon finely chopped shallot

1 cup heavy cream

2 tablespoons chopped fresh flat-leaf parsley

2 teaspoons kosher salt

¹/₄ teaspoon freshly ground white pepper

BEURRE BLANC–TYPE SAUCE

1 large shallot, finely chopped

¹/₂ cup fish stock (see sidebar, page 40)

¹/₄ cup white wine vinegar

¹/₄ cup dry white wine

1¹/₂ cups cold unsalted butter, cut into 1-inch pieces

¹/₂ teaspoon finely chopped lemon zest

1 teaspoon freshly squeezed lemon juice

Kosher salt and freshly ground white pepper

2 tomatoes, peeled, seeded, and cut into 4 or 5 wedges for garnish (page xx)

(continued)

Put the fish chunks in the freezer to partially freeze, 10 to 15 minutes. (Don't leave them longer, or they will freeze solid.)

In a large pot of salted boiling water, blanch the romaine leaves, pressing down to submerge them, for 30 seconds without returning to a boil. Drain in a colander and spread the leaves on a towel to dry.

In two batches, in a food processor, combine the fish, egg whites, wine, brandy, zests, lemon juice, ginger, and shallot and process until finely puréed. With the machine running, gradually add half of the cream to each batch, until the mixture is stiff enough to hold peaks. Combine the 2 batches in a bowl and stir in the parsley, salt, and pepper.

Preheat the oven to 375°F. Butter a 6-cup loaf pan. Line it with all but 2 of the romaine leaves, positioning them so the tips hang over the sides. Fill with the fish mixture, spreading it evenly with a spatula or your hands. Lay the 2 reserved leaves on top and fold the overhang up and over the top. Cover the pan with aluminum foil, pinching around the edges to seal.

Put the terrine in a larger pan and place in the oven. Add hot water to come one-third of the way up the sides of the terrine, and bake until firm to the touch in the center, 45 to 50 minutes. Remove from the oven and lift the terrine out of the water. Puncture the foil to allow steam to escape and set aside to cool for 2 hours. Serve at room temperature, or cool the terrine completely, refrigerate it for up to 3 days, and serve it cold without the beurre blanc.

To make the sauce, in a small saucepan, combine the shallot, fish stock, vinegar, and wine over medium-high heat. Bring to a boil and cook until reduced by half, about 5 minutes. Decrease the heat to medium-low and gradually whisk in the butter one piece at a time until emulsified. Stir in the lemon zest and juice and season with salt and pepper. Set aside over warm water to keep warm. Use without reheating or the sauce will break (see Annie's Tip, page 158).

To serve, unmold the terrine and cut it into 8 to 10 slices, keeping the green border. Arrange the slices on plates and drizzle with the warm sauce. Garnish with the tomato wedges and serve right away.

FISH STOCK

To make 2 1/2 cups of a quick and easy fish stock, place about 1/2 pound of trimmings and bones from nonfatty white fish (such as halibut, trout, or snapper) in a pot. Add 1/4 of a small yellow or white onion, 1/2 of a bay leaf, a sprig of fresh thyme or a small pinch of dried thyme, and 1 whole clove. Add water to cover by 1 inch and bring to a boil over medium-high heat. Decrease the heat to medium, partially cover, and simmer for 30 to 35 minutes, until the onion is cooked through and the liquid is slightly reduced. Strain through a fine mesh sieve into a bowl and allow to cool completely before using. The stock may be refrigerated for up to 2 days or frozen for up to 2 weeks.

CHILLED UDON NOODLES
with Shrimp and Shiitake Mushrooms
Serves 4

In a kind of Asian pasta salad with California overtones, Annie chills thick, wheaty udon noodles and tosses them with a zesty, almost Thai dressing. Dried udon can be found on many supermarket shelves, and fresh udon is often available in the refrigerated produce section.

Serve with a COASTAL SAUVIGNON BLANC

8 ounces fresh or dried udon noodles

1 teaspoon plus 1 tablespoon peanut oil, plus extra
   for coating

3/4 pound medium shrimp, peeled and deveined, tails on

8 ounces shiitake mushrooms, stemmed and sliced
   1/4 inch thick

Kosher salt

DRESSING

2 tablespoons minced garlic

2 teaspoons finely chopped fresh ginger

4 scallions, including green parts, thinly sliced

1/2 cup chopped cilantro

2 jalapeño chiles, seeded and finely chopped

1/2 teaspoon crushed red pepper flakes

1/4 cup peanut oil

1/4 cup rice wine vinegar

1/4 cup low-sodium soy sauce

Cook the noodles in boiling salted water until tender, 5 minutes for fresh, 7 minutes for dried. Drain, coat with peanut oil to prevent sticking, and allow to cool. Refrigerate for at least 1 hour, or until chilled.

In a sauté pan, heat the 1 teaspoon peanut oil over high heat. Add the shrimp and sauté until barely firm and turning pink, about 2 minutes. Transfer to a bowl and allow to cool. Refrigerate until chilled. In the same pan, heat the 1 tablespoon peanut oil over medium-high heat and add the mushrooms. Sprinkle with salt and sauté until wilted and beginning to turn golden, about 3 minutes. Remove from the heat and set aside at room temperature until cool, or up to 1 hour.

In a large bowl, combine all the dressing ingredients and mix well. Add the noodles, shrimp, and mushrooms. Toss together and serve.

SHRIMP AND FLAGEOLET BEANS
with Baby Arugula and Red Bell Pepper Aioli

Serves 6

Annie created this starter for the 2001 Napa Valley Wine Auction. She chose flageolets because they cook up soft and sweet, the essence of legume goodness, without collapsing into a mush; they pair well with seafood, especially shrimp; *and* they hold up well, so can be prepared in advance. This is a recipe with lots of components so a game plan is included to keep the procedure simple.

Flageolets are available in gourmet food markets and natural foods stores. White cannellini beans or great Northern beans would both be excellent substitutes.

Serve with a FUMÉ BLANC

SHRIMP

1 pound jumbo shrimp (16 to 20 count), shelled and deveined, tails on

1 teaspoon finely chopped lemon zest

2 teaspoons thinly sliced shallot

1/2 teaspoon finely chopped serrano or jalapeño chile

2 teaspoons chopped fresh flat-leaf parsley

1 teaspoon chopped fresh thyme

1 tablespoon extra virgin olive oil

1/4 teaspoon kosher salt

1/4 teaspoon freshly ground black pepper

FLAGEOLETS

1 1/2 cups flageolet beans

1 tablespoon extra virgin olive oil

3 tablespoons finely chopped yellow onion

1/2 teaspoon minced garlic

1/2 cup finely chopped fennel

1 small carrot, peeled and cut into 1/4-inch dice

1 teaspoon finely chopped fresh thyme

6 cups water

1/2 bay leaf

1 1/2 teaspoons kosher salt

RED BELL PEPPER AIOLI

1 large egg

1 red bell pepper, roasted and peeled (page xx)

2 tablespoons freshly squeezed lemon juice

1 clove garlic, minced

1 2/3 cups extra virgin olive oil

1 teaspoon kosher salt

VINAIGRETTE

1 tablespoon balsamic vinegar

1 teaspoon sherry vinegar

1 tablespoon finely chopped shallot

1/2 teaspoon finely chopped lemon zest

2 tablespoons extra virgin olive oil

1 cup packed baby arugula leaves

1 cup cherry tomato halves

To prepare the shrimp, toss them with the zest, shallot, chile, parsley, thyme, oil, salt, and pepper in a bowl. Cover and refrigerate for at least 4 hours or up to overnight.

Soak the flageolets overnight in water to cover. (Or, use the quick-soak method: bring the beans and water to cover to a boil for 1 minute. Remove from the heat and let stand for 1 hour.) Drain and rinse.

To cook the beans, heat the oil in a large, heavy pot over medium-high heat. Add the onion, garlic, fennel, carrot, and thyme. Decrease the heat to medium-low, and sauté the vegetables until wilted, 10 minutes. Add the flageolets, water, and bay leaf. Bring to a boil over high heat, then decrease the heat to maintain a simmer. Cook, uncovered, until the beans are soft, about 2 hours. Remove from the heat, stir in the salt, remove the bay leaf, and let the beans cool in the liquid. Use right away, set aside at room temperature for up to 2 hours, or refrigerate in the liquid for up to 3 days. (Note: the beans may also be cooked in a pressure cooker for 25 minutes after coming to pressure, plus 5 minutes standing time before adding the salt.)

To make the aioli, blend the egg in a food processor. Add the bell pepper, lemon juice, and garlic, and process until smooth. With the machine running, gradually add the oil until emulsified. Stir in the salt. Cover and refrigerate until ready to use, or up to 2 days.

To make the vinaigrette, whisk all the ingredients together in a small bowl.

To cook the shrimp, heat a nonstick sauté pan over medium-high heat. Add the shrimp and cook, turning each with tongs, until barely pink and firm, 3 to 5 minutes. Use right away or set aside at room temperature for up to 1 hour.

To serve, drain the beans and toss with the shrimp in a large bowl. Add the vinaigrette and toss to mix. Gently fold in the arugula and cherry tomatoes. Mound on 6 plates and garnish with a dollop of the aioli.

GAME PLAN

Up to 3 days ahead:
* Cook the flageolets, allow to cool, and refrigerate.

Two days ahead:
* Make the red bell pepper aioli, cover, and refrigerate.

One day ahead:
* Marinate the shrimp and refrigerate.

Two hours ahead:
* Make the vinaigrette and set aside at room temperature.
* Prepare the arugula leaves and cut the cherry tomatoes in half.

One hour ahead:
* Cook the shrimp (they don't need to be brought to room temperature before cooking), and set aside at room temperature.

Just before serving:
* Drain the flageolets (they don't need to be rbrought to room temperature before using).
* Toss the shrimp and flageolets together with the other ingredients.

LOBSTER TARTLETS
with Leek and Fennel Confit, Haricots Verts, and Lobster Sauce

Serves 4

For the opening of the To Kalon cellars in March 2001, the state-of-the-art underground oak-barrel fermentation rooms at the Robert Mondavi Winery, Annie served these lobster tartlets as the first course of a splendid sit-down meal. As befits such an extravagant dish, the recipe calls for an extravagant amount of prep work. To guide the home cook in getting to the finish in professional style, Annie offers her game plan notes, starting from the day before.

Serve with a CHARDONNAY

1 (1¼-pound) live lobster

LOBSTER SAUCE

1½ tablespoons extra virgin olive oil

1 leek, white part only, coarsely chopped

½ celery stalk, coarsely chopped

½ carrot, peeled and coarsely chopped

1 tablespoon tomato paste

½ cup Fumé Blanc or other dry white wine

PASTRY DOUGH

1¼ cups all-purpose flour

¾ teaspoon kosher salt

¾ cup cold unsalted butter, cut into ½-inch bits

1 egg yolk beaten with 3 tablespoons ice water

LEEK AND FENNEL CONFIT

2 tablespoons unsalted butter

2 tablespoons water

½ cup chopped leeks, white part only

½ cup chopped fennel

Kosher salt and freshly ground black pepper

¼ pound haricots verts, stem ends trimmed

½ teaspoon finely chopped shallots

2 tablespoons champagne vinegar

⅓ cup extra virgin olive oil

1 cup micro-greens or mixed baby greens

8 tiny cherry tomatoes, halved, for garnish

To cook the lobster, bring a large pot of salted water to a rolling boil over high heat. Drop in the lobster, cover, and cook for 7 minutes, counting from the start, not from when the water comes back to a boil. With kitchen tongs, transfer the lobster to a plate and allow to cool enough to handle.

Preheat the oven to 400°F. Pull the small swimmeret legs off the lobster body and place on a baking sheet. Twist the large claws off the lobster, crack the shells, and remove the meat intact. Add the claw shells to the baking sheet and place the claw meat in a bowl. Cut the body lengthwise down the belly side, remove the meat, and cut it into ¾-inch pieces. Put in the bowl with the claw meat, cover, and refrigerate. Add the body shells to the baking sheet and roast until bright red and slightly golden brown, about 25 minutes.

To make the sauce, in a large sauté pan, heat the oil over medium-high heat. Add the leek, celery, and carrot and sauté until golden, about 5 minutes. Stir in the tomato paste, wine, and roasted lobster shells. Add water to come three-quarters of the way up the sides of the ingredients and bring to a boil. Decrease the heat to maintain a gentle simmer and cook until reduced to about 1½ cups, about 30 minutes. Pass through a fine mesh sieve, return to medium-high heat, and cook until reduced to about ½ cup, 10 to 15 minutes.

(continued)

To make the pastry dough, combine the flour and salt in a food processor. Add the butter and pulse briefly until the mixture is in pea-sized bits. Add the egg yolk mixture to the flour and pulse until blended enough to gather together. Form into a ball and wrap in plastic wrap. Press into a thick disk and refrigerate for at least 30 minutes or up to overnight. Remove the dough from the refrigerator and let rest at room temperature for 15 minutes before rolling out.

To make the pastry shells, preheat the oven to 375°F. On a floured work surface, roll the dough out and cut it into four 5-inch-diameter rounds. Fit the rounds into four 3-inch tartlet pans. Prick the bottom of each shell with a fork and bake until golden, 13 to 15 minutes. Remove from the oven and set aside.

To make the confit, heat the butter and water together in a sauté pan over medium heat until the butter melts. Add the leeks and fennel, season with salt and pepper, and cook until most of the liquid evaporates and the vegetables are soft, about 5 minutes. Remove from the heat and set aside.

In a large pot of salted boiling water, cook the haricots verts until limp but not soft, 5 to 6 minutes. Drain and set aside.

Just before serving, preheat the oven to 375°F. In a small bowl, whisk together the shallots, vinegar, and oil. Toss the lettuces with some of the vinaigrette, just enough to moisten the leaves.

To assemble the tartlets, remove the lobster meat from the refrigerator and let sit for 15 minutes to take off the chill. Fill each shell with one-fourth of the leek and fennel confit. Arrange one-fourth of the lobster meat, haricots verts, and cherry tomato halves over the mixture in each tartlet. Place the tartlets in the oven and heat for 5 minutes.

To serve, transfer the warmed tartlets to 4 plates. Drizzle some of the champagne vinaigrette over the top. Strew the dressed greens over all and encircle with a little of the reduced sauce. Serve right away.

GAME PLAN

One day ahead:
- Make the pastry dough and line the tartlet shells. Wrap the tartlets in plastic wrap and refrigerate.
- Cook the lobster and make the sauce. Cover separately and refrigerate.

Several hours before serving:
- Bake the pastry shells and set them aside at room temperature.
- Make the leek and fennel confit and set aside at room temperature.
- Cook the haricots verts and set aside at room temperature.
- Make the dressing and set aside at room temperature.
- Cut the cherry tomatoes in half.

Just before serving:
- Heat the sauce.
- Toss the greens with the dressing.
- Bake the tarts and assemble the dish.

ANNIE'S CRAB CAKES
with Tartar Sauce

Serves 8

One day, as Annie was wondering how to make a batch of crab cakes lighter, she had the idea that adding egg whites might fluff and moisten the mixture without making it soggy. It was one of those Eureka! moments, and that's how she makes her crab cakes now. She garnishes them with a classic tartar sauce; that didn't need any fixing.

Serve with a SAUVIGNON BLANC *or* CHARDONNAY

TARTAR SAUCE

1¹/₂ cups lemon mayonnaise (page 36)

¹/₄ cup finely chopped scallions, including green parts

¹/₂ cup finely chopped fresh flat-leaf parsley

¹/₃ cup finely chopped French cornichons

¹/₂ teaspoon coarsely ground black pepper

CRAB CAKES

2 tablespoons unsalted butter

¹/₂ cup finely chopped celery

¹/₂ cup finely chopped yellow onion

1 pound fresh crabmeat, picked over for shell

2 cups fine bread crumbs (page xix)

¹/₄ cup chopped fresh flat-leaf parsley, plus 8 sprigs
     for garnish

1 tablespoon chopped fresh thyme

1 tablespoon chopped fresh chives

1 teaspoon Worcestershire sauce

1 tablespoon Dijon mustard

1 teaspoon Tabasco sauce

4 eggs, separated

Kosher salt

Vegetable oil, for frying

To make the tartar sauce, combine all the ingredients in a bowl and mix with a fork. Cover and refrigerate up to overnight.

To make the crab cakes, preheat the oven to 375°F. Melt the butter in a sauté pan over medium-high heat. Add the celery and onion and sauté for 5 minutes, until wilted. In a large bowl, combine the celery, onion, crab, bread crumbs, the chopped parsley, the thyme, chives, Worcestershire sauce, mustard, and Tabasco and mix well with a fork or your hands. Stir in the egg yolks. Whip the egg whites to stiff peaks and gently fold into the crab mixture. Season with salt. Form into 8 balls approximately 2¹/₂ inches in diameter.

To cook the crab cakes, lightly grease a nonstick sauté pan with oil and place over medium-high heat. Brown half the cakes on one side for about 3 minutes. Transfer to a baking sheet, browned side down. Repeat with the remaining cakes. Bake in the oven until firm and slightly golden, about 8 minutes.

Serve the crab cakes on plates, garnished with a spoonful of tartar sauce and a sprig of parsley.

JUMBO SHRIMP
with Celery, Roma Tomatoes, and Watercress
Serves 6

When the wedding party assembled for Annie's son Quinn's rehearsal dinner, it was a hot day in the Napa Valley, some might say too hot to cook. Annie, the "caterer," rose to the occasion with this light-on-the-cooking, elegant opener.

Serve with a FUMÉ BLANC *or* PINTO GRIGIO

1¹/₂ pounds jumbo shrimp (16 to 20 count), shelled and deveined, tails on

1 tablespoon kosher salt

5 celery stalks, very thinly sliced

2 Roma tomatoes, peeled, seeded, and julienned (page xx)

10 kalamata olives, pitted and coarsely chopped (page xx)

1 tablespoon chopped fresh flat-leaf parsley

2 tablespoons freshly squeezed lemon juice

¹/₄ cup extra virgin olive oil

Kosher salt and freshly ground black pepper

2 bunches hydroponic watercress, or 6 cups tender tops from regular watercress

Put the shrimp in a sauté pan, add the salt and water to cover, and place the pan over high heat. Just as the water comes to a boil, remove it from the heat and drain the shrimp. In a bowl, combine the shrimp, celery, tomatoes, olives, parsley, lemon juice, oil, and salt and pepper to taste. Toss well. Arrange the watercress on 6 plates. Top with the shrimp salad and serve.

Patio dining at the Vineyard Room.

BREADED SCALLOPS
with Rémoulade Sauce and Micro-Greens

Serves 4

Micro-greens are essentially lettuce sprouts. Annie gathers them fresh from the garden outside the kitchen door at the winery and uses them to lend a delicate finishing touch to crunchy, breaded scallop medallions and nippy rémoulade sauce. Mixed baby lettuces can substitute for the micro-greens.

Serve with a FUMÉ BLANC

RÉMOULADE SAUCE

1 large egg

1 egg yolk

2 tablespoons Dijon mustard

1 cup vegetable oil

2 tablespoons prepared horseradish

1/4 lemon, seeded

1/4 cup chopped scallions, including green parts

1 tablespoon white wine vinegar

Dash of Tabasco sauce

1 tablespoon Worcestershire sauce

1 tablespoon minced garlic

2 teaspoons kosher salt

1 tablespoon ketchup

1/4 cup chopped fresh flat-leaf parsley

SCALLOPS

Peanut or grapeseed oil, for frying

1 pound sea scallops, muscle removed, halved crosswise to make 1/2-inch-thick rounds

1 egg, well-beaten

1 cup very fine bread crumbs (page xix)

1/4 cup micro-greens, for garnish

To make the rémoulade sauce, blend the egg and egg yolk together in a food processor. With the machine running, add the mustard and then gradually add the oil in a thin stream. One at a time, blend in the horseradish, lemon, scallions, vinegar, Tabasco, Worcestershire sauce, garlic, salt, ketchup, and parsley until the mixture is homogenized and the lemon rind is finely chopped. Cover and refrigerate up to overnight.

To prepare the scallops, preheat the oven to 375°F. Line a baking sheet with a double layer of paper towels. Pour the oil into a large, heavy sauté pan to a depth of 1/2 inch. Heat over medium-high heat.

Dip the scallops into the beaten egg and coat with bread crumbs on all sides. Fry the scallops, in batches so as not to crowd them, until golden on both sides, 30 seconds per side. Transfer to the prepared baking sheet as you go. Place the scallops, still on the baking sheet, in the oven and cook for 3 minutes, until firm to the touch.

To serve, arrange 3 pieces of scallop on each plate and drizzle the rémoulade sauce over them. Garnish each serving with a large pinch of micro-greens in the center and serve.

Salads:
Side to Main

S ALAD IS A THEME that plays throughout Annie's and Margrit's cuisine. Both often use a handful of dressed greens tossed with a tangy vinaigrette to add a spry taste and verdant color to their entrée plates. (Margrit notes that "after some years, Bob agreed it would be okay to have the salad as garnish alongside the entrée rather than before or after it.") For alfresco dining, the salad might be a composition that includes meat, fish, or poultry with vegetables and greens, all arranged together to make a light meal or buffet dish. This chapter is a veritable treasure chest of ways to combine salad ingredients—some cooked, some raw—and includes three special side salads, one of bread, one of pasta, and another of potato, that are especially good for picnic fare.

GREEN SALAD

Serves 6 as a first course, 10 to 12 as garnish

For salad greens, Annie is partial to baby lettuces while her mother more often chooses sturdier leaves, like escarole or romaine. Any will do for this recipe which, as well as garnish, can serve as a separate course.

BASIC VINAIGRETTE

1/4 cup red wine vinegar, preferably Margrit's homemade

1 tablespoon finely chopped shallots

Pinch of kosher salt

Pinch of freshly ground black pepper

1/3 cup extra virgin olive oil

12 cups mixed salad greens

To make the vinaigrette, combine the vinegar, shallots, salt, and pepper in a small bowl. Gradually whisk in the oil until the mixture is emulsified. Use right away or set aside at room temperature for up to several hours, whisking again before using.

Put the salad greens in a large bowl and drizzle with the vinaigrette. Toss ever so gently so as not to bruise the leaves and serve right away.

MARGRIT'S HOMEMADE VINEGAR

"Maybe thirty or more years ago, I discovered a 'mother' in a commercial wine bottle. This is the prized viscous sediment occasionally found in the bottom of a wine and is used as the source of vinegar. I started my first vinegar by using two bottles of wine mothers, one white and one red. They both developed, but I liked the red better. I kept adding mother, but began using only Cabernet Sauvignon. After about one year, I had a good magnum of red wine vinegar. I expanded a bit by using this mother starter for two or three magnums more. Now, years later, the vinegar is still from these original starters. (I used the older one up and keep adding leftover wine to the newer bottles.) Once a year I check for new mothers: it depends on the year. If there are such deposits, I transfer the vinegar and strain out the mother. I tried developing vinegar in small wooden casks but decided it came out too woody. Because Cabernet Sauvignons are already wood aged, there is enough wood flavor, so I keep the vinegar in the magnum bottles. Room temperature seems to be just fine. If you decide to try making your own vinegar, use a ball of gauze to close the bottle (don't use a cork), because a little oxygen is necessary for an aerobic fermentation."

PANZANELLA

Serves 4 to 6 as a side dish

The annual Napa Valley Wine Auction picnic is a gala affair with hundreds of people dining *sur l'herbes* on the sunny grounds of Meadowood Resort. During this charity event a good time is had by all, while exceedingly valuable reserve wines are auctioned, with proceeds going to Queen of the Valley Hospital. For the 2001 auction, Annie thought, what better combination than bread and wine? What better dish than panzanella to accompany the wine tastings? For the occasion, Annie used two hundred loaves of bread and served two thousand people. Here, she's reduced the proportions to serve a modest four to six.

Serve with a SANGIOVESE

½ loaf (about ½ pound) day-old French or Italian bread, cut into 1-inch-thick slices

2 tablespoons plus ½ cup extra virgin olive oil

1 English cucumber, peeled, seeded, and cut into ½-inch dice

Kosher salt

2 cloves garlic, minced

⅓ cup red wine vinegar

5 tomatoes (1½ to 2 pounds), seeded and cut into ½-inch cubes, juices reserved

1 red onion, cut into ½-inch dice

½ cup loosely packed fresh basil leaves, torn

Leaves from 1 small head radicchio, torn into bite-sized pieces (2 to 3 cups)

Leaves from 1 small bunch frisée, torn into bite-sized pieces

Freshly ground black pepper

½ cup (2½ ounces) crumbled feta cheese, preferably French feta

Preheat the oven to 375°F. Brush the bread with the 2 tablespoons oil, spread on a baking sheet, and toast until slightly golden and dried out, about 15 minutes. Remove from the oven, allow to cool enough to handle, then tear into 1-inch pieces. Set aside.

Spread the diced cucumber on a paper towel and sprinkle with salt. Set aside to drain for 20 minutes, then rinse in a colander. Pat dry.

In a large bowl, whisk together the garlic, vinegar, and the ½ cup oil. Add the cucumber, tomatoes, onion, basil, radicchio, frisée, and bread. Toss to mix and season with salt and pepper. Let stand until the bread has absorbed some of the juices, 15 to 20 minutes. Sprinkle the cheese over the top and serve right away.

PANZANELLA FOR A CROWD

For such a large quantity of bread salad, Annie had about ten volunteers, plus the kitchen staff (six people) from the Meadowood Resort, and three or four more close friends to help. She started ordering everything about six weeks prior and received the goods five days before the event. There were long tables devoted only to bread cutting, another table for tomatoes, another for the lettuces, and so on. In a very intensive last-minute preparation, all hands-on, everything was actually put together about a half hour before the panzanella was served because the bread would get too soggy if done more in advance.

MARGRIT'S MACARONI SALAD
with Tomatoes, Mushrooms, and Basil Vinaigrette
Serves 4 to 6 as a side dish

Margrit's macaroni salad is a full-to-overflowing bowl of elbow noodles plumped with mushrooms and tomatoes, dressed with an assertive vinaigrette and bound with Parmesan cheese. Sometimes she uses corkscrew, or other similar-shaped pasta, instead of elbow macaroni.

Serve with a FUMÉ BLANC

8 ounces small elbow macaroni

1 teaspoon extra virgin olive oil

MUSHROOMS

Extra virgin olive oil, for coating the pan

1/4 pound shiitake or cremini mushrooms, stemmed and sliced 1/4 inch thick

1 clove garlic

Pinch of kosher salt

BASIL VINAIGRETTE

1 large shallot, finely chopped

1 teaspoon balsamic vinegar

1/4 cup light olive oil

1/4 cup chopped fresh basil

1 pound ripe tomatoes, peeled and coarsely chopped into 1/2-inch chunks (page xx)

2/3 cup freshly grated Parmesan cheese

Kosher salt and freshly ground black pepper

In a large pot of salted boiling water, cook the pasta according to the package instructions until al dente. Drain, toss with the oil to prevent sticking, and transfer to a large bowl. Set aside at room temperature.

To cook the mushrooms, coat a nonstick sauté pan with oil and place over medium-high heat. Add the mushrooms, garlic, and salt. Sauté, stirring frequently, until the mushrooms are limp and slightly golden, 2 to 3 minutes. Set aside.

To make the vinaigrette, combine all the ingredients in a small bowl and whisk to mix.

To assemble the salad, add the mushrooms, vinaigrette, and tomatoes to the macaroni and toss to mix. Add 1/3 cup of the cheese, season with salt and pepper, and toss again. Serve at room temperature or chilled, with the remaining cheese on the side.

A Fourth of July Family Barbecue

On the Fourth of July, the family party is at Annie's house. Nestled at the foot of the gently sloping hills outside Santa Rosa, with a large deck and a pool to jump into for cooling off on a hot day, it's the perfect place for a barbecue. Annie turns out a buffet of summer delights, and everyone helps. The food is laid out picnic style with white and red wines informally set on the table.

Jumbo Shrimp (page 48, the shrimp only)
with Rémoulade Sauce (page 49)

Tomato-Pesto Pizza (page 11)

Green Salad (page 53)

Margrit's Macaroni Salad with Tomatoes, Mushrooms,
and Basil Vinaigrette (page 55)

Châteaubriand with Parsley Sauce (page 89)

Grilled Corn on the Cob (page 87)

Bing Cherry Crisp (page 185, variation)

Robert Mondavi Chardonnay

Robert Mondavi Merlot

AMERICAN-STYLE POTATO SALAD

Serves 8 to 10 as a side dish

Potato salad is beloved picnic fare for both Annie and Margrit. Annie often serves this American-style potato salad for family Fourth of July get-togethers. See pages 128 and 153 for two other potato salads.

DRESSING

2 egg yolks

2 tablespoons freshly squeezed lemon juice

2 tablespoons white wine vinegar

1 clove garlic, minced

1 tablespoon coarse-grain mustard

1/2 teaspoon dry mustard

1 teaspoon kosher salt

1/2 teaspoon freshly ground black pepper

1 cup extra virgin olive oil

SALAD

4 pounds red, white, or yellow potatoes

1/2 pound bacon

1/2 cup thinly sliced scallions, including green parts

1/2 cup finely chopped red onion

1/2 cup chopped fresh flat-leaf parsley

2 celery stalks, chopped

6 hard-cooked eggs, coarsely chopped

1 tablespoon freshly squeezed lemon juice

Kosher salt and freshly ground black pepper

To make the dressing, combine the egg yolks, lemon juice, vinegar, garlic, wet and dry mustards, salt, and pepper in a food processor and process until blended. With the machine running, gradually add the oil until emulsified. Transfer the dressing to a small bowl. Use right away or cover and refrigerate up to overnight.

Put the potatoes in a saucepan and cover with cold water. Bring to a boil over high heat, decrease the heat to medium-high, and cook until tender, about 25 minutes. Drain and set aside until cool enough to handle.

While the potatoes cool, fry the bacon in an ungreased sauté pan over medium-high heat, turning occasionally, until crisp, about 10 minutes. Transfer to paper towels to drain.

Peel the potatoes and cut them into 1/2-inch dice. Place in a large bowl. Coarsely chop the bacon and add it to the bowl. Add the scallions, red onion, parsley, celery, and chopped eggs. Toss gently to mix, add the dressing, and toss gently again. Stir in the lemon juice and salt and pepper to taste. Cover and refrigerate until chilled, then serve right away.

SLIGHTLY ASIAN ROASTED CHICKEN SALAD

Serves 6 as a main course

Roasted chicken opens a world of salad possibilities. With the variation suggestion below, here are two of Margrit's ways to dress roasted chicken for an ambrosial salad plate. If you're in a pinch for time, simply simmer 4 chicken breast halves in lightly salted chicken stock combined with a dry white wine—3 cups stock to 1 cup wine—until opaque throughout, about 10 minutes. Allow to cool and continue with the recipe.

Serve with a SAUVIGNON BLANC *or* FUMÉ BLANC

1 (3¹/₂- to 4-pound) chicken

¹/₂ cup white sesame seeds

¹/₂ cup slivered almonds

1 teaspoon finely chopped fresh ginger

1 shallot, finely chopped

2 teaspoons finely chopped or slivered lemon zest

3 tablespoons freshly squeezed lemon juice

1 tablespoon low-sodium soy sauce

1 tablespoon sesame oil

¹/₄ cup light olive or peanut oil

1 teaspoon kosher salt

¹/₂ teaspoon freshly ground black pepper

2 ripe avocados

1 large tomato, peeled and cut into ¹/₂-inch dice (page xx)

6 cups torn romaine or other lettuce leaves

6 sprigs cilantro, for garnish

Preheat the oven to 400°F. Put the chicken in a roasting pan and roast until the thigh meat is no longer pink and the skin is crackly and golden, 45 minutes to 1 hour, depending on the size. Set aside until cool enough to handle.

While the chicken roasts, spread the sesame seeds on a baking sheet and toast in the oven until golden, about 5 minutes. Separately toast the almonds on a baking sheet until they begin to turn golden, about 3 minutes.

In a small bowl, combine the ginger, shallot, zest, lemon juice, soy sauce, sesame oil, olive oil, salt, and pepper. Whisk to mix.

To make the salad, peel, seed, and cut the avocados into 1-inch cubes. Cut the chicken meat off the bones and slice or tear into bite-sized strips. Put in a bowl and toss with the sesame seeds. Add the avocados, tomato, and dressing and gently toss. Arrange the lettuce on a platter or 6 plates. Mound the chicken mixture on the leaves, sprinkle the almonds over the top, garnish with a cilantro sprig, and serve.

VARIATION

To vary the Asian theme, use peanuts instead of almonds, garlic instead of shallot in the dressing, and add thinly sliced scallions, a pinch of crushed red pepper flakes, and cilantro leaves to the chicken mixture. Replace the tomato and avocado with julienned cucumber.

GRILLED CHICKEN BREAST SALAD
with Romaine Lettuce, Kalamata Olives, and Blue Cheese

Serves 4 as a main course

For a main-course salad, Annie sets grilled whole chicken breasts atop romaine lettuce. To add extra flavor, she marinates the chicken in some of the dressing before grilling. For the cheese, she likes Point Reyes blue from nearby Marin County because it's creamy and not too salty.

Serve with a PINOT NOIR

DRESSING

1/2 cup extra virgin olive oil

3 tablespoons red wine vinegar

1 tablespoon Dijon mustard

1 teaspoon finely chopped shallot

1 small clove garlic, minced

Pinch of kosher salt

Freshly ground black pepper

4 small skinless, boneless chicken breast halves

4 ounces pancetta, cut into 1/4-inch pieces

6 cups baby romaine lettuce leaves

1 cup kalamata olives, pitted (page xx)

2 cups small cherry tomatoes, halved

3/4 cup crumbled blue cheese

To make the dressing, whisk together the oil, vinegar, mustard, shallot, garlic, salt, and pepper in a small bowl. Put the chicken breasts in a dish, add 2 tablespoons of the dressing, and turn to coat all over. Cover and refrigerate for 2 to 4 hours. Remove from the refrigerator 20 minutes before cooking.

Prepare a medium-hot fire in a charcoal grill or preheat a gas grill to medium-high. Grill the breasts, turning once or twice, until golden on the outside and no longer pink but still moist in the center, 14 to 16 minutes. Transfer to a plate and let rest for 5 minutes.

In a small sauté pan over medium heat, fry the pancetta until just barely crisp, about 5 minutes. Transfer to paper towels to drain.

Toss the lettuce with the remaining dressing. Add the pancetta, olives, tomatoes, and cheese and gently toss again. Divide among 4 plates and place a chicken breast on top of each serving. Serve right away, while the chicken is still warm.

GRILLED FLANK STEAK
with Capers and Lemon Zest on a Bed of Salad Greens

Serves 4 as a main course

Annie serves grilled flank steak *en salade* on summer days when it's too hot to cook indoors. She cross-hatch cuts the steak to keep it from curling so it can be neatly sliced, and also because she thinks it looks pretty.

Serve with a ZINFANDEL

1 pound flank steak

Extra virgin olive oil, for coating, plus 1/3 cup for dressing

Kosher salt and freshly ground black pepper

1 tablespoon capers, rinsed

1 teaspoon finely chopped lemon zest

1 tablespoon minced garlic

1 large red bell pepper, thinly sliced

1 large tomato, cut into small wedges

1/3 cup freshly squeezed lemon juice

6 cups torn salad greens

Prepare a medium-hot fire in a charcoal grill, preheat a gas grill to medium-high, or preheat the broiler. Score the steak on one side in a cross-hatch pattern, coat with oil, and sprinkle with salt and pepper on both sides. Place on the grill or in the broiler and cook, turning once, for 3 to 4 minutes on each side for rare to medium rare. Remove from the heat and set aside for at least 20 or up to 40 minutes to allow the juices to settle.

Cut the steak crosswise into thin slices and place in a bowl. Add the capers, zest, garlic, bell pepper, tomato, lemon juice, and the 1/3 cup oil and toss to mix. Spread the greens on a serving platter or 4 plates. Top with the steak mixture and serve right away.

ANNIE'S CAESAR SALAD
with Pan-Roasted Garlic and Coddled-Egg Dressing

Serves 4 as a first course

It's a long way from 1924 Tijuana, the reputed birthplace of Caesar salad, to twenty-first-century northern California, where it has taken on cult status to the extent that it appears on the menu of almost every café and bistro. That's because people love it. Annie offers a version true to its roots, and adds the improvisation of roasting the garlic and partially cooking the egg (see Annie's Tips). She never "holds the anchovies." In fact, she unabashedly drapes fillets of them across the top of the salad. For a full meal, top it with sliced smoked or plain-cooked chicken.

Serve with a CHARDONNAY

½ cup extra virgin olive oil

½ baguette, cut into ½- to ¾-inch cubes
   (about 1½ cups)

3 large cloves garlic

1 large egg

½ teaspoon white wine vinegar

2 tablespoons freshly squeezed lemon juice

½ teaspoon kosher salt

⅛ teaspoon freshly ground black pepper

Dash of Worcestershire sauce

12 cups inner romaine lettuce leaves, chilled

½ cup freshly grated Parmesan cheese

8 flat anchovy fillets (optional)

In a sauté pan, heat ¼ cup of the oil over medium-low heat. Add the bread and garlic and toss to coat. Cook until the bread and garlic are golden, 7 to 8 minutes, shaking the pan every 2 or 3 minutes. Using a slotted spoon, transfer to paper towels to drain.

Bring a small saucepan of water to a boil. Carefully add the egg and boil gently for 1 minute. Drain and run cold water into the pan until tepid. Crack the egg into the bowl of a food processor, including the white clinging to the shell, which you can scrape off with a spoon. Add the vinegar, lemon juice, and roasted garlic, and process until homogenized. With the machine running, gradually add the remaining ¼ cup oil, then the salt, pepper, and Worcestershire sauce.

Put the lettuce in a large salad bowl. Add the dressing and cheese and toss to mix. Add the croutons and toss to mix. Garnish with the anchovies and serve.

ANNIE'S TIPS

Roasting the garlic and toasting the croutons with it over low heat has the double advantage of smoothing the garlic's sharpness and bringing out its nutty flavor, while the croutons become fragrant and crisp throughout without burning.

Coddling the egg for 1 minute heats it through enough to slightly thicken the white while leaving the yolk runny. It makes the egg enrichment even richer.

A Wedding Rehearsal Dinner

Continuing the custom of the groom's family providing the meal for the wedding rehearsal dinner as well as her family tradition of coming together around the table, Annie catered this festive outdoor barbecue for her son Quinn and his bride to be, Molly, at La Famiglia Winery.

Jumbo Shrimp with Celery, Roma Tomatoes,
and Watercress (page 48)

Robert Mondavi La Famiglia Pinot Grigio

Skirt Steak with Roasted Pepper–Shiitake
Mushroom Salsa (page 87)

Annie's Caesar Salad (page 62)

Robert Mondavi La Famiglia Sangiovese

Peach and Blackberry Crisp (page 185)

Robert Mondavi La Famiglia Moscato Bianco

SMOKED SALMON AND CELERY ROOT SALAD
with Two Vinaigrettes

Serves 6 as a main course

Celery root is a staple in the cooking of both Annie and Margrit, used regularly in stocks and stews and mashed with potatoes for a side dish (page 149). That tradition was Annie's inspiration for this recipe, which she made for a Thanksgiving event sponsored by the *San Francisco Chronicle* one year.

Even with all the fresh herbs available in markets today, chervil is a bit hard to find. If it's not available, use a mixture of fresh tarragon and flat-leaf parsley as a substitute rather than dried chervil. The julienne blade of a food processor works great to cut the celery root into the proper shape for this salad.

Serve with a CHARDONNAY

ROASTED RED BELL PEPPER VINAIGRETTE

1/2 red bell pepper, roasted, peeled, and cut into 1/4-inch dice (page xx)

1/2 English cucumber, peeled, seeded, and cut into 1/4-inch dice

3/4 teaspoon finely chopped shallot

1/2 tablespoon chopped fresh flat-leaf parsley

1 teaspoon freshly squeezed lemon juice

1/2 tablespoon extra virgin olive oil

1/2 teaspoon kosher salt

SALMON ROLLS

1 large celery root, peeled and julienned

1/4 cup crème fraîche (page xx) or sour cream

1/2 teaspoon Dijon mustard

2 tablespoons heavy cream

2 tablespoons freshly squeezed lemon juice

2 tablespoons chopped fresh chives

Kosher salt and freshly ground black pepper

1 pound thinly sliced smoked salmon

CHERVIL VINAIGRETTE

1 1/2 tablespoons white wine vinegar

1 1/2 teaspoons freshly squeezed lemon juice

1 1/2 teaspoons finely chopped shallot

1 tablespoon chopped fresh chervil

1/3 cup extra virgin olive oil

1/4 teaspoon kosher salt

Pinch of freshly ground white or black pepper

8 cups torn sturdy salad greens, such as escarole, frisée, or watercress, or a mixture

---

GAME PLAN

Three days ahead:
- Roast the pepper.

One day ahead:
- Squeeze 3 tablespoons lemon juice (1 teaspoon for the roasted pepper vinaigrette, 2 tablespoons for the salmon rolls, and 1 1/2 teaspoons for the chervil vinaigrette).
- Finely chop 1 large shallot and divide in half for each vinaigrette
- Make the red pepper vinaigrette and refrigerate it.
- Make and refrigerate the salmon rolls.
- Wash and dry the salad greens.

Just before serving:
- Make the chervil vinaigrette.

To make the red pepper vinaigrette, combine all the ingredients in a small bowl and mix well. Refrigerate for at least 30 minutes or up to overnight.

To make the salmon rolls, combine the celery root, crème fraîche, mustard, cream, lemon juice, and chives in a bowl. Season with salt and pepper and toss to mix. Lay out slices of the smoked salmon on a cutting board. Spread each with a thin layer of the celery root mixture. Roll into a cylinder, patching any torn spots with a small, extra piece of salmon. Place the rolls on a plate, cover, and refrigerate to firm for 20 minutes or up to overnight.

To make the chervil vinaigrette, combine all the ingredients in a small bowl and whisk to mix. Set aside at room temperature for up to 1 hour.

To serve, toss the salad greens with the chervil vinaigrette. Place a mound of the greens in the center of each plate. Cut the salmon rolls into approximately 2-inch pieces and place 3 around the salad on each plate. Spoon some of the red pepper vinaigrette next to each salmon roll and serve right away.

POACHED SALMON SALAD
with Haricots Verts, Baby Artichokes, and Cucumber-Chardonnay Vinaigrette

Serves 6 as a main course

Annie enjoys adding a whimsical touch to her dishes with edible flower petals she plucks from her herb and flower gardens both at home and at the Vineyard Room. Here, peppery orange nasturtiums or delicate-tasting chive flowers brighten verdant vegetables and soft pink salmon.

Serve with a CHARDONNAY

SALMON

1/2 cup sliced leeks, including light green parts

6 sprigs thyme

6 sprigs flat-leaf parsley

1 teaspoon kosher salt

4 cups water

1/2 cup Chardonnay

1 1/2 pounds salmon fillets, pin bones removed, cut into 6 pieces

VEGETABLES

1/4 pound haricots verts, stem ends trimmed

12 baby artichokes, outside leaves removed, tops cut down to the light green part

2 tablespoons extra virgin olive oil

CUCUMBER-CHARDONNAY VINAIGRETTE

1/2 English cucumber, peeled, seeded, and finely diced

1 tablespoon finely chopped shallot

1 tablespoon Chardonnay

2 tablespoons white wine vinegar

1/3 cup extra virgin olive oil

Kosher salt and freshly ground black pepper

8 cups mixed salad greens

Petals from 6 unsprayed nasturtiums or chive flowers

To poach the salmon, combine the leeks, thyme, parsley, salt, water, and wine in a pot and bring to a boil over high heat. Add the salmon, decrease the heat, and simmer until the salmon is opaque on the outside and medium rare in the center, about 6 minutes. Transfer to a platter and set aside to cool.

While the salmon cools, blanch the haricots verts in a large pot of salted boiling water until al dente, about 4 minutes. Remove with a wire strainer, transfer to a bowl, and set aside. Blanch the artichokes in the same pot of boiling water until softened, 5 minutes. Drain and pat dry. In a sauté pan, heat the oil over medium-high heat. Add the artichokes and sauté until browned and tender, about 5 minutes. Set aside.

To make the vinaigrette, combine all the ingredients in a bowl and whisk to mix. Set aside at room temperature for no more than 2 hours, or it will become watery.

To serve, lightly moisten the greens with some of the vinaigrette and place on 6 plates. Break the salmon into large chunks and set atop the lettuce. Toss the haricots verts with some of the vinaigrette and set alongside the salmon. Arrange the artichoke hearts around the salmon and haricots verts and sprinkle any remaining vinaigrette over all. Garnish with the flower petals and serve.

BROILED MONKFISH AND ASPARAGUS SALAD
with Red Wine Vinaigrette

Serves 4 as a main course

Produce markets in northern California offer fresh asparagus for much of the year, and Annie takes advantage of the bounty in many ways. She purées fat spears for asparagus soup (page 26), cuts medium spears on the diagonal and tosses them in salads, and quickly wilts pencil-thin spears to serve alongside grilled poultry and meat dishes. Here, she blanches asparagus tips to accompany monkfish in a light luncheon salad.

Monkfish, sometimes called poor man's lobster, should have the texture of lobster when cooked: firm all the way through but still a little moist in the center. Annie broils the monkfish for this salad because grilling overwhelms the fresh flavor of the other ingredients.

Serve with a FUMÉ BLANC

MONKFISH

2 tablespoons extra virgin olive oil

1 tablespoon chopped fresh basil

1 tablespoon freshly squeezed lemon juice

1 pound monkfish fillets, cut into 4 portions

Kosher salt

RED WINE VINAIGRETTE

2 tablespoons dry red wine

1 teaspoon freshly squeezed lemon juice

2 tablespoons red wine vinegar

1/2 teaspoon balsamic vinegar

1/4 cup extra virgin olive oil

1/4 teaspoon freshly ground black pepper

20 small asparagus spears, trimmed

4 cups packed mixed salad greens

2 ripe tomatoes, preferably 1 golden, 1 red, peeled and cut into 4 wedges (page xx)

4 thin slices lemon, for garnish

In a nonreactive dish large enough to hold the fish pieces in 1 layer, combine the oil, basil, and lemon juice. Add the fish and turn to coat all over. Sprinkle lightly with salt on both sides. Cover and refrigerate for at least 30 minutes or up to 1 hour.

To make the vinaigrette, in a small bowl, combine all the ingredients and whisk to mix. Set aside for up to 1 hour.

In a large pot of salted boiling water, cook the asparagus until limp, 3 minutes. Drain and rinse under cool water until no longer hot. Set aside on a paper towel.

To cook the fish, preheat the broiler. Broil the fish until firm but still moist in the center, 2 minutes on each side. Transfer to a platter and let rest for 5 minutes.

To assemble the salad, toss the salad greens with the vinaigrette, reserving a little for the asparagus. Spread the greens on 4 plates. Arrange the asparagus and fish over the greens and moisten with the remaining vinaigrette. Garnish with the tomato wedges, place a lemon slice on top of each piece of fish, and serve.

Pasta and Risotto

O RZO, COUSCOUS, BULGUR WHEAT, a mix of Arborio rice with butternut squash—all are candidates for Annie's improvisations on the theme of risotto. For Margrit, pasta is part of dinner any day she's cooking at home—homemade pasta of course. That's because, as she says, "when you're married to an Italian, you make pasta." Following is a collection of Margrit's and Annie's pasta and risotto dishes, including an Asian-inspired ravioli that can be used alone for a light meal or as a side dish to serve alongside a meat, fish, or poultry entrée.

MARGRIT'S HOMEMADE PASTA

Serves 4 as a side dish, 6 for pasta in brodo

For Margrit, making pasta at home is not a chore. Watching her turn out a batch is like viewing a time lapse video of then and now for pasta making. She uses a food processor for mixing the dough, which she then kneads by hand. A pasta machine rolls the dough to the right thickness and then cuts the sheets into even strands. The strands are dried the old-fashioned way, draped over a mechanical wooden clothesline that Bob has rigged up, which can easily be pulled out for use and then garaged under the counter when the pasta is finished. If you don't have such a handy drying rack, hang the pasta over a laundry line or chair backs.

2 cups all-purpose flour, plus extra for kneading

1 large egg

3 egg yolks

2 tablespoons extra virgin olive oil

About 1 tablespoon cold water

In a food processor, combine the 2 cups flour, egg, egg yolks, and oil. Pulse until the ingredients come together, 30 seconds to 1 minute. Dribble in up to 1 tablespoon water until the mixture sticks together to make a stiff dough.

Transfer the dough to a lightly floured surface and knead until smooth, 5 to 6 minutes. Cut into 4 sections, loosely cover with plastic wrap, and let rest for 20 to 30 minutes.

Using a pasta machine, roll out each section of the dough 3 or 4 times, narrowing the width of the rollers each time, until the pasta is about 1/16 inch thick. Set the blade to cut the width of pasta you want (1/4 inch wide for fettuccine, 1/16 inch wide for angel hair). Run the pasta sheets through the machine to cut into strands. Carefully drape the strands across a dowel, laundry line, or back of a chair and let dry for at least 30 minutes. Use within several hours, while still somewhat supple.

FETTUCCINE
with Roasted Vegetables

Serves 8 as a first course, 4 as a main course

Like other vegetables, fennel grows sweeter and more flavorful when roasted. Here, the anisey bulb is added to Annie's vegetable medley for fettuccine. Unless she's pressed for time, Annie makes her own pasta. If that's not feasible, she uses Rustichella d'Abruzzo brand dried pasta.

Serve with a FUMÉ BLANC

1/3 cup extra virgin olive oil

4 large cloves garlic, minced

10 Roma tomatoes (about 1 1/2 pounds), halved lengthwise

3/4 pound asparagus, trimmed and peeled

4 fennel bulbs (2 to 2 1/2 pounds), each cut into 8 wedges

1 recipe (1 pound) Annie's pasta dough, cut into fettuccine (page 74)

1 cup Fumé Blanc

1/4 cup chopped fresh chives

Kosher salt and freshly ground black pepper

1/3 cup freshly grated Parmesan cheese

Preheat the oven to 450°F. In a small bowl, mix together the oil and garlic. Arrange the tomatoes, asparagus, and fennel in a single layer on a rimmed baking sheet and coat with 2 to 3 tablespoons of the garlic oil. Roast for 5 minutes, until the vegetables begin to wilt. Turn the vegetables over and brush with an additional tablespoon or so of the garlic oil. Roast for 10 minutes more, or until limp. Remove the asparagus and cut into 1 1/2-inch pieces. Return the tomatoes and fennel to the oven and continue roasting for 10 minutes, until the tomatoes are soft and the fennel is tender.

Meanwhile, cook the fettuccine in a large pot of salted boiling water until al dente. Drain and return to the pot over medium heat. Add the wine and remaining garlic oil and cook until the liquid is slightly reduced, about 2 minutes. Add the roasted vegetables, any collected juices, and chives. Stir to mix and season with salt and pepper. Serve, accompanied with the cheese on the side.

PENNE
with Tomatoes, Olives, and Feta

Serves 8 as a first course, 4 as a main course

Margrit's variation on pasta primavera is a versatile pasta dish. It can be put together in a flash (she emphasizes that "we don't want to cook the tomatoes very much"), and served as a first course or, in double the portion, as a main dish. All kinds of wines go with it.

Serve with a CHARDONNAY, PINOT NOIR, MERLOT, *or* YOUNG CABERNET SAUVIGNON.

1 pound penne pasta

1 teaspoon plus 1 tablespoon extra virgin olive oil

3 cloves garlic, chopped

5 scallions, including light green parts, chopped

2 cups cherry tomato halves

Kosher salt and freshly ground black pepper

1/2 cup finely shredded fresh basil

1/2 cup coarsely chopped fresh flat-leaf parsley

1 cup kalamata olives, pitted (page xx)

1 cup (5 ounces) crumbled feta cheese, preferably French feta

Cook the pasta in a large pot of salted boiling water according to the package instructions, until al dente. Drain and return to the pot while still moist. Toss with the 1 teaspoon oil to keep the penne from sticking together. Set aside in a warm place.

While the pasta cooks, make the sauce: In a sauté pan, heat the 1 tablespoon oil over medium heat. Add the garlic and scallions and sauté until wilted, 1 minute. Add the tomatoes, season with salt and pepper, and cook until the tomatoes begin to wilt, 1 minute. Remove from the heat and stir in the basil, parsley, and olives.

To serve, toss the tomato mixture with the pasta and transfer to a serving bowl. Garnish with the feta cheese, and serve.

KABOCHA SQUASH RAVIOLI
with Sage Butter Sauce

Serves 6 as a first course

Kabocha squash, a relative newcomer in produce markets, is prized for its nutty, sweet pulp. Like butternut or delicata squash, it mashes into a smooth purée that's perfect for a ravioli filling, and either of those can substitute for kabocha. Any extra filling can be formed into patties, dusted with flour, and sautéed for a squash fritter side dish.

Serve with a CHARDONNAY

ANNIE'S PASTA DOUGH

1 cup all-purpose flour, plus extra for kneading and rolling

1 teaspoon kosher salt

2 large eggs, well beaten

FILLING

1/2 small kabocha squash

Extra virgin olive oil, for coating

Kosher salt and freshly ground black pepper

1 sprig thyme

1/2 russet potato

1 clove garlic, minced

1/2 teaspoon chopped fresh thyme

1 tablespoon heavy cream

SAGE BUTTER SAUCE

1/4 cup unsalted butter

3 tablespoons finely shredded fresh sage

1/4 cup chicken stock (page xix)

1 tablespoon chopped fresh flat-leaf parsley, for garnish

To make the pasta dough, mix the flour and salt together in a bowl. Make a well in the center and add the eggs. With a fork, slowly whisk the flour into the eggs to make a homogeneous mixture. Transfer to a floured work surface and knead into a smooth dough, about 5 minutes. Lightly grease a bowl with olive oil. Put the dough in the bowl and turn to coat all over. Cover with a towel and set aside in a warm place to rest for 30 minutes or up to several hours.

To prepare the filling, preheat the oven to 375°F. Coat the cut side of the squash with oil, sprinkle with salt and pepper, and place the thyme sprig in the cavity. Place, cut side down, on a baking sheet, along with the potato. Bake until the squash and potato are soft all the way through, about 55 minutes. Remove from the oven and allow to cool.

Scoop out the flesh from the squash and potato and place in a bowl. Mash with a masher or fork until blended and somewhat puréed but still with some texture. Stir in the garlic, chopped thyme, and cream and season with salt and pepper.

To make the ravioli, divide the pasta dough in half. Using a pasta machine, roll out each section of dough 3 or 4 times, narrowing the width of the rollers each time, until the pasta sheet is about 14 inches long. On one of the pasta sheets, drop tablespoonfuls of the filling 2 inches apart in 2 rows. Brush the area around each filling mound with water. Top with the second pastry sheet and press firmly around each mound. With a round pastry cutter or paring knife, cut around each mound to make rounds or squares

of ravioli. Dust the ravioli with flour and set aside without stacking them. At this point, the ravioli may be covered and set aside in the refrigerator for up to 6 hours. Remove from the refrigerator 20 minutes before cooking.

To make the sauce, brown the butter in a sauté pan over medium heat, about 3 minutes. Add the sage and stock and cook until thickened, about 1 minute. Keep warm while cooking the ravioli.

In a large pot of salted boiling water, cook the ravioli for 2 minutes after the water returns to a boil. Using a slotted spoon, transfer to 6 plates. Spoon sauce over each serving, sprinkle with parsley, and serve right away.

SPAGHETTINI
with Tomato-Herb Sauce and Sautéed Shrimp

Serves 8 as a first course, 4 as a main course

For her spaghettini with tomato-herb sauce, Annie concocts an unusual medley of fresh herbs that includes tarragon and basil. Both mildly licorice-flavored herbs accent the anise taste of the fennel bulb and counterbalance the sweetness of the shrimp and acid of the tomatoes.

Serve with a FUMÉ BLANC

3/4 cup plus 2 tablespoons extra virgin olive oil

1/2 cup finely chopped fennel bulb

4 large shallots, finely chopped

6 tomatoes (11/2 pounds), peeled, seeded, and cut into 1/4-inch dice (page xx)

1/4 cup freshly squeezed lemon juice

1/2 teaspoon kosher salt

1/4 teaspoon freshly ground black pepper

1/2 cup chopped mixed fresh flat-leaf parsley, tarragon, chives, and basil

1 pound spaghettini pasta

11/2 pounds medium shrimp, peeled, deveined, and tails removed

In a large, heavy sauté pan, heat the 3/4 cup oil over medium heat. Stir in the fennel and shallots. Cook, stirring from time to time so they don't brown, until softened, about 10 minutes. Add the tomatoes, lemon juice, salt, pepper, and all but 2 tablespoons of the herbs. Cover and simmer over low heat for 40 minutes.

In a large pot of salted boiling water, cook the pasta according to the package instructions, until al dente. Drain and return to the pot while still moist. Stir in a few drops of olive oil so the strands don't stick together and set aside in a warm place.

In a large sauté pan, heat the 2 tablespoons oil over medium-high heat. Add the shrimp and sauté, stirring, just until pink, about 3 minutes.

To serve, toss the pasta with the sauce and shrimp. Transfer to a serving bowl, garnish with the remaining 2 tablespoons chopped herbs, and serve.

SHRIMP RAVIOLI IN GINGER BROTH

Serves 4 as a first course

Ready-to-use wonton skins, or wrappers, available in Asian markets and increasingly in the refrigerated Asian foods section of most supermarkets, are a gem for the home and professional cook. Annie uses them to wrap shrimp and poaches the resulting dumplings in a ginger-fragrant broth.

Serve with a CHARDONNAY

BROTH

4 cups chicken stock (page xix)

1/4 cup Chardonnay

1 tablespoon finely chopped fresh ginger

1/2 teaspoon kosher salt

1/4 teaspoon freshly ground white pepper

FILLING

12 medium shrimp (6 to 8 ounces), peeled, deveined, and tails removed

1 tablespoon finely shredded fresh basil

1 tablespoon finely chopped fresh ginger

Pinch of kosher salt

Pinch of freshly ground white pepper

24 (2 1/2-inch-square) wonton wrappers

1 tablespoon finely shredded fresh basil

1/4 cup finely diced roasted red bell pepper (page xx)

To make the broth, combine all the ingredients in a soup pot. Bring to a boil over high heat, decrease the heat to low, cover, and simmer for 10 minutes.

To make the filling, cut the shrimp in half lengthwise. In a bowl, combine them with the basil, ginger, salt, and pepper. Stir to blend.

Lay the wonton wrappers out on a counter. Place a shrimp half in the center of each. Brush the edges with water. Fold one side of the wrapper over to form a triangle and pinch the edges together to seal.

Bring the broth to a simmer and add the dumplings. Cook until the dumplings float to the top, about 2 minutes. Gently stir in the basil and bell pepper. Ladle into 4 bowls or deep-rimmed plates and serve right away.

ORZO "RISOTTO"
with Tomatoes and Parmesan Cheese
Serves 6 as a side dish

In orzo risotto, the tiny seed pasta is boiled and cooked a second time in stock flavored with tomatoes. Annie serves it as a side dish with grilled or sautéed chicken or pork dishes, or perhaps lamb kebabs.

Serve with the wine accompanying the entrée, or a FUMÉ BLANC *if serving the risotto on its own*

1¹/₂ cups orzo pasta

1¹/₂ tablespoons extra virgin olive oil

1 yellow onion, finely chopped

3 cloves garlic, minced

1 cup chicken stock (page xix)

3 tomatoes, peeled, seeded, and diced (page xx), then drained

¹/₄ cup freshly grated Parmesan cheese

2 tablespoons chopped fresh flat-leaf parsley

1¹/₂ teaspoons kosher salt

Freshly ground black pepper

In a large pot of salted, briskly simmering water, cook the orzo until al dente, about 10 minutes. Drain and allow to cool for 5 minutes.

In a sauté pan, heat the oil over medium-high heat. Add the onion and garlic and sauté until softened, about 5 minutes. Stir in the orzo, stock, and tomatoes. Bring to a boil and cook, stirring often, until the liquid is absorbed, about 5 minutes. Stir in the cheese, parsley, salt, and pepper to taste. Serve right away.

BUTTERNUT SQUASH RISOTTO

Serves 6 as a first course, 8 as a side dish

Butternut squash lives up to its name: its pulp, when cooked, is butter smooth and nutty tasting. Not only that, it yields without argument to a vegetable peeler so you can peel it and cut it easily into the size desired for your recipe. As an added boon, it holds its shape in a risotto.

Serve with a CHARDONNAY

1/4 cup unsalted butter

1 yellow onion, finely chopped

3/4 pound butternut squash, peeled and cut into
   1/2-inch dice

1 large clove garlic

5 cups chicken stock (page xix), heated

1 1/2 cups Arborio rice

1/2 cup Chardonnay or other fruity dry white wine

Kosher salt and freshly ground black pepper

1/2 cup freshly grated Parmesan cheese

Melt the butter in a large, heavy pot over medium heat. Add the onion and squash and sauté, stirring, until slightly wilted, about 2 minutes. Add the garlic and 1/2 cup of the stock. Cover and cook for 10 minutes, until the squash is tender. Add the rice and stir until opaque, about 2 minutes. Add the wine and stir until absorbed, about 3 minutes. Decrease the heat to medium-low and add the remaining stock 1/2 cup at a time, stirring constantly and waiting until each addition has been absorbed before adding more. Continue stirring gently until the mixture is creamy and the rice is al dente, about 20 minutes total.

Season with salt and pepper and stir in the cheese. Serve right away.

Pasta and Risotto

COUSCOUS RISOTTO
with Shrimp, Garlic, and Tomatoes
Serves 6 as a first course, 4 as a main course

Annie attributes the inspiration for this risotto to a cooking class Barbara Kafka taught at the winery. It was the first time she had seen couscous cooked this way, and it works well: the tiny pasta granules turns out fluffy and flavorful, without needing to be steamed.

Serve with a COASTAL SAUVIGNON BLANC

COUSCOUS

1 tablespoon unsalted butter

2 tablespoons extra virgin olive oil

1 teaspoon ground cumin

1 yellow onion, finely chopped

3 cloves garlic, minced

1½ cups couscous

4 cups chicken stock (page xix), heated

Kosher salt and freshly ground black pepper

SHRIMP

3 tablespoons extra virgin olive oil

2 cloves garlic, minced

Pinch of crushed red pepper flakes

¼ cup Sauvignon Blanc or other dry white wine

5 Roma or 2 ripe red tomatoes, peeled, seeded, and coarsely chopped (page xx)

¼ cup water

1 pound medium shrimp, peeled and deveined, tails on

2 tablespoons chopped fresh flat-leaf parsley

To make the couscous, melt the butter with the oil in a saucepan over medium heat. Add the cumin and cook until it begins to smell toasty, about 1 minute. Stir in the onion and garlic and cook until translucent, about 2 minutes. Stir in the couscous. Increase the heat to medium-high and add 1 cup of the stock. Stir until it is absorbed, then add another cup, stir until it is absorbed, and so on until the stock is used up, 5 to 6 minutes total. Season with salt and pepper and set aside in a warm place.

To cook the shrimp, heat the oil in a large sauté pan over medium-high heat. Add the garlic and pepper flakes and stir for 30 seconds. Add the wine, tomatoes, and water, increase the heat to high, and cook until the liquid is almost gone and the tomatoes are soft, 4 to 5 minutes. Add the shrimp and cook, stirring, until they just turn pink, about 3 minutes.

To serve, transfer the couscous to a serving dish, spoon the shrimp mixture over, sprinkle the parsley on top, and serve.

MARGRIT'S SWISS RISOTTO
with Beef Marrow and Red Wine

Serves 6 as a first course, 4 as a side dish

Margrit freely admits that the Swiss use bouillon cubes shamelessly. Either cubes or a bottled paste can be used in this risotto made with beef broth, red wine, and marrow. To obtain the marrow, you must bake or poach some marrow bones. As for the butter content, Margrit states that the Swiss love butter and have a saying, "Add more butter and it will get better."

Serve with a MERLOT

3 cross-cut beef shank bones with large marrow holes
   (see Note)

1 tablespoon good-quality beef bouillon paste, or
   3 beef bouillon cubes

6 tablespoons unsalted butter

1 small yellow onion, finely chopped

1 small shallot, finely chopped

1 1/2 cups Arborio or Vialone rice

1 3/4 cups Merlot or other dry red wine

3/4 cup freshly grated Parmesan cheese

Put the marrow bones in a pot, add water to cover, and bring to a boil over high heat. Decrease the heat and simmer briskly for 30 minutes. Remove from the heat and strain into a bowl. Remove the marrow from the bones with a spoon and set aside. Discard the bones. Set the broth aside to cool and allow the fat to rise to the surface.

To make the risotto, skim the fat off the top of the reserved broth. Pour 1 1/4 cups of the broth into a small saucepan. Add the bouillon paste and heat over medium-high heat until the paste dissolves. Keep warm over very low heat.

In a saucepan, melt 4 tablespoons of the butter over medium heat. Add the onion, shallot, and marrow and cook until the onion and shallot are translucent but not browned, about 3 minutes. Increase the heat to medium-high, add the rice and stir until opaque, about 2 minutes. Add the wine and stir until the wine is absorbed, about 5 minutes. Add 1/4 cup of the warm broth and stir constantly until the liquid is absorbed. Repeat the process until all the broth is used; adjust the heat if necessary to prevent scorching the rice. After the last addition, continue cooking until the mixture is creamy and the rice is al dente. This will take a total of about 20 minutes.

Stir in the cheese and the remaining 2 tablespoons butter and serve right away.

NOTE

Instead of boiling the marrow bones to make a beef broth, you could bake the bones in a 350°F oven for 30 minutes, until the marrow is soft. Remove the marrow and set aside for the risotto, and then use 1 1/4 cups already-made beef stock if you have it on hand.

Meats

ALL MANNER OF MEATS, festooned with vegetables and sauces designed to suit the season, appear on Annie's and Margrit's tables. Among them are dishes that pay homage to slow cooking (braised lamb shanks, Ticino-style pot roast) and dishes that salute quick cooking (pork scaloppine with Chardonnay-caper sauce, veal sauté with shallot-lemon cream); dishes that derive from Margrit's European roots (stuffed veal rolls, spring lamb stew) and those that showcase Annie's cutting-edge California style (skirt steak with bell pepper and shiitake salsa, pork and white bean chili verde). Behind each dish there's a story—some are about the accompanying vegetables, some about the sauces and wine suggestions, some about how these dishes came to be in the Napa Valley kitchens of Annie and Margrit.

SKIRT STEAK
with Roasted Pepper–Shiitake Mushroom Salsa and Corn on the Cob

Serves 6

Annie reccommends this menu as perfect for a lazy summer day. The salsa can be made in advance, and the corn is grilled along with the steaks to make a full meal.

Serve with a SANGIOVESE *or* CHILLED FUMÉ BLANC

SKIRT STEAK

2 tablespoons extra virgin olive oil

2 teaspoons chopped garlic

1 tablespoon chopped fresh rosemary

2 pounds skirt steak, cut into 6 portions

6 ears corn, in the husk

Extra virgin olive oil

Kosher salt and freshly ground black pepper

ROASTED PEPPER SHIITAKE-MUSHROOM SALSA

1/2 pound shiitake mushrooms, stemmed

3 tablespoons extra virgin olive oil

Pinch of kosher salt

Pinch of freshly ground black pepper

1 small red bell pepper, roasted, peeled, and finely chopped (page xx)

1 avocado, finely chopped

2 tablespoons freshly squeezed lime juice

1 clove garlic, minced

2 scallions, including green parts, finely chopped

1 tablespoon chopped cilantro

To prepare the steaks, mix together the oil, garlic, and rosemary in a large dish. Add the steak pieces and turn to coat. Set aside at room temperature for 30 minutes, or refrigerate for up to 3 hours.

Peel the husks away from the corn ears without removing them completely. Pull out the corn silk, rub the corn with oil, and season with salt and pepper. Fold the husks back over the cobs. Set aside for up to 30 minutes.

To make the salsa, preheat the oven to 375°F. Toss the mushrooms with 2 tablespoons of the oil, salt, and pepper. Wrap in aluminum foil and place in the oven for 10 minutes, or until soft. Allow to cool, then unwrap and slice thin. In a bowl, combine the mushrooms, bell pepper, avocado, lime juice, garlic, scallions, cilantro, and the remaining 1 tablespoon olive oil and gently stir to mix. Use right away or refrigerate for up to 2 days.

To cook the corn and steaks, prepare a medium-hot fire in a charcoal grill or preheat a gas grill to medium-high. Place the corn over the hottest part of the fire and cook, turning 2 or 3 times, until the husks are charred and the kernels are tender, about 10 minutes. Move the corn to the side of the grill and place the steaks over the hottest part of the fire. Grill, turning once, until medium rare, about 2 minutes on each side. Transfer to a plate and set aside for 5 minutes to allow the juices to settle.

To serve, place the steaks on a large platter and spoon some of the salsa on top of each. Serve right away with the corn and extra salsa on the side.

FILET MIGNON *with Carrots, Shallots, and Cabernet Sauvignon Sauce*

Serves 6

Filets mignons suggest a chic dinner party. Annie likes to serve them gussied up with a rich, Napa Valley wine sauce. Despite its fanciness, the sauce is quite uncomplicated and easy to make. Having at hand a pallet of wines to choose from, she sometimes uses Zinfandel or Pinot Noir to vary the sauce for other beef or robust chicken dishes, or she selects a Chardonnay as the base for cloaking lighter chicken and fish dishes in the same way. The sauté of carrots and shallots adds color and flavor depth on the side, and she suggests an accompaniment of potato gratin (page 126) to complete the picture.

Serve with a CABERNET SAUVIGNON

CABERNET SAUVIGNON SAUCE

1/4 cup unsalted butter

1/2 cup finely chopped shallots

3 sprigs thyme

1 bay leaf

1 tablespoon freshly ground black pepper

1 (750-ml) bottle Cabernet Sauvignon

2 cups beef stock (page xix)

CARROTS AND SHALLOTS

3 tablespoons unsalted butter

3 carrots, peeled and cut into 1/4-inch dice

7 shallots, sliced 1/4 inch thick

3 sprigs thyme

1 small bay leaf

Kosher salt and freshly ground black pepper

1/4 cup fresh flat-leaf parsley leaves

Extra virgin olive oil

6 (6-ounce) beef filets mignons

To make the sauce, melt 2 tablespoons of the butter in a saucepan over medium heat. Add the shallots, decrease the heat to low, and cook, stirring occasionally, until golden, 8 to 10 minutes. Add the thyme, bay leaf, pepper, and wine and increase the heat to high. Bring to a boil and cook to reduce to 1/2 cup, 25 to 30 minutes, depending on the diameter of the pan. Add the stock, bring to a boil, then decrease the heat to medium-low. Simmer gently, skimming 2 or 3 times, for 30 minutes, or until thickened and reduced to about 1 cup. Remove from the heat and pass through a fine mesh sieve. Swirl in the remaining 2 tablespoons butter. Set aside over warm water to keep warm (see Annie's Tip, page 158).

To cook the carrots and shallots, melt the butter in a large sauté pan over medium heat. Add the carrots, shallots, thyme, bay leaf, and salt and pepper to taste. Decrease the heat to medium-low and cook until the carrots and shallots are tender, about 10 minutes. Remove the thyme sprigs and bay leaf. Stir in the parsley. Set aside and keep warm.

To cook the filets, heat a heavy sauté pan large enough to hold the steaks without crowding over high heat (use 2 pans if necessary). Add just enough oil to lightly grease the pan(s) and sear the filets on one side for 1 minute. Decrease the heat to medium and cook for 2 more minutes. Turn the filets over and cook for 2 to 3 minutes on the second side for rare or medium rare. Remove from the heat and let sit for 2 to 3 minutes to allow the juices to settle.

To serve, spoon a pool of sauce onto 6 plates. Set a filet in the middle of the sauce and spoon the carrots and shallots around it. Serve right away.

CHÂTEAUBRIAND *with Parsley Sauce and Crisp Rosemary Potatoes*

Serves 6

A hefty cut of steak rubbed with rosemary. Potatoes that sport a bit more of the spiky-leafed herb. A piquant, classic Italian green sauce with an added stroke of red bell pepper color. This menu, served with a robust Barbera wine, is Annie's divine Napa Valley version of Tuscan steak and potatoes. Châteaubriand is the American cut from the top sirloin of the beef, rather than the French cut from the fillet. Even if not displayed in the meat case, most butchers will cut it for you on request.

Serve with a BARBERA

STEAK

3 tablespoons chopped fresh rosemary

1 tablespoon kosher salt

1½ teaspoons freshly ground black pepper

2 pounds Châteaubriand (top sirloin) steak, at least 1½ inches thick

1 tablespoon extra virgin olive oil, plus extra for greasing the pan

PARSLEY SAUCE

½ cup chopped fresh flat-leaf parsley

¼ cup finely chopped red bell pepper

4 shallots, finely chopped

4 large cloves garlic, minced

2 tablespoons capers, drained and chopped

⅓ cup extra virgin olive oil

1 tablespoon red wine vinegar

CRISP ROSEMARY POTATOES

3 pounds red potatoes

½ cup extra virgin olive oil

6 cloves garlic

2 teaspoons chopped fresh rosemary

1 teaspoon kosher salt

Freshly ground black pepper

To prepare the steak, mix together the rosemary, salt, and pepper. Rub the steak with the oil and press in the rosemary mixture on all sides. Refrigerate for at least 30 minutes or up to 4 hours.

To prepare the sauce, combine all the ingredients in a small bowl and whisk to mix. Set aside at room temperature for at least 30 minutes or up to 2 hours.

To prepare the potatoes, peel and cut them into 1-inch dice. Wash them in 2 or 3 changes of water, drain, and pat dry. Pour the oil into a large nonstick sauté pan over medium-high heat. When the oil is hot, add the potatoes, garlic, and rosemary. Stir to mix and coat the potatoes with the oil. Cover the pan and decrease the heat to medium. Cook until golden brown on the bottom, 8 to 10 minutes. Stir, add the salt, and stir again. Cover the pan and cook for 5 minutes more. Remove the lid and continue cooking, stirring frequently, until golden all over, about 5 minutes. Season with pepper.

To cook the steak, preheat the oven to 400°F. Grease a cast-iron or other heavy ovenproof sauté pan with oil. Heat over high heat, then add the steak and sear, turning once, until nicely browned, 3 minutes on each side. Place in the oven and finish cooking until medium rare, about 8 minutes. Remove and let rest for 15 minutes. (Note: Letting the steak rest after taking it from the oven is an important part of the recipe. Don't be tempted to rush the time, or your steak will not be as tender and succulent as it can be.)

To serve, cut the steak across the grain into ¼-inch-thick slices. Arrange the slices on 6 plates. Place a tablespoon or so of the sauce on top of the meat and add a pile of potatoes to the side. Serve right away, with a bowl of the extra sauce on the side.

T-BONE STEAK FLORENTINE
with Sautéed Zucchini and Mushroom Gratin

Serves 4

Faced with a choice among rib-eye, porterhouse, New York, or T-bone steaks, Annie goes for the T-bone. Though they're all good, for her the flavor of the T-bone is enhanced with the memory of sitting at an outdoor café in Florence, sipping red wine and enjoying the sun and art and people all around. To replicate the experience, she grills the steaks in the straightforward Florentine manner, with salt and pepper and a finishing touch of lemon juice and olive oil, then serves them with sautéed zucchini and a mushroom gratin. (The gratin also serves for more formal occasions, see the menu on the next page.)

Serve with a MERLOT *or* PINOT NOIR

MUSHROOM GRATIN

1/2 cup homemade bread crumbs (page xix)

3/4 cup (3 ounces) freshly grated Parmesan cheese

3 tablespoons chopped fresh flat-leaf parsley

1 teaspoon chopped fresh thyme

2 tablespoons unsalted butter

3 tablespoons chopped shallots

2 cloves garlic, chopped

8 ounces chanterelle mushrooms, sliced 1/2 inch thick

4 ounces shiitake mushrooms, stemmed and sliced 1/2 inch thick

4 ounces whole oyster mushrooms

1/2 cup Chardonnay

1 cup heavy cream

1 teaspoon kosher salt

1/2 teaspoon freshly ground black pepper

SAUTÉED ZUCCHINI

3 tablespoons extra virgin olive oil

4 zucchini, cut 1/3 inch thick on the diagonal

5 cloves garlic, coarsely chopped

Pinch of kosher salt

1 teaspoon chopped fresh oregano

1 tablespoon freshly squeezed lemon juice

STEAK

4 (3/4-pound) T-bone steaks, about 3/4 inch thick

Kosher salt and freshly ground black pepper

Juice of 1 lemon

Extra virgin olive oil, for drizzling

To make the gratin, preheat the oven to 450°F or preheat the broiler. In a small bowl, combine the bread crumbs, cheese, parsley, and thyme and mix well.

In a large sauté pan, melt the butter over medium-high heat. Add the shallots and sauté until translucent, about 2 minutes. Add the garlic and sauté for 1 minute. Add all the mushrooms and sauté until well wilted, about 5 minutes. Add the wine, cream, salt, and pepper and cook until the liquid is bubbly, 5 minutes. Using a slotted spoon, transfer the mushrooms to a bowl. Increase the heat to high and cook to reduce the sauce until thick enough to coat a spoon, 6 to 10 minutes. Return the mushrooms to the sauce and stir. Transfer the mixture to a 2-quart gratin dish and sprinkle the bread crumb mixture over the top. Place in the oven or under the broiler until the topping is toasted and the sauce is bubbling again, about 3 minutes. Set aside.

To make the zucchini, heat the oil in a large sauté pan over medium-high heat. Add the zucchini, garlic, and salt and stir to mix. Decrease the heat to low and cook gently, without stirring, until melted almost into a jam, about 15 minutes. Add the oregano and lemon juice, stir gently, and set aside.

A Family Christmas Dinner

When the party is at Margrit and Bob's home on Wappo Hill, an on-the-spot calligraphed menu with watercolor drawings by Margrit is part of the presentation. In tribute, she always lists the chef at the bottom of the menu, and for family Christmas, it's always, "everyone in the kitchen."

Crostini with Spicy Crab Salad (page 15)

Sauvignon Blanc

Rosemary and Mustard–Crusted Rack of Lamb (page 100)

Cauliflower Gratin (page 108)

Rösti Potatoes (page 95)

Wilted Escarole Salad (page 161)

Cabernet Sauvignon and Chardonnay

Christmas Steamed Bread Pudding (page 184)

Pears Poached in Moscato d'Oro (page 174)

Moscato d'Oro

To cook the steaks, prepare a medium-hot fire in a charcoal grill or preheat a gas grill to medium-high. Season the steaks with salt and pepper on both sides. Place them directly over the hottest part of the fire and grill until browned on the bottom, about 3 minutes. Turn them over and grill on the other side for 2 to 3 minutes for medium rare. Transfer to a platter and set aside to rest for 10 minutes.

To serve, place a steak on each of 4 large plates. Sprinkle with a little lemon juice and drizzle with some olive oil. Spoon some of the mushroom gratin around the steaks and add a large dollop of the zucchini alongside. Serve right away.

TICINO-STYLE POT ROAST
Braised with Merlot and Fresh Herbs

Serves 4 to 6

Along with roasted chicken, pot roast may be *the* every-Sunday American dish. It was also so in Ticino, the Swiss canton on Lake Maggiore where Margrit grew up. There, the meat is cooked with herbs and Merlot, their everyday wine, and it's a version of pot roast resplendent with flavor. If you don't have fresh herbs, use 1/2 teaspoon mixed dried herbs. Margrit suggests serving the pot roast with potatoes boiled in their skins.

Serve with a MERLOT

2 tablespoons unsalted butter

2 pounds boneless beef chuck roast

Kosher salt and freshly ground black pepper

1 carrot, peeled and chopped

1/4 celery root, peeled and chopped

1 leek, including light green part, sliced

2 whole cloves

3 cloves garlic, chopped

2 tomatoes, chopped

1/4 teaspoon fresh rosemary leaves

1/4 teaspoon fresh thyme leaves

1/2 teaspoon chopped fresh basil

1 cup beef stock (page xix)

1 cup Merlot

In a large stew pot, melt the butter over medium-high heat. Add the meat and sprinkle liberally with salt and pepper. Brown on both sides, turning once, about 5 minutes total.

Without removing the meat, add the carrot, celery root, leek, and cloves and stir to mix. Decrease the heat to medium and cook until the vegetables begin to wilt, about 2 minutes. Add the garlic, tomatoes, rosemary, thyme, basil, stock, and wine, stir to mix, and bring to a boil over high heat. Decrease the heat to medium-low, cover, and simmer for 1 1/2 hours, or until the meat is fork-tender. Remove from the heat and let rest, partially covered, for 30 minutes.

Transfer the meat to a plate and set aside in a warm place. Strain the liquid through a fine mesh sieve into a bowl, discarding the solids. Let sit for a few minutes to allow the fat to rise to the top, then skim. Return the skimmed liquid to the pot and cook over high heat until slightly thickened, about 15 minutes.

To serve, cut the meat into 1/4-inch-thick slices and arrange on a serving platter. Pour the reduced liquid over the meat and serve right away.

BEEF AND BLACK BEAN CHILI *with Queso Fresco*

Serves 4 to 6

The black beans of southern Mexican, Caribbean, and South American cooking have been roundly embraced by American cooks from the Southwest to California. Annie is no exception. Her black bean chili is made with beef and beef stock for extra heartiness. It's a fabulous concoction suitable for any festive get-together: it can easily be doubled or tripled for a large crowd; black beans don't require soaking; and making the chili a day in advance benefits the flavor.

Queso fresco is a mild Mexican fresh cheese. You can find it in Latino markets, cheese shops, and upscale supermarkets. Or, substitute farmer's or ricotta cheese spiked with a little feta.

Serve with a ZINFANDEL

1 cup dried black beans

3 cups water

Kosher salt

1/4 cup extra virgin olive oil

1 1/2 pounds beef stew meat (chuck or boneless short ribs), cut into 1/2-inch cubes

1 yellow onion, coarsely chopped

2 tablespoons coarsely chopped garlic

2 tablespoons pure chile powder

1/2 teaspoon ground cumin

4 cups beef stock (page xix)

3 jalapeño chiles, seeded and finely chopped

GARNISHES

1/2 cup crumbled queso fresco cheese

1/4 cup finely chopped yellow onion

1/4 cup cilantro leaves

12 warm corn or flour tortillas, for serving

ANNIE'S TIP

When browning meat for stew-type dishes, the key is to work in batches, adding only as many pieces as will fit in the pan without crowding. If crowded, the meat steams and loses juices rather than searing and becoming nicely colored.

Put the beans in a pot, add the water, and bring to a boil over high heat. Decrease the heat to medium and simmer until the beans are tender, adding extra water if necessary, 75 to 90 minutes, depending on the age of the beans. Stir in salt to taste. Use right away, or allow to cool in the liquid and refrigerate for up to 1 week. (Note: the beans may also be cooked in a pressure cooker for 25 minutes after coming to pressure, plus 5 minutes standing time before adding the salt.)

In a large pot, heat the oil over medium-high heat. Add the beef in small batches and cook for about 3 minutes, until brown all over, transferring each batch to a plate as it's done (see Annie's Tip). Add the onion and garlic to the pot and cook until they begin to wilt, about 1 minute. Add the chile powder and cumin and stir to mix. Return the beef and any collected juices to the pot, add the stock, and stir to mix. Bring to a boil, decrease the heat to medium-low, and simmer, uncovered, until the meat is fork-tender, about 45 minutes. Stir in the cooked beans, the jalapeños, and salt to taste. Simmer for 20 minutes, then remove from the heat and let rest for 15 minutes.

To serve, ladle the chili into a large serving bowl or soup bowls, garnish with the cheese, onion, and cilantro, and serve with the tortillas on the side.

VEAL SAUTÉ *with Shallot-Lemon Cream Sauce and Rösti Potatoes*

Serves 4

Thanks to Margrit's multilingual background, she sometimes refers to this dish as *zuri gschatzles*, sometimes as *émincé de veau,* and sometimes *vitello tritato alla zurighese.* They all translate as a quick veal sauté enriched with cream. Rösti, a latke-like large potato pancake, is her favored accompaniment. Partially cooking the potatoes and refrigerating them overnight before shredding is the key to perfect rösti.

Serve with a SAUVIGNON BLANC

RÖSTI POTATOES

3 large russet potatoes (about 2¹/₂ pounds total), scrubbed

3 tablespoons unsalted butter

¹/₂ teaspoon kosher salt

¹/₄ teaspoon freshly ground white pepper

2 tablespoons milk

VEAL SAUTÉ

1¹/₄ pounds veal cutlets, cut into 1-inch-wide strips

Kosher salt and freshly ground white pepper

3 tablespoons unsalted butter

4 shallots, finely chopped

1 tablespoon all-purpose flour

³/₄ cup dry white wine

³/₄ cup heavy cream

1 tablespoon finely slivered lemon zest

1 tablespoon finely chopped fresh flat-leaf parsley, for garnish

MARGRIT'S TIP

To coordinate the cooking times for the rösti and veal sauté, start the veal after the rösti has cooked for 20 to 25 minutes and is almost done. The sauté takes about 5 minutes.

To prepare the rösti, place the potatoes in a saucepan with water to cover. Bring to a boil and cook for 10 to 15 minutes, until semi-tender: still firm in the center but with the skin pulling away. Drain and allow to cool completely, then refrigerate overnight.

Peel the potatoes, then shred them on the large holes of a box grater. In a large sauté pan, melt the butter over medium-high heat. Add the potatoes, salt, and pepper, and stir to mix. Press into a round cake about ³/₄ inch thick. Sprinkle with the milk. Cover the pan and cook until the cake begins to sizzle, about 5 minutes. Decrease the heat to medium-low and cook for 30 minutes, until a golden crust has formed on the bottom.

When the rösti is almost done (see Margrit's Tip), season the veal strips liberally with salt and pepper. In a large sauté pan, melt the butter over high heat until it foams. Add the veal and cook very quickly, turning once, until no longer pink on the outside, about 1 minute total. Transfer to a plate and set aside in a warm place. Add the shallots to the same pan, decrease the heat to medium-high and cook until translucent, about 1 minute. Sprinkle the flour over the shallots, stir to mix, and add the wine. Stir and cook until the liquid is reduced by half, about 1 minute. Stir in the cream and zest. Continue cooking until the mixture is creamy, 1 to 2 minutes more. Correct the salt and pepper seasoning, add the veal, and stir to mix.

Transfer to a serving platter without further cooking and garnish with the parsley. Flip the rösti over onto another serving platter and serve everything right away, while still hot.

STUFFED VEAL ROLLS ALLA TICINESE

Serves 4

Margrit serves her Swiss veal rolls with buttered egg noodles and Merlot, traditional accompaniments. Though the recipe may seem complicated, she assures that it isn't (see Margrit's Tip).

Serve with a MERLOT

STUFFING

1 tablespoon unsalted butter

2 ounces pancetta or lean bacon, finely chopped

1/2 yellow or white onion, finely chopped

2 ounces fresh cremini or porcini mushrooms, finely chopped; or 1/3 ounce dried mushrooms, soaked in warm water for 20 minutes, squeezed dry, and finely chopped

1 cup coarsely chopped French or Italian bread

1 tablespoon chopped fresh flat-leaf parsley

1 teaspoon finely chopped lemon zest

8 (2- to 3-ounce) veal scaloppine, pounded 1/8 inch thick

Freshly ground black pepper

5 tablespoons unsalted butter

1/2 teaspoon chopped fresh rosemary

1/2 teaspoon chopped fresh thyme

1/3 cup dry red wine

1/2 yellow or white onion, finely chopped

2 large tomatoes, peeled, seeded, and coarsely chopped (page xx)

1/4 pound fresh cremini or porcini mushrooms, thinly sliced; or 1 ounce dried mushrooms, soaked in warm water for 20 minutes, squeezed dry, and thinly sliced

1/2 teaspoon kosher salt

8 ounces egg noodles

2 tablespoons chopped fresh flat-leaf parsley, for garnish

MARGRIT'S TIP

The stuffing and sauce call for many of the same ingredients. To expedite the preparation, have ready:

- 6 tablespoons butter (1 tablespoon for the stuffing, 3 tablespoons for sautéing, and 2 tablespoons for the noodles)
- 1 onion, chopped and divided into two piles
- 6 ounces fresh mushrooms, or 1 1/3 ounces dried mushrooms, rehydrated. Finely chop about a third of them for the stuffing and thinly slice the rest for the sauce.

To make the stuffing, melt the butter in a sauté pan over medium-high heat. Add the pancetta, stir, and cook until softened, 1 minute. Stir in the onion and mushrooms and cook until wilted, about 3 minutes. Transfer to a small bowl. Add the bread, parsley, and zest and stir to mix.

Lightly sprinkle the scaloppine on both sides with pepper. Spread one-eighth of the stuffing mixture evenly over the surface of each. Roll up the short way and secure with toothpicks. In a large sauté pan, melt 3 tablespoons of the butter over medium-high heat. Add the veal rolls and cook, turning to brown all around, about 2 minutes. Add the rosemary, thyme, and wine to the pan. Decrease the heat to medium-low, cover, and cook until the meat begins to firm, 5 minutes. Turn the rolls over, cover, and cook until firm but still pink in the center, about 5 minutes. Transfer the rolls to a plate and set aside in a warm place.

Add the onion to the same pan, stir to mix, and increase the heat to medium-high. Stir in the tomatoes, mushrooms, and salt and cook until the liquid is reduced and saucy, about 5 minutes.

Meanwhile, cook the egg noodles in a large pot of salted boiling water according to the package instructions. Drain, return to the pot, and stir in the remaining 2 tablespoons butter.

To serve, spoon the egg noodles onto 4 plates. Remove the toothpicks from the veal rolls and set 2 rolls atop the noodles on each plate. Spoon the sauce over the rolls, sprinkle with parsley, and serve right away.

BRAISED VEAL *with Sage, Rosemary, and Marsala*

Serves 4

Stews and braised dishes are a solid part of Margrit's home cooking, handed down from her mother and her mother's mother. Although her grandmother was not a particularly adventuresome cook, Margrit says, her own mother cooked like an angel. Though often rushed these days, moving from office to evening event or traveling for the winery, Margrit makes sure to take time for the slow-cooked dishes of her childhood. Like her mother, she serves this veal stew with spätzli, tiny Swiss noodle dumplings.

Serve with a PINOT NOIR

2 tablespoons extra virgin olive oil

1 tablespoon unsalted butter

1³/₄ pounds veal stew meat, cut into 1¹/₂-inch cubes

Kosher salt and freshly ground black pepper

6 large fresh sage leaves, finely chopped

2 teaspoons finely chopped fresh rosemary

¹/₂ cup Marsala

¹/₂ cup water

2 tablespoons chopped fresh flat-leaf parsley

1 recipe spätzli (page 144)

In a large sauté pan, combine the oil and butter and heat over medium-high heat until the butter melts. Add the veal, stir to coat the pieces, and season liberally with salt and pepper. Add the sage and rosemary, stir to mix, and cook until the veal is browned on all sides, 4 to 5 minutes. Pour in the wine and stir to mix. Cover the pan, decrease the heat to low, and simmer ever so gently for 40 minutes, or until the veal is tender. Check the pan from time to time and add a little water or light stock if the liquid has evaporated. Remove from the heat and set aside to rest for at least 15 to 30 minutes or up to 2 hours; reheat before serving.

To serve, transfer the veal to a platter. Set the pan over high heat, add the water, and stir to scrape up the browned bits from the bottom of the pan. Pour over the veal, sprinkle the parsley over the top, and spoon some spätzli around the veal. Serve right away.

Antique wine press at the Robert Mondavi Winery.

BUTTERFLIED LEG OF LAMB *with Mint Pesto and Bulgur Pilaf*

Serves 6

In a Middle Eastern–inspired dish, Annie grills lamb, serves it with bulgur pilaf, and adds pizzazz with a mint pesto. The pesto is good company not only for the lamb and bulgur combination but also for the Cabernet Sauvignon wine with its mint overtones.

Serve with a CABERNET SAUVIGNON

LAMB

6 large cloves garlic, minced or pressed

2 tablespoons chopped fresh rosemary

2 tablespoons chopped fresh sage

1/2 cup extra virgin olive oil

1 teaspoon kosher salt

1/2 teaspoon freshly ground black pepper

1 (6-pound) leg of lamb, boned and butterflied

BULGUR PILAF

2 tablespoons extra virgin olive oil

1 small white onion, finely chopped

2 cups coarse bulgur wheat

3 cups chicken stock (page xix)

MINT PESTO

1/2 cup packed fresh basil leaves

1 cup packed fresh mint leaves

1/2 cup fresh flat-leaf parsley leaves

1 tablespoon pine nuts

1 large clove garlic, coarsely chopped

1/2 teaspoon kosher salt

1/3 cup extra virgin olive oil

1/4 cup freshly grated Parmesan cheese

To prepare the lamb, mix together the garlic, rosemary, sage, oil, salt, and pepper in a dish large enough to hold the lamb opened flat. Add the lamb and turn to coat. Refrigerate for at least 3 hours or preferably overnight. Remove from the refrigerator 30 minutes before cooking.

Prepare a medium-hot fire in a charcoal grill or preheat a gas grill to medium-high. Place the lamb on the grill rack on the side of the grill, not directly over the coals. Cook, turning once, until done as you like, 20 minutes for rare, 30 minutes for medium rare. Transfer to a plate and let rest for 10 minutes to allow the juices to settle.

While the lamb cooks, prepare the pilaf. In a saucepan, heat the oil over medium-high heat. Add the onion and sauté until translucent, about 1 minute. Stir in the bulgur and continue sautéing for 3 minutes, or until the bulgur is lightly toasted. Add the stock and bring to a boil. Decrease the heat to low, cover, and simmer for 5 minutes. Remove from the heat and let sit, without removing the lid, until the stock is absorbed and the grains are tender, at least 10 minutes or preferably 30 minutes.

To make the pesto, combine the basil, mint, parsley, pine nuts, garlic, and salt in a food processor. Blend until the ingredients are coarsely chopped. With the machine running, gradually add the oil in a thin stream. Transfer to a bowl and mix in the cheese. Serve right away, cover tightly and set aside at room temperature for up to 1 hour, or refrigerate up to overnight.

To serve, slice the lamb across the grain into 1/4-inch-thick slices. Arrange the lamb on 6 plates and mound some pilaf to the side. Garnish the meat with some of the pesto and serve right away, with the extra pesto on the side.

ROSEMARY AND MUSTARD–CRUSTED RACK OF LAMB
with Fennel Ratatouille

Serves 4 to 6

Annie serves the rack chops with her rendition of ratatouille, made with fennel bulb and ground fennel. To grind the fennel, you need a spice grinder or else you can pulverize the seeds in a mortar and pestle. She cuts the vegetables into fine dice so that they virtually melt together, almost into a marmalade. Make sure to ask your butcher to french the racks: trimming the meat and fat from the top of each rib bone so that the rack can be easily divided into chops.

Serve with a CABERNET SAUVIGNON

FENNEL RATATOUILLE

1/2 cup extra virgin olive oil

2 tablespoons chopped garlic

1/2 cup finely diced yellow onion

1 cup finely diced fennel

1 cup finely diced red bell pepper

Kosher salt

1 cup finely diced zucchini

1/2 cup finely diced eggplant

1 cup finely diced tomatoes

1 teaspoon ground fennel seed

1 cup chopped fresh flat-leaf parsley

LAMB

Kosher salt and freshly ground black pepper

2 racks lamb (16 chops), frenched and trimmed of fat

1 tablespoon extra virgin olive oil

1 tablespoon Dijon mustard

1 teaspoon chopped fresh rosemary

1/2 cup not-too-fine bread crumbs (page xix)

To make the ratatouille, heat the oil in a sauté pan over medium heat. Add the garlic, onion, diced fennel, and bell pepper. Sprinkle with salt, stir to mix, and sauté, stirring frequently, until the vegetables are just tender, about 5 minutes. With a slotted spoon, transfer to a bowl, leaving the oil in the pan. Add the zucchini and eggplant to the pan, sprinkle with salt, and stir to mix. Sauté, stirring frequently, until just tender, about 3 minutes. With a slotted spoon, transfer to the bowl with the other vegetables, leaving any remaining oil in the pan. Decrease the heat to medium-low, stir the tomatoes into the pan, and cook until they collapse, 2 to 3 minutes. Add them to the bowl with the other vegetables and stir in the ground fennel and parsley. Use right away, set aside at room temperature for up to 4 hours, or cover and refrigerate for up to 5 days.

To cook the lamb, preheat the oven to 375°F. Sprinkle salt and pepper all over the racks. In a large ovenproof sauté pan, heat the oil over high heat. (Use 2 pans if necessary to avoid crowding.) Place the racks in the pan, meat side down, and sear well, about 2 minutes. Turn and sear the other side, about 2 minutes more. Remove from the heat, transfer the racks to a work surface, and set the pan aside. Smear the mustard over the top of the meat. Combine the rosemary and bread crumbs and press the mixture into the mustard. Return the racks to the pan, coated side up, and roast until the internal temperature is 125°F, about 20 minutes. Remove from the oven and let sit for 5 to 10 minutes to allow the juices to settle.

To serve, cut the racks into individual chops and arrange on a large platter or dinner plates, 3 chops per person. Mound the ratatouille in the center of the platter or place a generous dollop alongside the chops on each plate, and serve.

CABERNET SAUVIGNON–BRAISED LAMB SHANKS
with White Bean and Roasted Garlic Purée

Serves 4 to 6

Like a Provençal lamb daube, this is a slow-cooked dish. Annie makes it for the Vineyard Room on cold and rainy days because it adds warmth to the expansive dining room. She also serves it at home for the same reason, albeit in a smaller space. The bevy of vegetables melts during cooking to soften the wine and add depth to the sauce. While that happens, there's plenty of time to prepare the bean purée.

Serve with a CABERNET SAUVIGNON

WHITE BEAN AND ROASTED GARLIC PURÉE

2 cups dried white beans

1 head garlic

1 tablespoon extra virgin olive oil

1/2 teaspoon chopped fresh thyme

About 1/2 cup heavy cream, warmed

1 teaspoon kosher salt

LAMB

6 tablespoons extra virgin olive oil

4 (1- to 11/2-pound) lamb shanks, cut in half

Kosher salt and freshly ground black pepper

3 small leeks, including light green parts, thinly sliced

1 fennel bulb, cut into 1/4-inch dice

4 small carrots, peeled and cut into 1/4-inch dice

1 celery root, peeled and cut into 1/2-inch dice

1/4 pound pancetta or bacon, cut into 1/2-inch pieces

2 heads garlic, halved crosswise

2 bay leaves

4 sprigs thyme

3 cups chicken stock (page xix)

3 cups Cabernet Sauvignon

1 (28-ounce) can Italian plum tomatoes, drained and coarsely chopped

1/4 cup chopped fresh flat-leaf parsley, for garnish

Soak the beans overnight in water to cover. (Or, use the quick-soak method: bring the beans and water to cover to a boil for 1 minute. Remove from the heat and let stand for 1 to 4 hours.) Drain and rinse.

To cook the beans, place them in a pot and add water to cover by 3 inches. Bring to a boil over high heat, decrease the heat to medium, and simmer until tender, about 11/2 hours. Drain and set aside, or allow to cool in the liquid and refrigerate overnight. (Note: the beans may also be cooked in a pressure cooker for 25 minutes after coming to pressure, plus 5 minutes standing time off the heat.)

To roast the garlic, preheat the oven to 375°F. Cut off the top quarter of the garlic head to expose the cloves. Place on aluminum foil and pour the oil over the top. Fold up the foil to enclose the garlic and roast in the oven until squeezable, about 1 hour. Remove from the oven and allow to cool.

While the beans cook and the garlic roasts, prepare the lamb. In a large, ovenproof pot, heat 2 tablespoons of the oil over medium-high heat. Sprinkle the lamb shanks with salt and pepper and brown them in batches, about 5 minutes per batch. Transfer to a platter as they are completed. Pour off the fat and heat the remaining 4 tablespoons oil over medium heat. Add the leeks, fennel, carrots, celery root, pancetta, garlic, bay leaves, and thyme sprigs. Cook, stirring, until the vegetables are lightly browned, about 5 minutes. Return the shanks and any collected juices to the pot. Add the stock, wine, and tomatoes. Increase the heat to high, stir to mix, and bring to a boil. Cover, place in the oven alongside the garlic packet, and cook for 2 hours, turning once or twice, until the meat is pulling away from the bone.

When the shanks are done, remove from the oven. Separate the garlic heads into cloves and remove the papery husks from the pot. Let the shanks rest while finishing the bean purée.

Put the beans in a food processor. Squeeze the cloves out of the roasted garlic and add to the beans, along with the chopped thyme and 1/4 cup of the warmed cream. Process until almost smooth but still a little chunky. Process in just enough of the remaining cream to make a purée the consistency of mashed potatoes. Stir in the salt.

To serve, divide the bean purée among dinner plates. Place a lamb shank over the purée and spoon the sauce and vegetables over the shanks. Sprinkle parsley over the top and serve right away.

In an artful arrangement for a Robert Mondavi Winery essence tasting, these glasses display many of the aromatic and taste components of wine. Star anise, cinnamon bark, raspberries, rose petals, green apple, rosemary, and mint are some of the elements that, individually noticed, can open a taster's nose and palate to the particular nuances of a wine. In the center foreground is a chunk of an oak barrel that has been prepared for fermentation. The barrels are slightly charred inside to impart a smoky, oaky taste to the wine.

BUTTERFLIED LEG OF LAMB
Marinated in Mint Vinaigrette with Couscous Tabbouleh

Serves 8

Mint, lamb, and spring come together in Annie's take on how to celebrate the new season of the year. Tabbouleh is usually made with bulgur, but Annie thought . . . why not use couscous instead? To marinate the lamb, she selects apple cider vinegar for its soft, fruity flavor, less acid than red wine vinegar and less sweet than balsamic vinegar. She serves the dish without a sauce because it doesn't need one.

Serve with a CABERNET SAUVIGNON

LAMB

1/4 cup chopped fresh mint

1 tablespoon whole-grain mustard

1 teaspoon freshly ground black pepper

1/4 cup apple cider vinegar

1/2 cup extra virgin olive oil

Kosher salt

1 (6 1/2-pound) leg of lamb, boned and butterflied

COUSCOUS TABBOULEH

1 recipe basic couscous (page 131)

1/2 cup extra virgin olive oil

1/4 cup chopped fresh mint

2 tablespoons finely chopped fresh flat-leaf parsley

2 tablespoons finely chopped scallions, including light green parts

1/2 cup diced red bell pepper

1 English cucumber, peeled, seeded, and finely chopped

1/3 cup freshly squeezed lemon juice

To prepare the lamb, combine the mint, mustard, pepper, vinegar, and oil in a small bowl and whisk to mix. Put the lamb in a dish large enough to hold it opened flat, boned surface up. Spread the entire surface with the mint mixture, poking it into the pockets and crevices. Set aside in the refrigerator to marinate for at least 4 hours or preferably overnight. Remove from the refrigerator 30 minutes before cooking.

To prepare the tabbouleh, place the couscous in a bowl and toss with the oil, mint, parsley, scallions, bell pepper, cucumber, and lemon juice. Use right away, set aside at room temperature for up to 2 hours, or cover and refrigerate for up to 2 days. Return to room temperature before serving.

To cook the lamb, prepare a medium-hot fire in a charcoal grill or preheat a gas grill to medium-high. Lightly salt the lamb and place on the grill rack directly over the coals. Grill for 30 minutes, turning and basting with the marinade every 5 minutes or so, until medium rare. Transfer to a platter and set aside in a warm place for 15 minutes to allow the juices to settle.

To serve, slice the lamb across the grain. Arrange the slices on plates and mound some tabbouleh to the side. Spoon some of the meat juices over the lamb and serve right away.

SPRING LAMB STEW *with Baby Carrots and Fingerling Potatoes*

Serves 6

When Annie was growing up, Margrit's spring lamb stew was a family favorite. Then, it was made with full-sized carrots and small red potatoes to enhance the lamb. Now that both mother and daughter live in the Napa Valley with its abundance of artisan produce, they opt for baby carrots and fingerling potatoes instead. And the dish has come to include some of the Valley's renowned Chardonnay wine. Even though the stew is served with a Pinot Noir, Chardonnay is the choice for the sauce to keep the clarity of color and refine the sweetness of the lamb and spring vegetables without overwhelming their flavors. Bone-in lamb neck is the cut of choice for the stew because the meat is most tender at the bone.

Serve with a PINOT NOIR

STEW

2 tablespoons extra virgin olive oil

4 pounds lamb shoulder stew meat, with some bone

Kosher salt and freshly ground black pepper

1/4 pound pancetta, coarsely chopped

2 carrots, peeled and coarsely chopped

1 yellow onion, coarsely chopped

6 cloves garlic, unpeeled

8 cups chicken stock (page xix)

1 cup Chardonnay

2 cups drained canned whole tomatoes, broken up a bit

2 sprigs thyme

2 bay leaves

CARROTS AND POTATOES

24 baby carrots with 1/2 inch green top intact, peeled

1 1/2 pounds fingerling potatoes, preferably about 1 inch long, left whole, or halved lengthwise if larger

2 tablespoons chopped fresh flat-leaf parsley, for garnish

To make the stew, preheat the oven to 350°F. In a large, ovenproof casserole, heat the oil over medium-high heat. In batches, brown the lamb, seasoning with salt and pepper and turning with kitchen tongs to brown all over, about 3 minutes per batch. Transfer each batch to a platter as you go.

Pour off any extra fat and add the pancetta to the pan. Sauté over medium heat until soft but not crispy, about 2 minutes. Add the carrots, onion, and garlic. Cook until they begin to turn golden, about 5 minutes. Return the lamb to the pot. Add the stock, wine, tomatoes, thyme, and bay leaves. Stir to mix and bring to a boil over high heat. Skim off the foam as the liquid comes to a boil. Cover the casserole, place in the oven, and braise for 2 hours, or until the lamb is fork-tender.

To prepare the carrots and potatoes, bring a large pot of lightly salted water to a boil over high heat. Add the carrots and cook until al dente, about 5 minutes. With a wire strainer, transfer the carrots to a colander to drain. In the same pot, boil the potatoes until tender, about 7 minutes. Drain in a separate colander.

When the lamb is done, remove the casserole from the oven and let rest for 15 minutes. Uncover and transfer the lamb pieces to a bowl. Strain the juices through a fine mesh sieve into a separate bowl. Set aside for 30 minutes to allow the fat to rise to the top. Wipe out the casserole.

To serve, skim the fat off the juices. Return the juices to the casserole and cook for 5 minutes over high heat to reduce slightly. Add the lamb, carrots, and potatoes and simmer over low heat for 5 minutes, or until the vegetables and lamb are heated through. Dish some of the lamb, carrots, and potatoes onto 6 plates. Sprinkle the parsley over the top of each portion and serve.

PORK TENDERLOIN
with Creamy Polenta and Chunky Sun-Dried Tomato Ketchup

Serves 4

In this dish, Margrit's painterly influence on Annie's color sense is gloriously evident. Combining polenta with more finely ground cornmeal results in a texture that is pleasingly smooth, while the cream addition enriches the grains and makes an unctuous porridge.

Serve with a ZINFANDEL *or* PINOT NOIR

PORK TENDERLOIN

1 teaspoon chopped fresh rosemary

1 teaspoon chopped fresh thyme

1 clove garlic, chopped

2 tablespoons Dijon mustard

1 tablespoon extra virgin olive oil

Pinch of kosher salt

1/4 teaspoon freshly ground black pepper

1 (1- to 11/4-pound) pork tenderloin

SUN-DRIED TOMATO KETCHUP

3 oil-packed sun-dried tomatoes, julienned

2 teaspoons coarsely chopped shallot

2 tablespoons chopped fresh flat-leaf parsley

1 small clove garlic

2 teaspoons capers, rinsed

1 tablespoon balsamic vinegar

11/2 teaspoons red wine vinegar

1/4 cup extra virgin olive oil

CREAMY POLENTA

11/2 cups chicken stock (page xix)

11/2 cups water

2 tablespoons unsalted butter

1 teaspoon kosher salt

1/4 teaspoon freshly ground white pepper

1/2 cup polenta

1/2 cup yellow cornmeal

1/4 cup heavy cream

1/2 cup freshly grated Parmesan cheese

To prepare the tenderloin, combine the rosemary, thyme, garlic, mustard, oil, salt, and pepper in a large glass or other nonreactive dish. Add the tenderloin, turn to coat, and set aside at room temperature for 1 hour or refrigerate for at least 4 hours or up to overnight. Remove from the refrigerator 30 minutes before cooking.

To make the ketchup, combine the tomatoes, shallot, parsley, garlic, capers, and vinegars in a food processor and process until well mixed. With the machine running, gradually add the oil to make a thick sauce. Use right away or refrigerate for up to 3 days.

To cook the tenderloin, prepare a medium-hot fire in a charcoal grill or preheat a gas grill to medium-high. Preheat the oven to 375°F. Place the loin on the grill rack directly over the fire and cook, turning once, for 5 minutes on each side, or until nicely browned. Transfer to a baking sheet and finish cooking in the oven until firm to the touch but still a little pink in the center, about 10 minutes. Remove from the oven and set aside for 5 minutes to allow the juices to settle.

To make the polenta, combine the stock, water, butter, salt, and pepper in a saucepan and bring to a boil over medium-high heat. Gradually stir in the polenta and cornmeal and let the mixture return to a boil. Cook, stirring frequently, for 15 minutes, until thick and creamy. Remove from the heat and stir in the cream and cheese. Serve right away, or set aside in a larger pan partially filled with simmering water to keep warm.

To serve, spread the polenta on 4 plates. Cut the tenderloin into 1/2-inch-thick slices and arrange them over the polenta. Spoon the ketchup over the pork and serve.

PORK SCALOPPINE
with Chardonnay-Caper Sauce and Cauliflower Gratin

Serves 4

Boneless tenderloins of veal, chicken, or pork can all be pounded into scaloppine with excellent results. Here, Annie dresses pork tenderloin scaloppine in a white wine reduction with capers and scallions that would also suit chicken breasts or veal. She serves the dish with a cauliflower gratin that may be prepared in advance and served later at room temperature.

Serve with a CHARDONNAY

CAULIFLOWER GRATIN

1 head cauliflower, cut into florets

2 tablespoons unsalted butter

3 tablespoons all-purpose flour

1 1/2 cups hot milk

1/3 cup plus 2 tablespoons shredded Gruyère cheese

1/2 teaspoon kosher salt

1/4 teaspoon freshly ground black pepper

PORK SCALOPPINE

1 (1 1/4-pound) pork tenderloin

3 tablespoons unsalted butter

3 tablespoons extra virgin olive oil

Flour, for dusting the scaloppine

1/4 cup chopped scallions, including light green parts

1/2 cup Chardonnay

2 tablespoons capers, rinsed

Kosher salt and freshly ground black pepper

1 tablespoon chopped fresh flat-leaf parsley, for garnish

To prepare the gratin, pour 1 inch of water into a saucepan and bring to a boil over high heat. Add the cauliflower florets and cook for 3 minutes after the water returns to a boil, or until tender but still crunchy. Drain, rinse under cold water to stop the cooking, and set aside.

In a small saucepan, melt the butter over medium heat. Add the flour and stir with a wooden spoon to make a paste. Continue stirring for 2 minutes, or until it foams and turns buttery yellow but does not brown. Add 1 cup of the hot milk and whisk to blend. Increase the heat to medium-high and continue whisking until simmering. Whisk in the remaining 1/2 cup milk in dribbles, until thickened and creamy, 3 to 5 minutes. Remove from the heat and stir in the 1/3 cup cheese. Season with salt and pepper.

To cook the gratin, preheat the oven to 400°F. Lightly butter a 2-quart baking dish. Spread a thin layer of the sauce in the bottom of the dish. Place the cauliflower florets in the dish, arranging them heads up as much as possible to make a nice presentation. Spoon the remaining sauce over the florets and sprinkle with the 2 tablespoons cheese. Bake for 20 minutes, or until browned. Remove from the oven and set aside in a warm place.

To prepare the scaloppine, starting at the thick end, cut the tenderloin into 1/2-inch-thick slices up to the thin tail end. One at a time, pound the slices and the tail between 2 sheets of waxed paper with a meat pounder or mallet to 1/4 inch thick. Set aside in the refrigerator if necessary while the gratin finishes cooking.

To cook the scaloppine, melt 1 tablespoon of the butter with the oil in a large, nonstick sauté pan over medium-high heat. In batches, dust the scaloppine with flour and sauté as many pieces as will fit in the pan without overlapping, just until brown on both sides, about 1 1/2 minutes total. Transfer to a plate and set aside in a warm place.

Add the scallions to the pan and cook over medium heat until they begin to wilt, about 1 minute. Add the wine and cook until bubbly and slightly thickened, about

A Charity Event

Margrit and Bob are magnanimous donors when it comes to offering their Wappo Hill home as venue for charity auction prize dinners. Architecturally extraordinary, with a swimming pool in the living room, their home is also a family place, warm and welcoming as its owners. The family feeling extends to the kitchen where Annie is often at the stove, overseeing the cooking part while Margrit and Bob mingle and chat to make everyone feel at home. For one such event for the American Institute of Wine and Food in May 2002, the excitement was high because Julia Child was the cohost. This was Annie's menu for the evening.

Annie's Crab Cakes with Tartar Sauce (page 47)

Robert Mondavi Stags Leap District Sauvignon Blanc

Filet Mignon with Cabernet Sauvignon Sauce (page 88)

Mushroom Gratin (page 90)

1991 Robert Mondavi Cabernet Sauvignon Reserve

Meyer Lemon Cornmeal Cake (page 192)

2000 Robert Mondavi La Famiglia Moscato Bianco

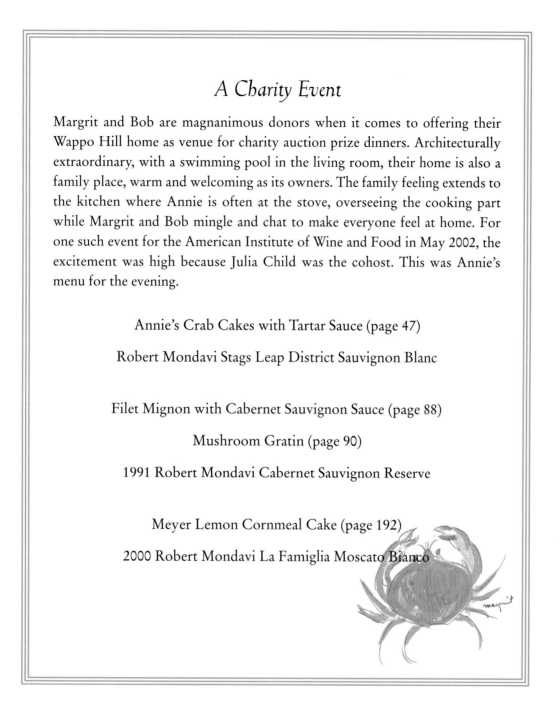

2 minutes. Stir in the capers and the remaining 2 tablespoons butter. Return the meat, along with its juices, to the pan. Sprinkle with salt and pepper and cook just until the meat is heated through, about 30 seconds.

To serve, arrange the scaloppine on a platter and spoon the sauce from the pan over them. Sprinkle with the parsley. Serve right away, with the cauliflower gratin on the side.

MUSTARD-MARINATED PORK LOIN
with French Green Lentils and Wilted Spinach

Serves 6 to 8

Every March, in an ode to mustard and the landscape, Napa Valley residents turn out for the annual Mustard Festival with as much enthusiasm as they do for the grape harvest events in September. Chefs make mustard sauce, rub meats with mustard for grilling, serve mustard in small crocks alongside frites, and stir it into vinaigrettes. Mustard is mixed with honey, with mayonnaise, and with ketchup for barbecue sauce. Annie joins in the fun and marinates pork loin with an herbed mustard mixture to flavor and tenderize the meat. The wilted spinach garnish adds an extra taste and a splash of color to the plate. The nutty-tasting green lentils cook up soft to the center while retaining their shape. Stir in the vinegar at the very end so its aroma and tang don't get lost.

Serve with a PINOT NOIR

PORK LOIN

3 pounds boneless pork loin roast

5 tablespoons extra virgin olive oil

3 tablespoons Dijon mustard

1 teaspoon chopped fresh thyme

2 teaspoons chopped fresh sage

1 large clove garlic, minced

Pinch of kosher salt

1/2 teaspoon freshly ground black pepper

FRENCH GREEN LENTILS

2 cups (about 1 pound) French green lentils

8 cups chicken stock (page xix)

3 yellow onions, 1 coarsely chopped and 2 finely diced

3 carrots, peeled, 1 coarsely chopped and 2 finely diced

4 large whole cloves garlic, plus 2 cloves garlic, minced

2 bay leaves

5 sprigs thyme, plus 2 teaspoons chopped fresh thyme

12 ounces pancetta, finely diced

1 tablespoon extra virgin olive oil

2 tablespoons balsamic vinegar

2 teaspoons kosher salt

1 teaspoon freshly ground black pepper

WILTED SPINACH

1/2 cup shallot–balsamic vinegar sauce (page 161)

10 cups baby spinach leaves

To prepare the pork loin, place it fat side up in a dish and make 1/2-inch slashes across the fat. In a small bowl, whisk together 3 tablespoons of the oil, the mustard, thyme, sage, garlic, salt, and pepper. Spread over the meat and refrigerate overnight. Remove from the refrigerator 30 minutes before cooking.

To prepare the lentils, combine them with the chicken stock in a large heavy pot. Tie the chopped onion, chopped carrot, whole garlic cloves, bay leaves, and thyme sprigs in a square of cheesecloth and add it to the pot. Bring to a boil over high heat, decrease the heat to medium-low, cover, and simmer for 25 minutes, or until the lentils are tender but still hold their shape.

Meanwhile, sauté the pancetta over medium heat in a sauté pan until it begins to turn golden and render its fat, about 5 minutes. Pour off the fat and add the oil. Stir in the diced onion, diced carrot, minced garlic, and chopped thyme. Sauté for 5 minutes, or until the vegetables soften.

Remove the cheesecloth bundle from the pot of lentils and add the sautéed vegetables. Cook, uncovered, over medium-high heat for 5 minutes. Stir in the vinegar, salt, and pepper. Set aside.

To cook the pork loin, preheat the oven to 375°F. Remove the meat from the marinade, reserving the marinade. In a heavy sauté pan, heat the remaining 2 tablespoons oil over medium heat. Add the meat and brown on all sides, about 12 minutes. Transfer to a baking sheet and brush with the reserved marinade. Roast for 30 minutes, or until an instant-read thermometer inserted in the center registers 145°F. Remove from the oven and let rest for 10 minutes.

To wilt the spinach, heat the vinaigrette in a stainless-steel bowl set over a pot of boiling water. When the vinaigrette begins to bubble, add the spinach, toss, and immediately remove from the heat (see Annie's Tip).

To serve, divide the lentils among dinner plates. Slice the roast 1/4 to 1/2 inch thick and arrange the slices over the lentils. Place a small handful of wilted spinach alongside the meat and serve.

ANNIE'S TIP

When making wilted salads, always use a mitten pot holder on one hand to grasp the bowl and use long-handled tongs in the other to toss the greens. That way, you don't risk burning yourself: the stainless-steel bowl gets hot very rapidly, and the greens need to be tossed quickly.

PORK, WHITE BEAN, AND TOMATILLO CHILI VERDE
with a Side of Green Beans

Serves 4

With roasted tomatillos and jalapeño, white beans, and a dash of Tabasco for a final kick at the end, Annie's chili verde is quite out of the ordinary. Whole-wheat tortillas and green beans on the side provide more of her own delicious touches.

Serve with a SANGIOVESE *or a* LIGHT ALE

1 cup dried small white beans

1 teaspoon kosher salt

1/4 cup extra virgin olive oil

2 pounds pork shoulder or boneless pork steaks, cut into 1 1/4-inch pieces

Freshly ground black pepper

1 red onion, chopped

4 cloves garlic, chopped

1 cup chicken stock (page xix)

8 tomatillos

1 large jalapeño chile

1/4 cup packed cilantro leaves

1 pound French green beans, stem ends trimmed

Dash of Tabasco sauce

1/4 cup tender cilantro sprigs, for garnish

3/4 cup crumbled queso fresco, for garnish

8 whole-wheat tortillas, warmed, for serving

Soak the white beans overnight in water to cover. (Or, use the quick-soak method: bring the beans and water to cover to a boil for 1 minute. Remove from the heat and let stand for 1 hour.) Drain and rinse.

To cook the beans, place them in a pot and add water to cover by 2 inches. Bring to a boil over high heat, decrease the heat to medium, and simmer until the beans are tender but still hold their shape, about 55 minutes. Stir in the salt. Drain and set aside, or allow to cool in the liquid and refrigerate for up to 3 days. (Note: the beans may also be cooked in a pressure cooker for 25 minutes after coming to pressure, plus 5 minutes standing time before adding the salt.)

Preheat the oven to 500°F. Heat 2 tablespoons of the oil in a large stew pot over medium-high heat. Add the pork in small batches and cook for about 3 minutes, seasoning with salt and pepper as you go, until brown all over (see Annie's Tip, page 94). Transfer each batch to a platter as it's done. Add the remaining 2 tablespoons oil and the onion to the pot. Cook, stirring to scrape up the browned bits from the bottom of the pan, until the onions are slightly wilted, about 2 minutes. Add the garlic and sauté for 1 minute, being careful not to let the garlic brown.

Return the pork and collected juices to the pot and add the stock. Bring to a boil, cover, decrease the heat to medium, and simmer for 25 minutes, until the meat is fork-tender.

While the meat cooks, put the tomatillos and jalapeño on a baking sheet and roast, turning frequently, until charred on all sides, about 12 minutes. Remove from the oven and allow to cool. Peel the papery husks from the tomatillos and pull off the stems. Peel the jalapeño, discarding the stem and seeds. In a food processor, combine the tomatillos, jalapeño, and cilantro leaves and purée. Add the purée to the pot with the meat, stir to mix, and continue simmering, uncovered, for 45 minutes.

While the chili simmers, blanch the green beans in a pot of salted boiling water until limp but still crunchy, about 8 minutes. Drain and set aside.

Stir the white beans into the chili and continue cooking for 10 minutes. Stir in the Tabasco and serve at once, garnished with the cilantro sprigs and crumbled cheese, and accompanied with the green beans and warm tortillas on the side.

GRILLED RABBIT
with Leeks, Mushrooms, Arugula, and Potato Gnocchi
Serves 6

In spring, when rains cause mushrooms to burgeon and the newly visible leeks are tender, the rabbit is young, and the evening is cool, this dish is perfect for a warm gathering of friends.

Annie's pillowy gnocchi are easy to make. You can prepare a batch, cook them several hours in advance, and reheat them just before serving. The potatoes should be passed through a food mill or potato ricer; if you have neither, use a fork, not a food processor or blender, which would make them gluey, not light and fluffy.

Serve with a PINOT NOIR *or* CHARDONNAY

RABBIT AND STOCK

2 (2- to 2¹/₂-pound) young rabbits

¹/₄ cup Dijon mustard

¹/₄ cup extra virgin olive oil

4 cloves garlic, mashed

8 sprigs thyme

2 tablespoons peanut oil

1 yellow onion, chopped

1 carrot, peeled and chopped

1 celery stalk, chopped

2 cloves garlic

6 cups chicken stock (page xix)

POTATO GNOCCHI

2 large russet potatoes

1 large egg, beaten

3 tablespoons unsalted butter, melted

¹/₄ cup freshly grated Parmesan cheese

¹/₂ cup all-purpose flour

1 teaspoon kosher salt

¹/₂ teaspoon freshly ground white pepper

Extra virgin olive oil, for drizzling

LEEKS AND MUSHROOMS

5 tablespoons unsalted butter

3 small leeks, including light green parts, sliced into ¹/₂-inch rounds

1 pound cremini, chanterelle, or shiitake mushrooms, or a combination, stemmed and cut into ¹/₂-inch slices

1 teaspoon minced garlic

¹/₂ teaspoon kosher salt

¹/₄ teaspoon freshly ground black pepper

2 tablespoons freshly squeezed lemon juice

3 cups arugula

To prepare the rabbit, cut off the front and back legs. Bone the center loin pieces and set the bones aside. In a large, nonreactive dish, combine the mustard, oil, mashed garlic, and 4 sprigs of the thyme. Add the rabbit pieces and turn to coat evenly. Set aside in the refrigerator.

To make the stock, using a cleaver or chef's knife, cut the rabbit bones into approximately 2-inch pieces. Heat the peanut oil in a large, heavy pot over high heat. Decrease the heat to medium-high, add the bone pieces, and cook until browned, 3 minutes. Decrease the heat to medium, add the onion, carrot, celery, and whole garlic

(continued)

cloves, and continue cooking until the vegetables are golden, 5 minutes. Add the stock and the remaining 4 sprigs thyme and bring to a simmer. Cook, partially covered, for 1½ hours. Strain through a fine mesh sieve into a bowl. Discard the solids and let the liquid cool for 15 minutes, then skim off the fat. There should be 3 cups; if there is more, place in a saucepan and boil over high heat until reduced to 3 cups.

To prepare the gnocchi, preheat the oven to 400°F. Bake the potatoes until tender, 50 to 55 minutes. Cut them in half while they are still hot, scoop out the flesh, and pass it through the fine plate of a food mill or a potato ricer into a bowl. Add the egg and butter and mix into the potatoes with a fork. Mix in the cheese, flour, salt, and pepper to make a moist dough. On a lightly floured surface, knead the dough until smooth. Divide the dough into 4 parts. Roll out the dough, one part at a time, into a rope about ½ inch in diameter. Cut the ropes into 1-inch pieces.

In a large pot of salted boiling water, cook the gnocchi in batches until they rise to the top, 2 to 4 minutes. Using a slotted spoon, transfer to a large bowl of ice water, then to another bowl. Drizzle with olive oil to prevent sticking. Set aside.

To cook the rabbit, prepare a medium-hot fire in a charcoal grill or preheat a gas grill to medium-high. Place the hind legs on the grill rack on the side of the grill, not directly over the hottest part of the fire. Grill, turning once, for 5 minutes on each side. Add the front legs on the side of the grill. Grill for 5 minutes. Turn over the front legs and the hind legs again and add the loins in the center

of the grill directly over the coals. Continue grilling, turning all the pieces once, until the meat is springy to the touch and the juices run rosy, about 5 minutes on each side.

To prepare the leeks and mushrooms, melt the butter in a large sauté pan over medium heat. Add the leeks and sauté until beginning to turn golden, about 3 minutes. Decrease the heat to low, stir in the mushrooms, and cook for 5 minutes, or until softened. Stir in the garlic and cook for 2 minutes. Stir in the reduced rabbit stock, salt, and pepper. Set aside and keep warm.

To serve, reheat the mushroom mixture and the gnocchi in separate pans. Spoon some of the mushrooms and leeks onto 6 plates, leaving behind some of the liquid. Place the rabbit on top. Stir the lemon juice and arugula into the remaining liquid and spoon over the rabbit. Add some gnocchi to the side and serve right away.

GAME PLAN

Up to 1 day ahead:
- Prepare the rabbit and set aside in the refrigerator.
- Make the stock and refrigerate.
- Bake the potatoes and make the gnocchi; refrigerate.

Several hours ahead:
- Cook the gnocchi and set aside to reheat.
- Cook the leeks and mushrooms and make the sauce. Set aside to reheat.

Just before serving:
- Grill the rabbit; reheat the gnocchi and sauce.

SAUTÉED RABBIT *with Fried Polenta*

Serves 4

Annie is partial to rabbit for its lean and delicate meat, which lends itself to so many grilled, stewed, and sautéed preparations. Because the meat is so low in fat, she keeps the pan covered while sautéing to retain moisture. For frying, she makes the polenta somewhat stiffer than for soft polenta (page 125) so it can easily be cut into neat squares or triangles.

Serve with a CHARDONNAY

POLENTA

6 cups water

1¹/₂ cups polenta

¹/₂ tablespoon kosher salt

Freshly ground black pepper

2 tablespoons unsalted butter

¹/₂ cup freshly grated Parmesan cheese

Extra virgin olive oil, for frying

1 tablespoon chopped fresh flat-leaf parsley, for garnish

RABBIT

¹/₄ cup Dijon mustard

1 tablespoon chopped fresh thyme

¹/₂ teaspoon kosher salt

¹/₄ teaspoon freshly ground black pepper

1 (2¹/₂- to 2³/₄-pound) rabbit, cut into 6 pieces

1 tablespoon unsalted butter

2 tablespoons extra virgin olive oil

1 tablespoon minced garlic

¹/₄ cup finely chopped shallots

¹/₂ cup chicken stock (page xix)

¹/₂ cup Chardonnay

To prepare the polenta, bring the water to a boil in a large saucepan. Add the polenta in a thin stream, stirring constantly. Add the salt, decrease the heat to medium-low, and cook for 20 minutes, stirring often, until smooth. Stir in the pepper, butter, and cheese and spread the mixture in a 9 by 13-inch baking dish. Allow to cool completely. Use right away, or cover and refrigerate for up to 3 days.

To prepare the rabbit, mix together the mustard, thyme, salt, and pepper in a large dish. Add the rabbit and turn to coat. Set aside at room temperature for up to 30 minutes or refrigerate for up to 4 hours.

To cook the rabbit, melt the butter with the oil in a large sauté pan over medium-high heat. Add the rabbit pieces and decrease the heat to medium. Cover the pan and cook, turning once, for about 12 minutes on each side, until nicely browned. Remove from the heat and transfer the rabbit to an ovenproof baking dish. Cover and keep warm in a 200°F oven while finishing the recipe. (There's no need to preheat the oven.) Place the sauté pan over high heat. Add the garlic and shallots and sauté until softened, 2 minutes. Add the stock and wine, stirring to scrape up the browned bits from the bottom of the pan. Cook to reduce for 3 minutes, or until slightly thickened, then cover and set aside in a warm place.

To fry the polenta, cut it into squares or triangles. Lightly oil a nonstick sauté pan and place over medium-high heat. In batches, fry the polenta, turning once, until crispy and golden around the edges, about 4 minutes total.

To serve, place a rabbit hind leg section on each of 2 plates, and a foreleg and a saddle piece on 2 other plates. Spoon the sauce over the rabbit and sprinkle chopped parsley over the sauce. Garnish each plate with fried polenta and serve.

Poultry

POULTRY DISHES ABOUND in the cooking of Annie and Margrit. Whole chickens, baby chickens, chicken parts, game hens, duck, and smaller bird cousins like quail and squab all appear frequently on their tables. In the Vineyard Room (pictured opposite), Annie serves poultry marinated and sautéed or grilled, then dresses the plate with fancy adornments like roasted baby vegetables, crisp wild rice cakes, perhaps a spoonful of sweet and tangy onion marmalade. When the occasion is casual, though, she might simmer a duck in a streamlined cassoulet and serve it buffet-style, or simply roast a whole chicken as she learned from Margrit. For her part, Margrit likes to stew chicken into an Italian-inspired bollito or a North African tajine, bake game hens for an easy get-together, or, one of her favorites, roast the Thanksgiving turkey for the family. In this chapter, you'll find all those personal and professional preparations plus a mouthwatering selection of accompaniments.

ROASTED CHICKEN
with Red Potatoes and Kalamata Olives

Serves 4

Anyone who cooks most likely has a favorite roasted chicken recipe, often accompanied with an unalterable conviction that it's "the best." Annie's preferred best way was handed down from her mother. The bird is rubbed all over with lemon and thyme, roasted at high heat, and basted two or three times during cooking. The basting is the important point. The result is a golden-skinned, succulent-fleshed chicken that can hold its own in any roast-chicken show. Here, the chicken gets a Mediterranean flourish, with potatoes and kalamata olives tossed into the roasting juices.

Serve with a PINOT NOIR

1 tablespoon freshly squeezed lemon juice

1/4 cup extra virgin olive oil

1 teaspoon chopped fresh thyme, or 1/2 teaspoon dried thyme

Kosher salt and freshly ground black pepper

1 (31/2-pound) chicken

11/2 pounds red, white, or Yukon Gold potatoes, halved crosswise

1/2 cup chicken stock (page xix)

1/2 cup chopped fresh flat-leaf parsley

1/2 cup pitted kalamata olives, pitted and coarsely chopped (page xx)

Preheat the oven to 400°F. In a small bowl, combine the lemon juice, 2 tablespoons of the oil, the thyme, a large pinch of salt, and several grinds of pepper. Rub the chicken inside and out with the mixture. Place on a rack in a roasting pan and cook, basting every 20 minutes, until the juices run golden, no longer pink. This will take from 60 to 75 minutes, depending on the size of the chicken.

While the chicken roasts, boil the potatoes in lightly salted water until tender, 10 to 15 minutes, depending on the size. Drain and allow to cool completely. Cut the potatoes into 1/2-inch slices.

When the chicken is done, transfer it to a platter and set aside in a warm place. Pour off the fat from the roasting pan and place the pan on the stove top over high heat. Stir in the stock and the remaining 2 tablespoons oil and bring to a boil. Add the potatoes, decrease the heat to medium-high, and cook for 2 minutes, or until the potatoes are heated through. Add the parsley, olives, and salt and pepper to taste and stir to mix.

To serve, carve the chicken into portions and arrange them on a platter. Spoon the potatoes and olives, along with any juices, around the chicken and serve.

BOLLITO OF CHICKEN
with Fingerling Potatoes, Asparagus, and Fava Beans

Serves 4

Margrit is often asked to supply recipes and menus for Robert Mondavi Winery publicity and ceremonial occasions. For an American Institute of Wine and Food event one year, she offered this classic Italian dish of simmered chicken and vegetables and this comment: "After really trying to come up with many fancy dishes Bob enjoys, I must admit that this simple dinner is his favorite. At heart, Bob is a simple person; there is still a lot of *paesano* in him." Margrit's personal touch to the traditional dish is the addition of celery root. She serves the bollito with boiled fingerling potatoes, fava beans, and asparagus, all drizzled with a vinegar dressing, another unique touch.

Serve with a MERLOT

BOLLITO

1 (5¹/₂-pound) roasting chicken

1 yellow onion, halved

¹/₄ celery root, peeled and cut into 2-inch pieces

2 carrots, peeled and cut into 2-inch pieces

¹/₂ green bell pepper, quartered

1 small jalapeño chile, halved

3 large cloves garlic

4 sprigs flat-leaf parsley

2 sprigs thyme

1 sprig oregano

3 quarts water, or to cover

Kosher salt and freshly ground black pepper

VEGETABLES

12 fingerling potatoes

12 asparagus spears, trimmed

1¹/₂ pounds fava beans, shelled

THREE-VINEGAR DRESSING

2 tablespoons red wine vinegar (see page 53 for Margrit's homemade vinegar)

¹/₂ tablespoon sherry vinegar

¹/₂ tablespoon balsamic vinegar

1 teaspoon freshly squeezed lemon juice

¹/₄ teaspoon kosher salt

¹/₈ teaspoon freshly ground black pepper

¹/₂ cup extra virgin olive oil

To make the bollito, combine all the ingredients in a large heavy pot and bring to a boil over high heat. Decrease the heat to medium and simmer, partially covered, for 45 minutes, or until the chicken is tender. Turn off the heat and let sit on the burner for at least 30 minutes or up to 1 hour.

While the chicken rests, prepare the vegetables. In a large pot of salted boiling water, cook the potatoes over high heat until tender, 8 to 10 minutes, depending on the size. Using a wire strainer, transfer the potatoes to a plate. Bring the water to a boil again, add the asparagus, and cook until limp but still bright green, about 5 minutes. Using a wire strainer, transfer the asparagus to the plate with the potatoes. Bring the water to a boil again, add the fava beans, and cook until the skins begin to wrinkle, about 3 minutes. Drain in a colander, rinse under cool water, and peel. Place on the plate with the potatoes and asparagus.

To make the dressing, combine all the ingredients in a small bowl or screw-top jar. Whisk or shake vigorously until emulsified. Use right away or store at room temperature for up to 2 days.

To serve, lift the chicken out of the pot and set on a plate. Strain the cooking liquid through a fine mesh sieve into a large bowl, discarding the solids, and reserve to use as a broth in another dish (such as Pasta in Brodo, page 22). Cut the chicken into serving pieces and divide the pieces among dinner plates. (Or, as Margrit most often does for casual family dinners, arrange on a platter.) Arrange the potatoes, asparagus, and fava beans around the chicken. Moisten the vegetables with the vinaigrette and serve right away.

FLATTENED CHICKEN
Stuffed with Zucchini, Mushrooms, and Ricotta Salata

Serves 4

Margrit's stuffed chicken is a homespun dish, but one with flair. The stuffing, which she sometimes varies by using Swiss chard in place of the zucchini, goes under the skin, and the bird is flattened so that it comes out almost like a galantine. She adds further ado by serving the dish with an elegant Robert Mondavi Winery Chardonnay at cellar temperature (55°F) or very lightly chilled.

Serve with a CHARDONNAY

STUFFING

1 tablespoon extra virgin olive oil

2 small zucchini, coarsely grated

¼ pound button mushrooms, thinly sliced

½ yellow onion, finely chopped

1 small clove garlic, minced or pressed

1 teaspoon chopped fresh marjoram

1 teaspoon chopped fresh flat-leaf parsley

¼ cup fine bread crumbs (page xix)

1 large egg, lightly beaten

¼ cup grated ricotta salata cheese

Kosher salt and freshly ground black pepper

1 (3½-pound) chicken

16 asparagus spears, trimmed and peeled

2 ripe tomatoes, cut into 4 wedges each

Preheat the oven to 375°F. To prepare the stuffing, heat the oil in a sauté pan over medium-high heat. Add the zucchini, mushrooms, onion, garlic, marjoram, and parsley and stir until the vegetables are wilted, about 3 minutes. Remove from the heat and stir in the bread crumbs, egg, and cheese. Season with salt and pepper and set aside to cool slightly.

To prepare the chicken, press down on the chicken breast with both hands hard enough to break the breastbone and flatten it. Using a boning knife or poultry sheers, cut through the breastbone from the inside to sever it in half, being careful not to cut all the way through the skin. Press down again to flatten it further. Push the stuffing under the skin of the chicken, beginning at the breast and working back and down the legs. Place the chicken on a baking sheet and roast for 50 minutes, or until the meat is no longer pink between the leg and thigh.

While the chicken roasts, blanch the asparagus in salted boiling water for 5 minutes, or until limp but still bright green. Drain and set aside.

To serve, cut the chicken into quarters and arrange on 4 plates. Garnish the plates with asparagus spears and tomato wedges and serve right away.

CHICKEN THIGHS
with Porcini, Tomato, and Black Olive Sauce on Soft Polenta

Serves 4 to 6

Every cook has at least one cupboard dish in the bag of tricks for days when there's no energy for shopping. If your pantry is well stocked, all you have to do is grab a few chicken thighs at the store, and dinner is ready within an hour. Margrit's philosophy is that the time you spend running around shopping for takeout meals can just as well be spent in your own kitchen. She's handed down that ethic to Annie, who always cooks dinner at home when she's not working. "It's as much about nurturing as needing," Annie says, "and there's time to take a breather and daydream while stirring the polenta."

Serve with a ZINFANDEL

1/2 ounce (about 1/2 cup) dried porcini mushrooms

SOFT POLENTA

5 cups water

1 tablespoon kosher salt

1 cup polenta or yellow cornmeal

3/4 cup (3 ounces) freshly grated Parmigiano-Reggiano cheese

CHICKEN

2 tablespoons extra virgin olive oil

6 boneless, skinless chicken thighs, cut into 1/2-inch-wide strips

1 yellow onion, finely chopped

2 cloves garlic, minced

2 cups coarsely chopped canned tomatoes, with juices

1 cup chicken stock (page xix

1 tablespoon shredded fresh basil

1 cup kalamata olives, pitted (page xx)

Kosher salt

2 tablespoons chopped fresh flat-leaf parsley, for garnish

Put the mushrooms in a small bowl, add hot water to cover, and set aside to plump for 15 to 30 minutes.

To make the polenta, bring the water to a boil in a deep, heavy saucepan over high heat. Add the salt and gradually pour in the polenta, whisking constantly so lumps don't form. When the polenta comes to a boil, decrease the heat to medium and cook, stirring with a wooden spoon every few minutes, until it begins to thicken, about 10 minutes. Stir in the cheese and continue cooking over medium heat for 5 minutes more, until thick like porridge and still spoonable. Cover and set aside in a warm place.

To cook the chicken, heat the oil in a large sauté pan over medium-high heat. Brown the chicken strips on all sides, in 2 batches to keep from crowding if necessary, about 2 minutes per batch. Transfer to a plate. Decrease the heat to medium, add the onion and garlic, and cook until soft, about 2 minutes. Return the chicken to the pan, add the tomatoes and stock, and stir to mix. Cover and cook for 10 minutes. Lift the mushrooms out of the soaking liquid, squeeze lightly, and add them to the pan with the chicken. Stir in the basil and cook, uncovered, for 15 minutes, or until the liquid is thick and saucy. Stir in the olives and add salt to taste.

To serve, spoon the polenta onto dinner plates. Top with the chicken and sauce, sprinkle the parsley over the top, and serve right away.

MARINATED CHICKEN BREASTS
with Potato-Turnip Gratin and Roasted Baby Beets

Serves 6

To make an attractive serving for informal Vineyard Room lunches, Annie uses boneless chicken breasts with the tasty drummette part of the wing attached. She leaves the skin on the breasts for flavor and succulence, gilds them with a zesty marinade, and serves a potato and turnip gratin as a peppy foil to the mild chicken meat.

Serve with a CHARDONNAY

CHICKEN

1 cup Chardonnay

1/4 cup brandy

1/4 cup white wine vinegar

1/4 cup Dijon mustard

3 large cloves garlic, chopped

1/4 cup extra virgin olive oil

12 small sprigs rosemary

1 teaspoon kosher salt

1/2 teaspoon freshly ground black pepper

6 small boneless chicken breasts, with drummettes attached (see Note)

BEETS

18 baby beets (about 1 inch in diameter), tops trimmed to 1 inch

1 1/2 tablespoons extra virgin olive oil

Kosher salt and freshly ground black pepper

2 tablespoons balsamic vinegar

POTATO-TURNIP GRATIN

3 turnips, peeled and sliced 1/4 inch thick

3 cups whole milk

3 large russet potatoes, peeled and sliced 1/4 inch thick

Kosher salt and freshly ground black pepper

1 cup heavy cream

NOTE

If you don't have a butcher who will cut the chicken breasts with wings attached, it's easy enough to do yourself. Purchase whole chickens and disjoint them with a boning or chef's knife into 5 sections: 2 breasts with wings attached, 2 leg/thigh sections, and the backbone. Remove the 2 first joints of the wings and use them, along with the backbone, to make stock (page xix). Reserve the legs and thighs for another recipe, such as Lemon and Black Pepper–Marinated Chicken (page 128).

To prepare the chicken breasts, combine the wine, brandy, and vinegar in a small saucepan and cook over high heat until reduced by half, about 5 minutes. Transfer to a dish large enough to hold the breasts in one layer. Add the mustard, garlic, oil, rosemary, salt, and pepper and stir to mix. Add the breasts and turn to coat. Cover and refrigerate overnight.

To prepare the beets, preheat the oven to 375°F. Place the beets in a baking dish and add the oil, a sprinkle each of salt and pepper, and a splash of water. Cover the dish with aluminum foil and bake until tender, about 1 hour. Remove, allow to cool enough to handle, then peel. Place the beets in a bowl, add the vinegar, and toss gently to coat.

While the beets are cooking, prepare the gratin. Lightly grease a 9 by 13-inch gratin dish with butter. Put the turnips in a saucepan with $1^1/_2$ cups of the milk. Put the potatoes in another saucepan with the remaining $1^1/_2$ cups milk. Season them both with salt and pepper and bring each to a boil over medium-high heat. Decrease the heat to medium and simmer until they are just tender, about 3 minutes for the turnips and 5 minutes for the potatoes. (Be sure not to overcook them, or the slices will fall apart.) Using a slotted spoon, transfer the slices to a baking sheet and allow to cool enough to handle. Discard the milk.

Overlap half the potato slices in the prepared dish. Sprinkle with salt and pepper. Overlap half the turnips on top of the potatoes. Sprinkle with salt and pepper. Make another layer of each, also seasoning with salt and pepper. Pour the cream over the top. Place in the oven with the beets and roast until golden, about 45 minutes.

To cook the chicken, prepare a medium-hot fire in a charcoal grill or preheat a gas grill to medium-high. Remove the chicken from the marinade and pat dry. Grill, turning once, over indirect heat—at the edges of, not directly over, the coals—until golden, about 10 minutes on each side.

To serve, divide the gratin among 6 plates. Place a chicken breast on top of the gratin and garnish with 3 beets on each plate. Serve right away.

LEMON AND BLACK PEPPER–MARINATED CHICKEN
with German Potato Salad and Phoebe's Black Bean Salsa

Serves 8

When Margrit's family assembles for a summer barbecue, each person contributes something creative to a menu that's simple to prepare and serve. Annie's chicken can be marinated for a day or two before grilling. Margrit's potato salad is dressed with a vinaigrette rather than mayonnaise and so there's no need to take the time to chill it; it's best served warm or at room temperature. The beans for Phoebe's salsa can also be cooked a day or two in advance and the remaining ingredients tossed in while the chicken and potato salad cook. That leaves plenty of time to gossip and catch up on family news.

Serve with a CHARDONNAY *and a* PINOT NOIR

CHICKEN

1/2 cup extra virgin olive oil

1/3 cup freshly squeezed lemon juice

1 tablespoon chopped fresh rosemary

2 teaspoons freshly ground black pepper

8 chicken leg and thigh sections

PHOEBE'S BLACK BEAN SALSA

2 cups cooked black beans (page 94)

1 1/2 cups fresh corn kernels (3 to 4 ears)

2 tomatoes, cut into 1/4-inch dice

1 red bell pepper, cut into 1/4-inch dice

1 green bell pepper, cut into 1/4-inch dice

1/2 cup finely chopped red onion

1 to 2 serrano or jalapeño chiles, thinly sliced, seeds and all

1/3 cup freshly squeezed lime juice

1/3 cup extra virgin olive oil

1/3 cup chopped cilantro

1/2 teaspoon ground cumin

1/2 teaspoon pure chile powder

1 teaspoon kosher salt

POTATO SALAD

2 1/2 pounds baby red potatoes, cut into 1/2-inch slices

1/4 cup red wine vinegar

1 tablespoon Dijon mustard

2 tablespoons finely chopped shallots

1 tablespoon kosher salt

1/2 teaspoon freshly ground black pepper

1/3 cup extra virgin olive oil

1/4 cup finely chopped fresh flat-leaf parsley

To prepare the chicken, combine the oil, lemon juice, rosemary, and pepper in a dish large enough to hold the chicken in 2 layers. Add the chicken and turn to coat all over. Cover and refrigerate overnight or up to 2 days. Remove from the refrigerator 30 minutes before grilling.

To make the salsa, combine all the ingredients in a large bowl. Set aside at room temperature for 1 to 2 hours to allow the flavors to blend. (May be made up to 1 day in advance and stored in the refrigerator.)

To make the potato salad, put the potatoes in a large pot and cover with water by 1 inch. Bring to a boil. Decrease the heat and simmer for about 6 minutes, or until the potatoes are tender but still holding their shape. Drain in a colander and set aside to cool until no longer steaming. Meanwhile, combine the vinegar, mustard, shallots, salt, and pepper in a large salad bowl. Whisk in the oil.

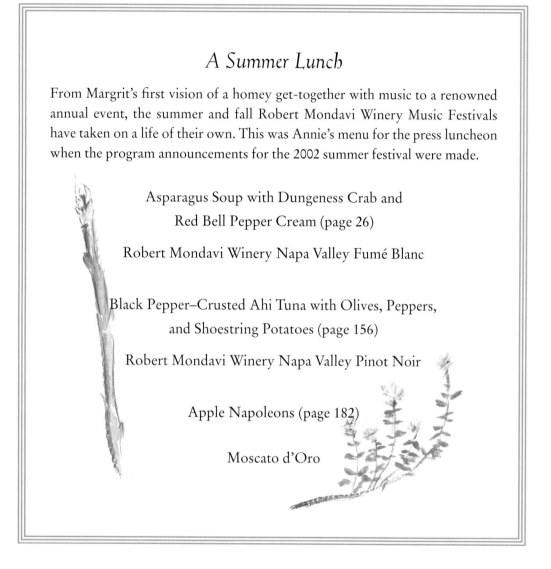

A Summer Lunch

From Margrit's first vision of a homey get-together with music to a renowned annual event, the summer and fall Robert Mondavi Winery Music Festivals have taken on a life of their own. This was Annie's menu for the press luncheon when the program announcements for the 2002 summer festival were made.

Asparagus Soup with Dungeness Crab and
Red Bell Pepper Cream (page 26)

Robert Mondavi Winery Napa Valley Fumé Blanc

Black Pepper–Crusted Ahi Tuna with Olives, Peppers,
and Shoestring Potatoes (page 156)

Robert Mondavi Winery Napa Valley Pinot Noir

Apple Napoleons (page 182)

Moscato d'Oro

While they're still warm, add the potatoes to the bowl and gently toss to mix. Sprinkle with the parsley.

To cook the chicken, prepare a medium-hot fire in a charcoal grill or preheat a gas grill to medium-high. Remove the chicken from the marinade, reserving the marinade. In a small saucepan, bring the marinade to a boil and cook for 5 minutes. Set aside to use as a basting sauce.

Place the chicken pieces on the grill rack. Cook, turning several times, until no longer pink at the joint between the leg and thigh, 35 to 40 minutes. Brush lightly with some of the reserved marinade each time the chicken is turned. (Have a spray bottle of water handy to douse flames that might flare up when the chicken is basted.) Transfer to a platter and serve with the salsa and potato salad alongside.

ACHIOTE-RUBBED POLLITOS *with Guacamole*

Serves 6

Pollitos, or "little chickens," weigh about 2½ pounds and are used often in Latino cooking. They used to be widely available and were known as broilers, distinct from the larger fryers of 3½ pounds or more. Game hens make a good substitute for pollitos. Achiote seeds can be found in Latino markets and many supermarkets. For her guacamole, Annie likes to keep the heat in the temperate zone, both out of deference to guests who can't tolerate chile heat and also because she wants the creamy sweetness of avocado to dominate.

Serve with a PINOT NOIR

3 (2½-pound) pollitos

¼ cup achiote seeds, finely ground in a spice grinder (see Annie's Tip)

3 tablespoons chopped fresh oregano, or 1 tablespoon dried oregano

⅓ cup champagne vinegar

8 cloves garlic, coarsely chopped

2 teaspoons kosher salt

2 teaspoons freshly ground black pepper

2 tablespoons extra virgin olive oil

GUACAMOLE

3 avocados, peeled, halved, and pitted

4 scallions, including light green parts, finely chopped

1 large jalapeño chile, seeded and finely chopped

1 ripe tomato, finely diced

1 large clove garlic, minced or pressed

¼ cup packed chopped cilantro

¼ cup freshly squeezed lime juice

¾ teaspoon kosher salt

Warm corn tortillas, for serving

To prepare the pollitos, cut them in half lengthwise and place them in a large roasting pan that will hold them in 1 tightly packed layer (you may need to use 2 pans). In a food processor, combine the achiote powder, oregano, vinegar, garlic, salt, pepper, and oil and process to a rough paste. Rub the paste over the pollito halves, turning to coat all over. Cover and refrigerate for at least 2 hours or preferably overnight. Remove from the refrigerator 30 minutes before cooking.

To cook the pollitos, prepare a medium-hot fire in a charcoal grill or preheat a gas grill to medium-high. Place the pollitos, bone side down, on the grill rack. Grill, turning every 10 minutes, until the meat between the thigh and leg is no longer pink, 30 to 35 minutes.

To make the guacamole, mash the avocados in a large bowl using a potato masher or sturdy wire whisk. Add the scallions, jalapeño, tomato, garlic, cilantro, lime juice, and salt and mix well with a fork. Use right away or cover tightly and set aside at room temperature for up to several hours.

To serve, place a pollito half on each of 6 plates. Add a large dollop of guacamole to the side of each and serve with warm corn tortillas.

ANNIE'S TIP

To replicate the color and flavor of achiote, use mild Hungarian paprika mixed with a pinch of ground turmeric.

TAJINE OF POUSSINS *with Aubergine*

Serves 4 to 6

Long after her days as an army wife, when she moved her household lock, stock, and barrel every few years, Margrit remains an inveterate traveler. She has a passion for exploring art, food, and cultures around the world. Once, when she had barely stepped off the plane from a trip to Morocco, it was her turn to host the bi-monthly lunch for her tennis group. Full of the sights and aromas of that heady cuisine, Margrit put together a Moroccan-inspired stew served over couscous with a Napa-style garnish of cilantro and lemon zest. On a hot day, serve the tajine with an icy-cold rosé; on a cool day, choose a Merlot.

Serve with a ROSÉ *or* MERLOT

1/4 cup unsalted butter

1 unpeeled globe eggplant, cut into 1/2-inch cubes

1 large yellow onion, chopped

4 cloves garlic, chopped

1/2 teaspoon kosher salt

2 teaspoons ground cumin

1 teaspoon good-quality curry powder

1 teaspoon pure chile powder

1/2 teaspoon ground coriander

2 poussins or game hens, quartered

2 yellow summer squash, cut into 1/2-inch pieces

4 smallish red potatoes, quartered

2 cups chicken stock (page xix)

2 cups coarsely chopped canned tomatoes, with juices

BASIC COUSCOUS

3 cups water

1/2 teaspoon kosher salt

1 tablespoon extra virgin olive oil

2 1/2 cups couscous

1/2 cup cilantro leaves, for garnish

1 tablespoon chopped lemon zest, for garnish

To prepare the tajine, melt the butter in a large casserole pot over medium-high heat. Add the eggplant, onion, garlic, and salt and stir to mix. Cook, stirring frequently, until the vegetables are wilted, about 5 minutes. Stir in the cumin, curry powder, chile powder, and coriander. Add the poussins, squash, potatoes, stock, and tomatoes with their juices. Gently stir to mix, and bring to a boil.

Cover the pot, decrease the heat to medium-low, and simmer for 20 minutes, or until the thigh meat is no longer pink. Uncover and simmer for 5 minutes, or until the liquid is reduced. Remove from the heat and set aside for 10 minutes.

To prepare the couscous, bring the water, salt, and oil to a boil in a pot over medium-high heat. Add the couscous, stir, and cover. Remove from the heat right away and let stand for 5 minutes. Fluff with a fork.

To serve, mound the couscous on dinner plates. Arrange the poussins and vegetables on top and moisten with broth. Garnish with cilantro and lemon zest and serve right away.

MARGRIT'S TIP

Poussins are essentially baby chickens, about 1 pound each. They are available fresh in upscale food markets and butcher shops that feature poultry. Fresh Cornish hens are a fine substitute, and better to use than frozen poussins.

HERB AND BUTTER–BRAISED POUSSINS
with Swiss Chard Gratin

Serves 4

Annie and Margrit look back with fondness on their time spent cooking together when Annie was growing up. These days, with their busy schedules, it's harder for them to find this time. When they do, Margrit might make braised poussins while Annie puts together a Swiss chard gratin, a recipe she learned from Margrit and refined from a Great Chefs cooking class at the winery. She innovates by including the greens, which were not in the original dish (Margrit prefers to use the stems only). But, differences in cooking style aside, Annie and Margrit enjoy being at the stove together in such treasured moments.

Serve with a PINOT NOIR

GRATIN

1¾ pounds white-ribbed Swiss chard

¼ cup unsalted butter

3 scallions, including light green parts, chopped

1 clove garlic, chopped

¼ cup heavy cream

Kosher salt and freshly ground black pepper

2 tablespoons all-purpose flour

1¾ cup milk

½ cup (2 ounces) shredded Gruyère cheese

POUSSINS

2 poussins (see Margrit's Tip, page 131)

Kosher salt and freshly ground black pepper

2 sprigs rosemary

2 large fresh sage leaves

1 cup unsalted butter

To prepare the gratin, preheat the oven to 375°F. Lightly grease an 8-inch-square glass or ceramic dish. Bring a large pot of water to a boil.

Cut the leaves off the chard stems. Keeping them in separate piles, coarsely chop the leaves and cut the stems crosswise into 1-inch pieces. Rinse and drain each pile.

Drop the stems into the boiling water and cook until tender, 6 to 8 minutes. Using a wire strainer, transfer to a colander and set aside to cool. In the same pot, blanch the leaves for 2 minutes. Drain into a separate colander, rinse under cold water, and set aside to cool.

In a large sauté pan, melt 2 tablespoons of the butter over medium-high heat. Squeeze the chard leaves dry, add to the pan, and sauté to evaporate any remaining moisture, about 2 minutes. Stir in the scallions and garlic, then the cream and salt and pepper to taste. Transfer to the prepared dish. Spread the chard stems over the top.

In a small saucepan, melt the remaining 2 tablespoons butter over medium-high heat. Add the flour, whisking to make a smooth paste. Slowly whisk in the milk and bring to a boil, stirring all the time. Decrease the heat to medium-low and cook, stirring frequently, until thickened, 10 to 12 minutes. Stir in ¼ cup of the cheese and season with salt and pepper. Pour into the dish with the chard. Sprinkle the remaining ¼ cup cheese over the top. Bake for 30 to 35 minutes, or until the top is slightly golden and the juices are bubbling up.

While the gratin bakes, prepare the poussins. Sprinkle them liberally with salt and pepper. Place a sprig of rosemary and a sage leaf in the cavity of each and flatten them with the palm of your hand. In a large sauté pan, melt the butter over medium heat. Add the poussins, breast side down, and cook for 10 minutes. Turn over and decrease the heat to medium-low. Continue cooking for 10 minutes, basting from time to time. Turn again and cook for 5 minutes. Turn one more time and cook until no longer pink at the thigh bone, about 5 minutes more. Be sure to lower the heat if the butter starts to burn. Transfer to a plate, set aside in a warm place, and let rest for 5 to 10 minutes while the gratin finishes cooking.

To serve, cut each poussin in half lengthwise and discard the herbs. Place the poussins, skin side up, on a serving platter. Pour the collected juices over the top and serve right away with the chard gratin on the side.

GRILLED POUSSINS, BABY LEEKS, AND ASPARAGUS
with Meyer Lemon Aioli

Serves 4

When it comes to poussins, Annie and Margrit agree: they are good all ways, from stewed with exotic North African spices to simply braised in herbs and butter. For a swank affair, Annie marinates and grills the baby chickens and garnishes the plates with an elegant duo of grilled vegetables and a refreshing Meyer lemon aioli.

Serve with a PINOT NOIR

POUSSINS

2 poussins, halved lengthwise (see Margrit's Tip, page 131)

2 tablespoons extra virgin olive oil

1 tablespoon chopped fresh marjoram

1 tablespoon chopped fresh thyme

1 tablespoon coarsely chopped garlic

1 tablespoon finely chopped Meyer lemon zest

1/2 teaspoon kosher salt

1/2 teaspoon freshly ground black pepper

MEYER LEMON AIOLI

1 egg yolk

2 tablespoons freshly squeezed Meyer lemon juice

1 teaspoon minced garlic

1 tablespoon chopped fresh chervil

1/4 teaspoon kosher salt

Pinch of freshly ground black pepper

1 cup extra virgin olive oil

8 baby leeks, including light green parts

1 pound asparagus, trimmed and peeled if large

Extra virgin olive oil

1 tablespoon finely chopped Meyer lemon zest, for garnish

To prepare the poussins, put the halves in a dish large enough to hold them in 1 layer (overlapping a little is okay). Add the oil, marjoram, thyme, garlic, zest, salt, and pepper. Turn to mix and coat evenly. Cover and refrigerate for at least 4 hours or preferably overnight. Remove from the refrigerator 30 minutes before cooking.

To prepare the aioli, combine the egg yolk, lemon juice, garlic, chervil, salt, and pepper in a food processor and process to blend. With the machine running, gradually add the oil in a thin stream. Use right away or cover and refrigerate for up to 2 days.

Bring a large pot of water to a boil. Drop in the leeks and blanch for 2 minutes. Using a wire strainer, transfer to an ice bath. Drain and set aside. In the same pot of water, blanch the asparagus for 2 minutes. Transfer to a fresh ice bath. Drain and set aside.

Prepare a medium-hot fire in a charcoal grill or preheat a gas grill to medium-high. Grill the poussins, breast side down, until nicely browned, about 5 minutes. Turn over the pieces and move to indirect heat on the edge of the grill. Cook until the thigh meat is no longer pink, about 20 minutes. Transfer the poussins to a platter and set aside in a warm place to rest for 10 minutes.

While the poussins rest, coat the asparagus and leeks with oil. Place them on the grill rack and cook, turning once or twice, until grill-marked all over, about 5 minutes.

To serve, place half a poussin on each of 4 plates. Arrange the grilled vegetables to the side of the poussins. Top with a spoonful of aioli and a sprinkling of lemon zest.

QUAIL MARINATED IN VERJUS AND HONEY
with a Mélange of Roasted Baby Vegetables

Serves 6

The *verjus* in the marinade adds a fruity essence to the meat, and the honey ensures that the birds will come out a deep golden color. Annie likes to sauté quail over high heat and then finish them on the grill. If the weather is not conducive to firing up the grill, her plan B is to finish the quail in a hot oven.

Serve with a PINOT NOIR

QUAIL

1/4 cup dry white wine

1/4 cup verjus (see Notes)

1/2 cup extra virgin olive oil

1 tablespoon honey

2 small shallots, thinly sliced

Rind of 1 lemon, cut into 2-inch by 1/2-inch strips

1 tablespoon chopped fresh thyme

1 teaspoon kosher salt

1/2 teaspoon freshly ground black pepper

6 semi-boned quail (see Notes)

NOTES

Verjus (French) or verjuice (English) is a sour liquid made from unripe grapes (in France) or from unripe crabapples (in Britain). Annie uses the grape version for marinades, sauces, and stews when she wants a fruity nip, a bit of tang. *Verjus* can be ordered from Navarro Winery at www.navarrowine.com or Fusion Foods at www.verjus.com.

A semi-boned quail has had the breastbone removed, while the other bones are intact. It's easy to eat, and can be flattened to cook more evenly. Sometimes, you can find the quail already semi-boned. If not, cut along the backbone of each quail and open it out. Then, remove the breastbone with a sharp boning knife. Or, if that's too much of a chore, leave the breastbone intact. As long as the quail is opened out, the cooking result will be much the same, just not as tidily easy to eat.

ROASTED BABY VEGETABLES

12 small red potatoes, quartered

6 small shallots

1/4 cup extra virgin olive oil

12 baby carrots, peeled

12 fresh shiitake mushrooms, stemmed

3 cups arugula

2 cups small cherry tomatoes

To prepare the quail, combine the wine, *verjus*, oil, honey, shallots, rind, thyme, salt, and pepper in 1 or 2 glass or ceramic dishes large enough to hold the quail in 1 layer. Stir to mix. Add the quail and turn to coat them all over. Cover and refrigerate for at least 3 hours or up to 6 hours.

To prepare the vegetables, preheat the oven to 375°F. In a bowl, toss the potatoes and shallots in 2 tablespoons of the oil. Spread on a baking sheet. In the same bowl, toss the carrots and mushrooms in the oil remaining in the bowl. Spread the carrots and mushrooms on a separate baking sheet. Place both baking sheets in the oven and roast until the carrots and mushrooms are wilted and tender, about 12 minutes. Remove the carrots and mushrooms from the oven and transfer to a bowl. Continue roasting the potatoes and shallots until tender, about 12 minutes more. Transfer to the bowl with the carrots and mushrooms and keep warm. In a sauté pan, heat the remaining 2 tablespoons oil over medium-high heat. Add the arugula and tomatoes and sauté until the arugula begins to wilt, about 3 minutes. Add to the roasted vegetables.

To cook the quail, prepare a medium-hot fire in a charcoal grill, preheat a gas grill to medium-high, or preheat the oven to 450°F. Place a large ovenproof sauté pan over high heat and lightly grease with olive oil. Remove the quail from the marinade, wiping off any excess, and sauté, breast side down, for 3 minutes. Transfer the quail to the grill or set them on a baking sheet, breast side up, and place in the oven. Cook for 2 minutes, or until the juices no longer run red but the breast meat is still rare. Transfer to a platter and set aside to rest for 3 minutes.

To serve, cut the quails in half lengthwise. Place 2 pieces of quail on each of 6 plates. Arrange the roasted vegetables around the quail and serve right away.

Two Picnic Lunches

After almost thirty years, Margrit and Annie are still immersed in the Robert Mondavi Winery music festivals. For the first concert, the music was jazz and Margrit made up an easy menu, complete with store-bought cake jazzed up with cognac and whipped cream. Today, the audience has grown from fifty to almost two thousand people and a new tradition has developed in which most people bring their own picnic to enjoy while sitting on the grand expanse of grass or under the eaves listening to the music. For those who don't bring their own food, Annie assembles a box lunch reminiscent of the first buffet she and Margrit set out on tables: the cake has been replaced with cheese, fruit, and Annie's shortbread cookies.

BUFFET LUNCH FOR THE SUMMER MUSIC FESTIVAL, 1972

Baked Chicken Quarters

Cauliflower Salad

Potato Salad

Totally Doctored Chocolate Cake

BOX LUNCH FOR THE SUMMER MUSIC FESTIVAL, 2002

Baked Game Hens (page 139)

Cauliflower Salad (page 139)

Potato-Watercress Salad (page 153)

Sugar-Coated Shortbread (page 195)

Cheese and Fruit

BAKED GAME HENS *with Cauliflower Salad*

Serves 6

When Annie and Margrit first cooked together professionally, they prepared a dish similar to this one for the premier Summer Music Festival. Now, since the festival meals are boxed rather than served buffet-style, Annie substitutes game hen halves for the original baked chicken quarters so that each person gets both white and dark meat.

Serve with a CHARDONNAY *or* PINOT NOIR

GAME HENS

3 game hens, halved

2 tablespoons freshly squeezed lemon juice

2 tablespoons chopped fresh oregano

2 cloves garlic, minced

2 teaspoons kosher salt

1 teaspoon freshly ground black pepper

CAULIFLOWER SALAD

1 head cauliflower, cored and very thinly sliced

1 red bell pepper, julienned

1/2 white onion, very thinly sliced

1 tomato, cut into 1/2-inch dice

1/2 cup chopped fresh flat-leaf parsley

2 tablespoons red wine vinegar

1/4 cup extra virgin olive oil

Pinch of kosher salt

1/4 teaspoon freshly ground black pepper

To prepare the game hens, combine them with the lemon juice, oregano, garlic, salt, and pepper in a large dish and turn to coat all over. Cover and refrigerate for 3 hours or up to overnight. Remove from the refrigerator 30 minutes before serving.

To make the cauliflower salad, in a large bowl, combine the cauliflower, bell pepper, onion, tomato, and parsley. In a small bowl, whisk together the vinegar, oil, salt, and pepper. Pour over the vegetables and toss to mix. Set aside at room temperature for 30 minutes or cover and refrigerate overnight.

To cook the game hens, preheat the oven to 425°F. Set the game hen halves, without crowding, on one or two baking sheets. Bake, turning once, until golden and the thigh meat is no longer pink, about 30 minutes. Remove from the oven and set aside to rest for 10 to 15 minutes.

To serve, place the game hen halves on a large platter. Serve picnic or buffet style, with the cauliflower salad in a bowl alongside.

ROASTED GAME HENS
with Chardonnay-Tarragon Sauce and Garlic Mashed Potatoes

Serves 4

Annie loves tarragon, especially with chicken. For simple roasted game hens, she infuses a white wine sauce with tarragon's anise flavor and lets the sauce carry the dish with no further fussing. Only some comforting mashed potatoes are needed to make a satisfying meal.

Serve with a CHARDONNAY

GAME HENS

2 (1-pound) Cornish game hens

Kosher salt and freshly ground black pepper

3 tablespoons unsalted butter

1 tablespoon extra virgin olive oil

1/2 cup Chardonnay

1/4 cup chopped fresh tarragon

GARLIC MASHED POTATOES

4 Yukon Gold potatoes (about 1 pound total), peeled and cut into 1-inch chunks

2 cloves garlic, minced or pressed

2 tablespoons unsalted butter

About 1 cup half-and-half

Kosher salt and freshly ground black pepper

Preheat the oven to 400°F. Sprinkle the game hens inside and out with salt and pepper. In a large ovenproof sauté pan, melt 1 tablespoon of the butter with the oil over medium-high heat. Add the game hens and sauté, turning frequently, until golden all over, about 12 minutes. (Prop the hens against each other or the side of the pan as you turn them so they get browned on all sides.) Set the hens breast side up and transfer the pan to the oven. Roast for 20 to 25 minutes, or until the skin is crisp across the top and the meat between the leg and thigh is no longer pink. Transfer to a platter and set aside in a warm place.

Pour off the fat from the sauté pan. Whisk in the remaining 2 tablespoons butter and the wine. Stir in the tarragon and cook over medium-high heat until reduced and thickened, about 3 minutes. Set over warm water to keep warm (see Annie's Tip, page 158).

While the hens roast, prepare the potatoes. Put the potatoes in a large pot, add water to cover by 1 inch, and bring to a boil over high heat. Boil until tender all the way through but not collapsing, 8 to 10 minutes. Drain and return to the pot while still moist. Add the garlic and butter and, without stirring, cover and set aside in a warm place to steam dry for 10 minutes.

Return the potatoes to high heat and add 3/4 cup of the half-and-half. With a potato masher or sturdy wire whisk, mix until the mixture is creamy but still a little chunky. Add up to 1/4 cup more half-and-half if the mixture is too dry. Season with salt and pepper. Keep warm.

To serve, cut the game hens in half. Mound some of the mashed potatoes on 4 plates. Set a game hen half on the potato bed. Strain the sauce through a fine mesh sieve over the hens and serve right away.

DUCK CASSOULET *with Lamb, Pork, and Sausage*

Serves 6 to 8

As with many of Annie's dishes, a particular occasion is the source of inspiration. This time it was for her brother, Babo, who wanted a simple cassoulet for his housewarming. Annie complied with this quicker version of the classic cassoulet. Untraditionally, she includes some Cabernet in the dish, and reduces the amount of fat normally called for, with no loss of flavor or succulence. It became a keeper in her repertoire, and in Babo's too. For a festive winter holiday buffet, she places the cassoulet pot on the table for guests to serve themselves.

Serve with a CABERNET SAUVIGNON

1 pound white cannellini or great Northern beans

Olive oil, for cooking

1 (4 1/2-pound) duck, cut into 8 serving pieces, trimmed of fat (see Note)

3/4 pound lamb kebab or stew meat, cut into 1/2-inch pieces

3/4 pound pork shoulder (pork-steak cut), trimmed of fat and cut into 1/2-inch pieces

1/4 pound bacon, coarsely chopped

3 yellow onions, chopped

6 cloves garlic, coarsely chopped

4 cups chicken stock (page xix)

1 cup Cabernet Sauvignon

2 tablespoons tomato paste

2 tablespoons chopped fresh thyme

Kosher salt and freshly ground black pepper

2 (1/4-pound) garlic sausages, sliced 1/2 inch thick

1 cup homemade bread crumbs (page xix)

Soak the beans overnight in water to cover. (Or, use the quick-soak method: bring the beans and water to cover to a boil for 1 minute. Remove from the heat and let stand for 1 to 4 hours.) Drain and rinse.

Preheat the oven to 325°F. Lightly grease a large ovenproof casserole pot with olive oil and place it over medium-high heat. Add the duck pieces, skin side down, and brown them, turning 2 or 3 times, until slightly golden on both sides, about 8 minutes total. Transfer to a plate. Pour off the fat in the pot. Add the lamb and pork pieces and brown all over, turning the pieces as needed, about 5 minutes. Transfer to the plate with the duck pieces.

Pour off the fat. Decrease the heat to medium, add the bacon, onions, and garlic, and stir until the onions are wilted, about 5 minutes. Return the duck, lamb, and pork to the pot, along with any collected juices. Add the beans, stock, wine, tomato paste, and thyme and stir to mix. Increase the heat to medium-high and bring to a boil. Cover and place in the oven. Cook for 2 1/2 hours, until the beans are very soft and the meat is meltingly tender.

Remove the pot from the oven. Season with salt and pepper and, ever so gently, stir in the sausage slices. Sprinkle the bread crumbs over the top and return to the oven, uncovered, until the crumbs have formed a crunchy crust across the top, about 20 minutes.

To serve, spoon the cassoulet onto dinner plates, making sure each plate gets some of each meat. Or, serve the cassoulet in its pot, buffet style.

NOTE

The duck should be separated into two legs, two thighs, and four breast halves. Reserve the backbone and wings to make stock.

ROASTED LIBERTY DUCK BREASTS
with Cabernet Sauvignon Sauce and Wild Rice Cakes

Serves 4

Annie uses Liberty duck breasts for her elegant composition showcasing Cabernet Sauvignon. Developed for Michael Wild's BayWolf Restaurant in Oakland by Liberty Farm in Sonoma County, these Peking-variety ducks are allowed to roam free on the farm. They have become the duck of choice for many northern California chefs. Regular Peking duck will work nicely for the recipe as long as the rub is left on for at least 6 hours (see Annie's Tips).

Serve with a CABERNET SAUVIGNON

DUCK

4 (6-ounce) boneless duck breasts halves

1 tablespoon kosher salt

3/4 teaspoon freshly ground black pepper

1 large clove garlic, coarsely chopped

1 large shallot, coarsely chopped

2 bay leaves, crumbled

2 tablespoons chopped fresh thyme

1 tablespoon extra virgin olive oil

ANNIE'S TIPS

Dry marinating, or curing, duck breasts before cooking adds flavor dimension and firms the skin so it achieves an appealing color during roasting. It's a technique that also works for duck leg/thigh sections, goose, and rabbit cooked in other ways, not necessarily roasted. It's important to brush off the salt and spices after 24 hours, even if not cooking until later. Then you can keep the meat refrigerated for another 24 hours and it won't be too salty.

You can make the wild rice cake batter up to 1 day in advance, but don't add the baking powder until you're ready to cook the cakes.

WILD RICE CAKES

1/2 cup wild rice (see Note, page 146)

1 1/2 cups water

Kosher salt

1/4 cup all-purpose flour

1/2 teaspoon baking powder

Freshly ground black pepper

1/3 cup whole milk

6 tablespoons unsalted butter, melted

2 large eggs, separated

CABERNET SAUVIGNON SAUCE

2 shallots, coarsely chopped

2 cups chicken stock (page xix)

1/3 cup Cabernet Sauvignon

1 tablespoon balsamic vinegar

1 tablespoon unsalted butter, cut into bits

Kosher salt and freshly ground black pepper

To prepare the duck breasts, score through the skin several times, taking care not to pierce through to the meat. In a dish large enough to hold the breasts in one tightly packed layer, combine the salt, pepper, garlic, shallot, bay leaves, and thyme. Add the breasts to the dish and turn to coat all over. Cover and refrigerate for at least 3 hours or up to 24 hours.

To prepare the rice cakes, rinse the rice and put it in a heavy pot with the water. Add a pinch of salt. Bring to a boil over high heat, decrease the heat to low, and cover. Simmer until tender but not mushy, 30 to 40 minutes, depending on the age and variety of the grains. Drain and set aside at room temperature or refrigerate overnight.

Combine the rice, flour, baking powder, and a pinch each of salt and pepper in a bowl. Combine the milk and 4 tablespoons of the melted butter in a separate bowl. Beat the egg yolks into the milk and butter and stir the mixture into the dry ingredients. Beat the egg whites until stiff peaks form and fold them into the batter. In a large non-stick sauté pan, heat the remaining 2 tablespoons melted butter over medium-high heat. In batches, drop table-spoonfuls of the batter into the pan and cook until browned on the bottom, about 2 minutes. Flip over and brown on the other side, about 2 minutes more. Transfer to a baking sheet as you go. Set aside.

To cook the duck, preheat the oven to 375°F. In a large sauté pan, heat the oil over medium-high heat. Wipe off the duck pieces and place as many as will fit without overlapping, skin side down, in the pan. Sear until nicely browned on the bottom, 6 to 8 minutes. (You will need to do this in batches or use 2 pans.) Transfer, skin side up, to a baking sheet large enough to hold the breasts without touching. Place in the oven and roast until medium rare, about 10 minutes. Remove from the oven and let rest for 5 minutes.

While the duck roasts, make the sauce. Add the shallots to the duck sauté pan and cook over high heat until golden and beginning to crisp, about 5 minutes. Stir in the chicken stock and cook over high heat until reduced to about 3/4 cup, about 10 minutes. Add the wine and vinegar and cook to reduce again to about 3/4 cup, about 10 minutes. Swirl in the butter and season with salt and pepper. Pour through a fine mesh sieve into a clean saucepan. Set over warm water to keep warm (see Annie's Tip, page 158).

To serve, slice the duck breasts into 3 or 4 lengthwise strips. Arrange on 4 plates and spoon the sauce over the top. Place 3 wild rice cakes on each plate and serve at once.

Detail of the St. Francis statue at the winery.

GRILLED SQUAB
with Cabernet Sauvignon–Onion Marmalade and Spätzli

Serves 4

Squabs are pigeons, one of the tastiest small birds, highly prized in Continental cooking of the early twentieth century. They are also a specialty of Chinese cuisine, so if you have a Chinese market nearby, look for them there. Annie's recipe for the dumplinglike noodles called *spätzli* in Switzerland (*spätzel* in Germany) was inherited from her maternal grandmother. Here, Annie dresses them in the time-honored way with melted butter to make a side dish for the squab, but sometimes she adds her own modern twist and embellishes them with asparagus and wild mushrooms to serve as a separate pasta course.

Serve with a CABERNET SAUVIGNON

CABERNET SAUVIGNON–ONION MARMALADE

1/2 cup unsalted butter

2 leeks, including tender green parts, thinly sliced

1 red onion, halved crosswise and thinly sliced

1 yellow onion, halved crosswise and thinly sliced

3/4 cup Cabernet Sauvignon

1/4 cup balsamic vinegar

1 teaspoon finely chopped fresh thyme

Pinch of kosher salt

Pinch of freshly ground black pepper

SPÄTZLI

11/4 cups all-purpose flour

1/4 teaspoon kosher salt

2 large eggs

3/4 cup milk

2 tablespoons unsalted butter, for serving

4 squabs, with giblets

1 large shallot, coarsely chopped

1 bay leaf

2 sprigs flat-leaf parsley

2 sprigs thyme

1/4 cup balsamic vinegar

1 tablespoon finely chopped shallot

2 tablespoons cold unsalted butter, cut into 1/2-inch pieces

Extra virgin olive oil, for coating

Kosher salt and freshly ground black pepper

GAME PLAN

One day ahead:
- Prepare the squabs and make the stock. Cover, and refrigerate them separately.

Several hours ahead:
- Make the spätzli batter, cover, and refrigerate.
- Make the marmalade, cover, and set aside at room temperature or refrigerate overnight.

Forty-five minutes ahead:
- Prepare the grill.
- Remove the squabs from the refrigerator.
- Make the sauce and keep warm.

Just before serving:
- Cook the squabs.
- Cook the spätzli.

To make the marmalade, melt the butter in a large nonreactive saucepan over medium heat. Add the leeks and both onions and cook, stirring frequently, until very soft, about 15 minutes.

Stir in the wine and vinegar. Simmer over low heat, stirring from time to time, until almost all of the liquid has evaporated, about 40 minutes. Increase the heat to medium and cook for 5 minutes more, or until the onions are almost caramelized. Add the thyme, salt, and pepper, stir, and set aside to cool.

To make the spätzli, combine the flour and salt in a bowl. Beat the eggs with the milk, and gradually stir this mixture into the flour, beating until smooth. The consistency will be like a thick pancake batter. Let stand for 30 minutes, or cover and refrigerate overnight.

To prepare the squabs, cut off the necks and remove the backbones. Refrigerate the squabs. Put the necks, backbones, gizzards, and hearts in a saucepan and discard the livers.

Add the shallot, bay leaf, parsley, and thyme to the pan with the squab parts. Add water just to cover, bring to a boil over medium-high heat, and cook until reduced by two-thirds, about 5 minutes. Strain through a fine mesh sieve, return to the pan, and cook to reduce to $1/4$ cup, about 3 minutes. In another saucepan, combine the balsamic vinegar and shallot over high heat and cook to reduce until almost dry, about 1 minute. Whisk in the reduced squab broth and the butter, a bit at a time, until emulsified. Set over warm water to keep warm (see Annie's Tip, page 158).

Prepare a medium-hot fire in a charcoal grill, preheat a gas grill to medium, or preheat the broiler. Bring a pot of salted water to a boil for cooking the spätzli, using a pot on which a metal colander can rest above the water level.

To cook the squabs, open them out, coat both sides with oil, and season with salt and pepper. Grill or broil the squabs, turning once or twice, for about 10 minutes for medium rare. Transfer to a plate and let rest while cooking the spätzli.

To cook the spätzli, place a metal colander over the pot of boiling water. Using a soup ladle or rubber spatula, push the batter through the holes of the colander into the water. As soon as the noodles rise to the top, about 30 seconds, drain them, and immediately place in a bowl of ice water. Drain again right away. Melt the butter in the same pot over medium heat, add the spätzli, and stir to coat and warm.

To serve, place a squab on each of 4 plates. Spoon some of the sauce over each squab and place a dollop of onion marmalade alongside each. Surround with spätzli and serve right away.

PHEASANT AND WILD RICE "SOUP"

Serves 6

Not exactly a soup, but not a plate dish either, Annie describes her pheasant and wild rice creation as the perfect meal for welcoming in the New Year with a round of friends. Farm-raised pheasant brings the dish within reach for those who don't hunt or have hunter friends. The wild rice should be hand-harvested from Minnesota. It's the best because the grains open out all the way to their inner core, releasing their grassy flavor in soft, nutty bites (see Note).

Serve with a PINOT NOIR

PHEASANT AND STOCK

1 (1½-pound) pheasant

1 carrot, peeled and cut into thirds

1 celery stalk, cut into thirds

¼ yellow onion

2 bay leaves

1½ cups water

¾ cup wild rice, rinsed

1 tablespoon unsalted butter

½ pound chanterelle mushrooms, sliced ¼ inch thick

Kosher salt and freshly ground black pepper

1 carrot, peeled and cut into ¼-inch dice

1 celery stalk, cut into ¼-inch dice

¼ yellow onion, cut into ¼-inch dice

1 cup sliced Swiss chard leaves (½-inch ribbons)

1 teaspoon chopped fresh thyme

1 tablespoon chopped fresh flat-leaf parsley

NOTE

Hand-harvested wild rice is available from Indian Harvest at www.indianharvest.com, 800-346-7032, or from Christmas Point at www.christmaspoint.com, 800-726-0613.

To cook the pheasant and make the stock, put the pheasant in a large pot with the carrot, celery, onion, and bay leaves. Add water to cover by 1 inch and bring to a boil over high heat. Decrease the heat to medium and simmer, uncovered, skimming occasionally, for 1½ hours.

Drain the pheasant and vegetables over a bowl, reserving the stock. Discard the vegetables and bay leaf. Remove the skin from the pheasant, pull the meat off the bones, and cut into thin strips.

To prepare the wild rice, bring the water to a boil in a saucepan. Add the rice, return to a boil, cover, and simmer until the grains are tender and open, 40 minutes. Remove from the heat and drain any remaining water. Set aside.

In a saucepan, melt the butter over medium-high heat. Add the mushrooms, season with salt and pepper, and cook until slightly golden and almost dry, about 5 minutes.

Pour 2 cups of the reserved stock into the original pot and cook over high heat to reduce to 1 cup, 15 to 20 minutes. Add the diced carrot, celery, and onion. Bring to a boil, cover, decrease the heat to medium, and cook until tender, 15 minutes. Add the remaining stock, the wild rice, mushrooms, chard, and pheasant meat. Bring to a boil, decrease the heat to low, and simmer for 5 minutes. Stir in the thyme and parsley, season with salt and pepper, and serve right away.

MARGRIT'S THANKSGIVING TURKEY
with Bread Stuffing, Potato–Celery Root Purée, and Broccoli–Red Pepper Salad
Serves 8

Shortly after marrying an American army officer, Swiss-born Margrit spent her first Thanksgiving on an army base in Germany during the Second World War. She celebrated the occasion with make-do goods from the base commissary: canned cranberry sauce and frozen (long-frozen) turkey. European home ovens at the time were not designed to hold a whole big American turkey, so the mess hall cooked the birds in their industrial-sized ovens and people came to pick them up and transport them home. Margrit opened the can of jellied cranberry sauce and whipped up some mashed potatoes while someone went out to fetch the turkey. But all the turkeys were gone! So the family made do with canned ham. Today, at home in the Napa Valley, she is the acknowledged Chief Turkey Roaster, and the grandchildren wouldn't consider it Thanksgiving without her turkey, fresh from the farm now.

After years of cooking the Thanksgiving bird the traditional way, with the stuffing in the cavity, Margrit has decided that it's best to cook them separately so the stuffing comes out browned on top. To moisten the stuffing and add meaty flavor, she simmers up a jalapeño-spiked giblet broth and adds a little more jalapeño to the stuffing itself for a truly Californian Thanksgiving dish.

Serve with a CHARDONNAY *and a* PINOT NOIR

TURKEY

Kosher salt and freshly ground black pepper

1 (14- to 16-pound) turkey

1/2 cup unsalted butter, at room temperature

2 sprigs rosemary

4 sprigs thyme

BROTH

Neck, gizzard, and wing tips from the turkey

1/2 small yellow onion

1 clove garlic

1 small carrot

1 small jalapeño chile

3 sprigs flat-leaf parsley

STUFFING

Unsalted butter, at room temperature

1 (12-ounce) baguette or other French bread, cut crosswise in half then lengthwise in half again

1 yellow onion

3 cloves garlic

1 bunch celery

1 pound porcini, chanterelle, cremini, or button mushrooms

1 small jalapeño chile

1/2 cup chopped fresh flat-leaf parsley

1 tablespoon chopped fresh rosemary

1 teaspoon chopped fresh thyme

1 teaspoon chopped fresh sage

2 teaspoons kosher salt

1 teaspoon freshly ground black pepper

Liver and heart from the turkey, chopped

1/2 cup unsalted butter, melted

3 large eggs

1/2 cup dry sherry

BROCCOLI-RED PEPPER SALAD

4 cups broccoli florets

1/4 cup red wine vinegar

1 tablespoon finely chopped shallots

1/2 teaspoon kosher salt

1/4 teaspoon freshly ground black pepper

1/2 cup extra virgin olive oil

2 red bell peppers, roasted, peeled, and julienned (page xx)

POTATO–CELERY ROOT PURÉE

2 russet potatoes, peeled and cut into 1-inch pieces

2 celery roots, peeled and cut into 1-inch pieces

1/2 cup heavy cream

3 tablespoons unsalted butter

2 teaspoons kosher salt

1 teaspoon freshly ground black pepper

1 to 2 tablespoons freshly squeezed lemon juice

To cook the turkey, preheat the oven to 375°F. Liberally salt and pepper the turkey inside and out. Place a double layer of cheesecloth over the breast and spread liberally with the butter. Place the rosemary and thyme sprigs over the butter and cover with another layer of cheesecloth. Set the turkey on a rack in a roasting pan and place in the oven. Roast for 15 minutes per pound, 3 1/2 to 4 hours, depending on the size of the turkey, or until an instant-read thermometer registers 165°F when inserted in the thigh. For the last 30 minutes, remove the cheesecloth so the breast can brown. Remove from the oven, tent with aluminum foil, and let rest in the roasting pan for at least 20 minutes or up to 40 minutes before carving.

While the turkey roasts, make the broth. Combine all the ingredients in a saucepan and add water to cover. Bring to a boil over high heat. Decrease the heat to medium-low and cook to reduce to about 1 cup, about 30 minutes. Strain through a fine mesh sieve into a bowl and set aside. Discard the solids.

To prepare the stuffing, butter the bread and toast in the 375°F oven until golden on top, 10 minutes. Remove and allow to cool completely.

Chop the onion, garlic, celery, mushrooms, and jalapeño (a food processor is okay as long as the vegetables are not chopped too small). Transfer to a large bowl. Cut the bread into 1/2-inch cubes and add to the bowl. Add the parsley, rosemary, thyme, and sage. Toss to mix and season with salt and pepper. Add the chopped liver and heart, melted butter, eggs, sherry, and the turkey broth. Mix well. Lightly butter a 9 by 13-inch baking dish. Spread the stuffing in the dish, cover with aluminum foil, and bake alongside the turkey until crisp on top, about 1 1/2 hours.

To make the salad, blanch the broccoli in salted boiling water for 3 to 5 minutes, or until bright green. Immediately drain and run under cold water to stop the cooking. In a small bowl, combine the vinegar, shallots, salt, and pepper and mix well. Gradually whisk in the oil until emulsified. Put the broccoli and peppers in a serving bowl and pour in the dressing. Toss gently. Set aside for up to 1 1/2 hours.

To make the purée, cook the potatoes and celery root in lightly salted boiling water over high heat until soft, about 10 minutes. Drain and return to the pot while still moist. Add the cream and butter and mash with a potato masher or sturdy wire whisk over low heat, stirring to prevent sticking, until thick and smooth, about 5 minutes. Whisk in the salt, pepper, and lemon juice to taste. Cover and keep warm over a hot water bath for up to 1 hour.

To serve, carve the turkey and present it family-style on a large platter with the stuffing, broccoli salad, and purée in separate dishes on the side.

GAME PLAN

One day ahead:
- Make the turkey broth, cover, and refrigerate.
- Prepare the bread, vegetables, and herbs for the stuffing and toss them together. Cover and refrigerate.
- Roast the red bell peppers for the salad; cover and refrigerate.

Four hours ahead:
- Roast the turkey.

Two hours ahead:
- Finish the bread stuffing and bake it alongside the turkey.

One hour before serving:
- Make the salad.
- Make the purée.

Seafood

WHILE LIVING IN SEA-SURROUNDED JAPAN and river-blessed Germany and traveling widely throughout Europe with its multitudinous lakes, streams, and waterways, Annie acquired a taste for fish and shellfish. In the 1980s, she assisted Jean Troisgros in a Great Chefs class at the Robert Mondavi Winery. He mentioned that his favorite food was fish and sauce, which opened Annie's mind to the creative possibilities of seafood. That revelation led her to such innovations as bedding a salmon fillet on thinly sliced Brussels sprouts with a beurre blanc, napping halibut with scallop sauce, and dolloping cilantro pesto on sea-fresh mussels. In addition to the many seafood small plates and salads found in this book, this chapter offers some of Annie's most delightful fish and shellfish creations, along with another special treat, Margrit's sautéed trout, a nostalgic favorite of both mother and daughter.

PAN-ROASTED HALIBUT
with Sun-Dried Tomato Vinaigrette and Potato-Watercress Salad

Serves 4

In halibut season, from late spring to early fall, chefs go wild for the firm, mild-tasting fish, using it in everything from sushi to salad to fish stew. In one of her favorite pairings, Annie serves a simply roasted halibut fillet with fingerling potatoes and anoints the fish with a spunky vinaigrette.

Serve with a FUMÉ BLANC

POTATO-WATERCRESS SALAD

1 pound (2¹/₂-inch-long) fingerling potatoes, quartered

1 teaspoon minced garlic

1 teaspoon Dijon mustard

2 tablespoons champagne vinegar

¹/₄ cup extra virgin olive oil

Kosher salt and freshly ground black pepper

1 cup watercress leaves

SUN-DRIED TOMATO VINAIGRETTE

¹/₄ cup finely shredded fresh basil

1 tablespoon capers, rinsed

1 tablespoon chopped oil-packed sun-dried tomatoes

1¹/₂ teaspoons minced garlic

3 tablespoons freshly squeezed lemon juice

¹/₃ cup extra virgin olive oil

HALIBUT

1 tablespoon extra virgin olive oil

1¹/₂ pounds skinless halibut fillets, cut into 4 portions

Kosher salt

To make the potato salad, put the potatoes in a pot and cover with water by 1 inch. Add a pinch of salt and bring to a boil over high heat. Cook until the potatoes are tender, 12 to 13 minutes. Drain and allow to cool for 5 minutes. In a bowl, whisk together the garlic, mustard, vinegar, and oil. Season with salt and pepper and add the potatoes. Toss to mix, then fold in the watercress. Set aside at room temperature.

To make the vinaigrette, combine the basil, capers, sun-dried tomatoes, garlic, and lemon juice in a small bowl. Whisk in the oil and set aside.

To cook the halibut, preheat the oven to 375°F. In a cast-iron skillet or ovenproof nonstick sauté pan, heat the oil over medium-high heat. Lightly sprinkle the halibut pieces with salt on both sides and put them in the skillet. Sear, turning once, until slightly golden on both sides, about 2 minutes on each side. Transfer the skillet to the oven and cook until the fish is just beginning to flake, about 6 minutes.

To serve, place a halibut piece on each of 4 plates. Top with a spoonful of the vinaigrette and arrange some of the potato salad alongside. Serve right away.

HALIBUT *with Vegetable Confetti and Scallop Sauce*

Serves 4

Annie describes her vegetable confetti as a transition dish between winter and spring. It's just the moment to capture the last of the celery root and the first of the asparagus and combine them with bright, always available, cherry tomatoes and crunchy celery. The scallops are a quick way to make a fish broth that Annie finds far preferable to bottled clam sauce.

Serve with a CHARDONNAY

SCALLOP SAUCE

1/2 pound sea scallops

2 tablespoons extra virgin olive oil

2 shallots, chopped

1 small clove garlic, chopped

2 leeks, including white and light green parts, chopped

1/4 cup Chardonnay

1 tablespoon white wine vinegar

1/2 cup heavy cream

3 1/2 tablespoons unsalted butter

Juice of 1/2 lemon

Kosher salt and freshly ground black pepper

VEGETABLE CONFETTI

8 thin asparagus spears, trimmed and cut into
    1-inch lengths

1 large celery stalk, julienned

1/2 large celery root, peeled and julienned

1 tablespoon unsalted butter

16 cherry tomatoes

1 tablespoon extra virgin olive oil

1 1/2 pounds skinless halibut fillets, cut into 4 portions

1 tablespoon chopped fresh chives, for garnish

To prepare the sauce, put the scallops in a saucepan, add water to cover, and bring to a boil over medium-high heat. Decrease the heat and simmer until the liquid is reduced to about 1/2 cup, about 30 minutes. Remove from the heat, discard the scallops, and reserve the liquid.

In a large sauté pan, heat the oil over medium heat. Add the shallots, garlic, and leeks and sauté until softened, about 5 minutes. Add the reserved scallop broth, wine, and vinegar. Increase the heat to medium-high and cook to reduce by half, about 10 minutes. Add the cream and continue to cook until the sauce thickens slightly and is very bubbly, about 3 minutes. Pour into a blender or food processor and purée as finely as possible. Strain through a fine-meshed sieve and return to the blender. Add the butter and blend well. Stir in the lemon juice and season with salt and pepper. Set aside and keep warm over warm water (see Annie's Tip, page 158).

To prepare the vegetables, bring a large pot of water to a boil over high heat. Add the asparagus, celery, and celery root and blanch for 2 minutes. Drain into a colander and transfer to a bowl. In a sauté pan, melt the butter over medium-high heat. Add the tomatoes and sauté until softened and wrinkled, 3 minutes. Transfer to the bowl with the other vegetables, toss well, and keep warm.

To cook the halibut, preheat the oven to 375°F. In a heavy skillet, heat the oil over high heat. Sear the halibut until golden on the bottom, 2 to 3 minutes. Turn over the fish and place the pan in the oven. Cook just until the fish begins to flake, 6 minutes.

To serve, place a piece of halibut on each of 4 plates. Pour some sauce around each and garnish with the vegetables. Sprinkle the chives over the top and serve.

GRILLED SWORDFISH
with Roasted Tomatillo–Avocado Salsa and Basmati Rice

Serves 4

Because of the overfishing of swordfish, this delightful dish has become almost archival in Annie's repertoire. But she offers it here in the hope that the day will come when responsible fish-harvesting practices will make swordfish once again plentiful and okay for eco-minded chefs to serve. In the meantime, she suggests substituting halibut or monkfish. The salsa, like a loose guacamole or a dense sauce, is Annie's innovative combination of the two and offers a plus: the tomatillo keeps the avocado from discoloring, so you can store it in the refrigerator overnight and it will remain bright green.

Serve with a PINOT NOIR

SWORDFISH

4 (3/4-inch-thick) swordfish steaks

2 cloves garlic, minced

3 tablespoons extra virgin olive oil

1 tablespoon freshly squeezed lemon juice

Kosher salt

BASMATI RICE

1 1/2 cups basmati rice

1/2 tablespoon kosher salt

1 teaspoon finely chopped fresh oregano

3 cups water

ROASTED TOMATILLO–AVOCADO SALSA

1/2 pound tomatillos, papery husks removed, rinsed

2 jalapeño chiles, seeded and chopped

1/4 cup cilantro leaves

1 avocado, chopped

2 scallions, including green parts, chopped

Kosher salt

To prepare the swordfish, put the steaks in a dish with the garlic, oil, lemon juice, and a liberal pinch of salt. Turn to coat all over. Set aside at room temperature for 15 minutes or refrigerate for up to 2 hours. Remove from the refrigerator 30 minutes before cooking.

To make the rice, combine it with the salt, oregano, and water in a pot over medium-high heat. Bring to a boil, decrease the heat to low, cover, and simmer ever so gently for 25 minutes, or until the grains are tender. Remove from the heat and set aside, still covered, on a back burner to steam dry while preparing the salsa and cooking the fish.

Prepare a medium-hot fire in a charcoal grill or preheat a gas grill to medium-high. To make the salsa, put the tomatillos on the grill rack and cook, turning once, until they begin to char, about 10 minutes total. Remove and set aside until cool enough to handle. In a food processor, combine the tomatillos, jalapeños, cilantro, and avocado and purée just until a little bit chunky. Stir in the scallions and salt to taste. Set aside, or cover and refrigerate overnight.

To cook the swordfish, place the steaks on the grill rack and cook, turning once, until opaque on the outside but still a little pink in the center, 8 to 10 minutes total. Transfer to a plate and let rest for 5 minutes.

To serve, place a fish steak on each of 4 plates. Top with a spoonful of salsa and mound some rice to the side. Serve right away with the extra salsa on the side.

BLACK PEPPER–CRUSTED AHI TUNA
with Olives, Peppers, and Shoestring Potatoes

Serves 4

Annie likes to serve meaty fishes, such as salmon and tuna, with a light-bodied red wine. She explains, "The whites don't stand up to the intensity of the fishes' texture and flavor, but the tannins in the heartier reds, like Cabs or Zins, overpower the fishes' delicacy. A Pinot Noir, however, satisfies all the considerations." Here, she accompanies tuna with a side of shoestring potatoes.

Serve with a PINOT NOIR

4 (5- to 6-ounce) ahi tuna steaks, each 1 inch thick
Coarsely ground black pepper

SHOESTRING POTATOES

4 large russet potatoes
Peanut oil, for frying
Kosher salt

VEGETABLES

2 tablespoons extra virgin olive oil
1 red onion, thinly sliced
2 red bell peppers, thinly sliced
3 large cloves garlic, minced
1 tablespoon chopped fresh thyme
1/2 jalapeño chile, seeded and finely chopped
1/2 cup kalamata olives, pitted and halved lengthwise (page xx)
Kosher salt

1 tablespoon extra virgin olive oil

Generously coat both sides of the tuna steaks with black pepper. Set aside at room temperature for 30 minutes or refrigerate for up to 4 hours.

To prepare the potatoes, peel them and cut off the rounded ends and sides to make rectangular shapes. Cut the potatoes lengthwise on a mandoline slicer using the 1/4-inch julienne blade. Or, use a food processor with the julienne blade or cut into matchsticks with a chef's knife. Place the matchsticks in a large bowl of cold water as you go. Change the water 3 or 4 times until all the starch is removed and the water is clear. Drain, then spin in a salad spinner in batches until completely dry, or spread the matchsticks out in a single layer on paper or cloth towels and pat dry. Cook right away, or set aside for up to 1 hour.

To cook the potatoes, line a baking sheet with paper towels. Pour peanut oil into a large, high-sided pot to one-third full. Heat the oil over high heat until a potato piece dropped in sizzles and rises to the top right away (375°F). Add one-third of the potatoes to the hot oil and fry until golden, about 5 minutes. Remove the potatoes with a wire strainer, shaking gently over the pot to remove excess oil, and place on the baking sheet. Repeat with two more batches of potatoes, making sure the oil is hot again before each batch. Sprinkle with salt and set aside in a 200°F oven (no need to preheat it).

To cook the vegetables, heat the olive oil in a large sauté pan over medium-high heat. Add the onion and bell peppers, stir to coat, and cook just until softened, 2 to 3 minutes. Stir in the garlic and cook for 1 minute. Stir in the thyme, jalapeño, olives, and salt to taste. Cook for 1 minute more, until the vegetables are wilted but still hold their shape. Remove from the heat and set aside.

To cook the tuna, heat the olive oil in a large cast-iron skillet or heavy nonstick sauté pan over high heat. Add the tuna and sear, turning once, until crusty on the outside and still rare in the middle, about 2 minutes on each side. Remove from the heat and let sit for 5 minutes.

To serve, arrange the tuna steaks on each of 4 plates. Spoon some of the vegetable mixture over the top of each steak, draping a bit of it over the sides. Place a handful of the shoestring potatoes alongside and serve right away.

ANNIE'S TIPS

Soaking the starch out of potatoes once they're cut is a technique to make the fries come out crispy.

As the tuna steaks sear, the black pepper releases sinus-clearing vapors, so have the overhead vent on or a window or door open as you cook.

SALMON FILLETS
with Whole-Grain Mustard Beurre Blanc and Brussels Sprouts

Serves 4

East coast or west and lots of places in between, salmon is almost always in the market, easily available and very fresh. There are even recreational day-boat trips in case you'd like the thrill of catching your own. Caught or bought, farmed or wild, the flavor of this lord of the near-in ocean waters is incomparable. In accordance, Annie uses salmon in a variety of glorious preparations, from smoked and poached to seared and roasted. For a winter holiday special, she serves indoor-grilled salmon on Brussels sprouts and blankets them with a tangy mustard beurre blanc. Straining the shallots out of the beurre blanc after reducing allows the whole-grain mustard to be the textural highlight of the sauce.

Serve with a PINOT NOIR

1¹/₂ pounds salmon fillets, skin and pin bones removed,
    cut into 4 portions
1 tablespoon extra virgin olive oil
Kosher salt and freshly ground black pepper

WHOLE-GRAIN MUSTARD BEURRE BLANC
¹/₂ cup Chardonnay
¹/₄ cup white wine vinegar
¹/₄ cup finely chopped shallots
1 cup unsalted butter, cut into ¹/₄-inch pieces,
    at room temperature
¹/₄ cup whole-grain mustard
Kosher salt and freshly ground black pepper

1 pound Brussels sprouts, wilted outer leaves removed,
    sliced ¹/₄ inch thick
¹/₄ pound thinly sliced pancetta, coarsely chopped
1 tablespoon chopped fresh flat-leaf parsley, for garnish

To prepare the salmon, brush each portion with oil and lightly sprinkle with salt and pepper. Set aside at room temperature for up to 1 hour or refrigerate for up to 4 hours. Remove from the refrigerator 30 minutes before cooking.

To make the beurre blanc, combine the wine, vinegar, and shallots in a saucepan and reduce over high heat until 2 tablespoons of liquid remain, about 2 minutes. Pass through a fine-meshed sieve and return to the pan over medium heat. Slowly whisk in the butter piece by piece. Whisk in the mustard and season with salt and pepper. Use right away or set aside over warm water for up to 30 minutes (see Annie's Tip).

To cook the Brussels sprouts, bring a large pot of water to boil, add the Brussels sprouts, and blanch for 1¹/₂ minutes without returning to a boil. Drain and rinse under cold water. Set aside in the colander. Heat a sauté pan over medium-high heat until hot, add the pancetta, and cook until slightly crisp, about 5 minutes. Add the Brussels sprouts and sauté for 2 minutes, or until barely soft but still bright green.

ANNIE'S TIP

Delicate sauces, such as beurre blanc and butter-thickened wine reductions (page 88), can't be reheated or they fall apart. Annie has a number of methods for keeping them warm for up to 2 hours while the rest of the dish is finished:

- over a double boiler half-filled with warm water
- on a ledge over the stove top
- in a thermos!

To cook the salmon, prepare a medium-hot fire in a charcoal grill, preheat a gas grill to medium-high, or place a grill pan over medium-high heat. Place the salmon on the rack or in the pan and cook, turning once, until medium rare, 3 to 4 minutes on each side.

To serve, spread the Brussels sprouts on each of 4 plates. Set a piece of salmon on top of the Brussels sprouts, drizzle the beurre blanc over the salmon, and sprinkle with the parsley. Serve right away.

SALMON FILLETS *with Orzo Salad and Olive-Eggplant Salsa*

Serves 4

Annie usually serves the salmon, salad, and salsa as a composition, but each can be used on its own. For instance, the orzo salad would complement a simple roasted chicken or round out a picnic plate of sausages. The salsa can be spooned alongside other meaty fish, such as swordfish or halibut, used to top crostini, or served as a dip for pita triangles. The salmon, grilled to perfection under her direction, can be served with just a squeeze of lemon.

Serve with a CHARDONNAY

1¹/₂ pounds skinless salmon fillets, pin bones removed,
    cut into 4 portions

1 tablespoon finely chopped scallions

1 tablespoon chopped fresh basil

1 tablespoon chopped fresh oregano

1 teaspoon finely chopped lemon zest

1 teaspoon kosher salt

2 tablespoons extra virgin olive oil

OLIVE-EGGPLANT SALSA

¹/₂ cup finely diced unpeeled eggplant

Extra virgin olive oil, for coating

2 Roma tomatoes, seeded and cut into ¹/₄-inch dice

¹/₄ cup finely diced red onion

2 scallions, including green parts, finely chopped

2 teaspoons chopped fresh basil

¹/₄ cup capers, drained and chopped

¹/₄ cup kalamata olives, pitted and coarsely chopped
    (page xx)

¹/₄ cup freshly squeezed lemon juice

¹/₂ cup extra virgin olive oil

ORZO SALAD

1 cup orzo pasta

¹/₂ cup chopped fresh flat-leaf parsley

1 tablespoon chopped fresh basil

¹/₄ cup water

¹/₄ cup white wine vinegar

¹/₄ cup extra virgin olive oil

Kosher salt and freshly ground black pepper

Place the salmon fillets in a glass or ceramic dish large enough to hold them in one layer. Add the scallions, basil, oregano, zest, salt, and oil and turn to coat all over. Cover and set aside at room temperature for 1 hour or refrigerate for up to 4 hours.

To make the salsa, preheat the oven to 425°F. Toss the eggplant with a little oil to coat it. Spread on a baking sheet and bake until tender, about 10 minutes. Transfer to a bowl and add the tomatoes, onion, scallions, basil, capers, olives, lemon juice, and oil. Stir to mix. Set aside at room temperature for at least 15 minutes or up to 1 hour to allow the flavors to blend, or cover and refrigerate overnight.

To make the orzo salad, cook the orzo in salted boiling water according to the package directions until al dente. Drain and transfer to a bowl.

In a food processor, combine the parsley, basil, and water and pulse until blended. Transfer to the bowl with the orzo. Add the vinegar and oil and toss to mix. Stir in salt and pepper to taste. Set aside while cooking the salmon.

To cook the salmon, prepare a medium-hot fire in a charcoal grill or preheat a gas grill to medium-high. Wipe the oil off the fillets and place them on the grill rack directly over the coals. Grill, turning once, until slightly golden on the outside and medium rare in the center, about 2 minutes on each side. Transfer to a plate and let rest for 5 minutes.

To serve, place a salmon fillet on each of 4 plates. Spoon a mound of orzo salad alongside and top each fillet with a spoonful of the salsa. Serve right away, with the remaining salsa on the side.

SALMON FILLETS
with Wilted Escarole in Shallot–Balsamic Vinegar Sauce

Serves 4

There are differences of opinion on the topic of wild versus farmed salmon, especially now that wild salmon is becoming more available in fish markets. Some prefer farmed salmon for its more delicate flavor and fatter flesh. In this dish, Annie prefers wild salmon for the opposite reasons: it's stronger-tasting and leaner, and blends more artfully with a sharp vinaigrette-type sauce. The sauce without the escarole is excellent on grilled steak.

Serve with a CABERNET SAUVIGNON

SALMON

1½ pounds salmon fillets, skin and pin bones removed, cut into 4 portions

Extra virgin olive oil, for coating

Kosher salt and freshly ground black pepper

SHALLOT–BALSAMIC VINEGAR SAUCE

2 large shallots, thinly sliced

1 clove garlic, minced

2 tablespoons balsamic vinegar

1½ tablespoons Cabernet Sauvignon

¼ cup extra virgin olive oil

Leaves from 1 head escarole lettuce, cut lengthwise into thin strips

To cook the salmon, preheat the oven to 375°F. Heat a large cast-iron skillet or ovenproof sauté pan over medium-high heat. Coat the salmon pieces with oil, season with salt and pepper on both sides, and place in the skillet. Sear until browned on the bottom, 3 minutes. Turn the pieces over and transfer the skillet to the oven. Roast until the salmon is firm on the outside but still rosy in the center, 3 to 5 minutes. Set aside in a warm place.

To prepare the sauce, combine the shallots, garlic, vinegar, and wine in a sauté pan over medium-high heat. Bring to a boil and remove from the heat. Whisk in the oil, add the escarole, and toss to mix.

To serve, place a piece of salmon on each of 4 plates. Top with some of the wilted escarole and serve.

WHITEFISH POT-AU-FEU IN CHARDONNAY BROTH
with Gremolata

Serves 4

Though Annie created this dish to spotlight the prized Chilean sea bass, for the moment, she, along with numerous other chefs and seafood purveyors, declines to offer it until there is no longer imminent danger of its being fished out of existence. In the meantime, another sea bass or grouper makes a fine candidate for lightly stewing in her Chardonnay wine broth. The bay leaf must be a Greek laurel leaf rather than the California variety, which is too pungent for the broth.

Serve with a CHARDONNAY

GREMOLATA

1 tablespoon finely chopped lemon zest

3 cloves garlic, minced

1/4 cup finely chopped fresh flat-leaf parsley

POT-AU-FEU

4 cups water

1/2 cup Chardonnay

1 tablespoon champagne vinegar

2 carrots, peeled and julienned

1 fennel bulb, julienned

1 yellow onion, thinly sliced

1 leek, including light green part, julienned

2 celery stalks, julienned

4 sprigs thyme

1 bay leaf

6 black peppercorns

Kosher salt

2 pounds (3/4-inch-thick) whitefish fillets, such as sea bass, grouper, or halibut, cut into 4 portions

8 crostini (page 14), for garnish

1 cup aioli (page 168), for garnish

To make the gremolata, combine all the ingredients in a small bowl and toss to mix. Set aside.

To make the pot-au-feu, combine the water, wine, vinegar, carrots, fennel, onion, leek, and celery in a large pot and bring to a boil over high heat. Add the thyme, bay leaf, and peppercorns. Cover, decrease the heat to low, and simmer until the vegetables are al dente, about 10 minutes.

Remove the thyme and bay leaf and season with salt. Bring to a simmer and add the fish. Cover and cook over medium-low heat until the fish flakes easily when prodded with a fork, 6 to 8 minutes.

To serve, transfer the fish to 4 shallow bowls or deep plates. Ladle the broth and vegetables over the top. Sprinkle with the gremolata. Set 2 crostini around the edge of each bowl, add a large spoonful of aioli, and serve right away.

TROUT IN THE SWISS STYLE

Serves 4

Annie suggested a trout dish from Margrit to round out this chapter. When it was time to test the recipe, Margrit was out of the country, but Annie, so familiar with Margrit's cooking, had no problem filling in the specifics of how her mother would do the dish. On her return, Margrit was tenderly pleased with the inclusion of her beloved trout from the cold Alpine Maggia River, "the best in the world," and more pleased that Annie's rendition was so exact, down to the buttered asparagus.

Serve with a RIESLING

1 pound asparagus, trimmed

4 (6-ounce) boneless trout, or 2 (1¼-pound) steelhead trout

Kosher salt

3 lemons, 1 thinly sliced, and 2 cut into wedges

4 sprigs thyme

¼ cup unsalted butter

1 tablespoon extra virgin olive oil

All-purpose flour, for dusting

Freshly ground black pepper

Peel the asparagus stalks with a vegetable peeler if they are large. Blanch in a large pot of salted boiling water until limp, 4 to 8 minutes, depending on the size of the asparagus. Drain and set aside.

To cook the trout, liberally sprinkle them with salt inside and out. Squeeze the lemon slices over the inside and outside and place the squeezed slices in the cavities of the trout, along with the thyme sprigs. Use right away, set aside at room temperature for up to 30 minutes, or refrigerate for up to 1 hour.

In a large sauté pan or cast-iron skillet, combine 2 tablespoons of the butter and the oil. Place over medium-high heat until the butter bubbles. Dust the trout with flour, shaking off any excess. In 2 batches, so as not to crowd them, sauté the trout for 8 to 12 minutes, depending on the size, or until the skins are crisp and the meat at the backbone is just barely pink. Transfer to a large platter, remove the thyme and lemon slices, and set aside in a warm place.

To serve, melt the remaining 2 tablespoons butter in a clean sauté pan over medium-high heat. Add the asparagus and season with salt and pepper. Heat through for 1 minute, then remove from the heat. Arrange the asparagus around the trout and garnish the platter with the lemon wedges. Serve right away.

RED SNAPPER BAKED IN TOMATO–NIÇOISE OLIVE SAUCE
with Saffron Rice and Avocado Fans

Serves 4

In a fusion dish of southern France meets Mexico via Spain in California, Annie bakes snapper in a Mediterranean sauce. The rice has an Iberian touch of saffron, and avocado fans provide a south-of-the-border accent. She often cooks snapper at home because it's inexpensive, quick to prepare, and readily available very fresh since high demand ensures rapid turnover even in supermarkets.

Serve with a PINOT NOIR

SAFFRON RICE

1/4 cup unsalted butter

2 tablespoons finely chopped yellow or white onion

1 1/2 cups long-grain white rice

Large pinch of saffron threads

1/2 cup dry white wine

2 1/2 cups chicken stock (page xix)

1/2 tablespoon kosher salt

RED SNAPPER

2 tablespoons extra virgin olive oil

1 red onion, finely chopped

2 large ripe tomatoes, roasted, peeled, and chopped (page xx), with juices

1/2 jalapeño chile, seeded and finely chopped

2 tablespoons chopped fresh flat-leaf parsley

1 teaspoon chopped fresh basil

Kosher salt and freshly ground black pepper

1 3/4 pounds red snapper fillets, cut into 4 portions

Juice of 1 lemon

1/2 cup niçoise olives, pitted and halved (page xx)

1 ripe avocado

To make the rice, melt 2 tablespoons of the butter in a pot over medium-high heat. Add the onion and sauté until translucent, 2 minutes. Stir in the rice, then the saffron, wine, stock, and salt. Bring to a boil, decrease the heat to low, cover, and simmer for 25 minutes, until tender. Remove from the heat and set aside, still covered, on a back burner to steam dry while preparing the snapper.

To cook the snapper, preheat the oven to 375°F. In a large sauté pan, heat the oil over medium-high heat. Add the onion and cook until softened, about 3 minutes. Stir in the tomatoes and their juices, jalapeño, parsley, basil, and salt and pepper to taste. Place the fillets in a lightly oiled baking dish large enough to hold them in one layer. Drizzle with the lemon juice and sprinkle with salt and pepper. Spoon the tomato mixture over the top and cover with aluminum foil. Bake for 15 minutes. Remove the foil and strew the olives over the top. Continue baking, uncovered, for 2 minutes, until the sauce is bubbling and the fish is flaky.

To serve, gently stir the remaining 2 tablespoons butter into the rice. Spread a bed of rice on each of 4 plates. Place a portion of the fish and sauce atop the rice. Peel, pit, and thinly slice the avocado lengthwise. Arrange a fan of avocado slices to the side on each plate. Serve right away.

MUSSELS *with Cilantro Pesto*

Serves 8 as a first course, 4 as a main course

From late November through March, mussels, wafting a clean ocean fragrance, appear on Annie's table as an appetizer or main meal. She prefers the attractive and meaty green-lip mussels jet-fresh from New Zealand or the equally sea-fresh black mussels from Prince Edward Island. With either variety, she enhances their lively taste with the Mexican flavors of poblano chiles and cilantro.

Serve with a FUMÉ BLANC

CILANTRO PESTO

2 cups cilantro sprigs, without large stems

1/2 cup flat-leaf parsley sprigs, without large stems

1 jalapeño chile, seeded and coarsely chopped

2 large cloves garlic, coarsely chopped

2 tablespoons pine nuts

2 teaspoons freshly squeezed lemon juice

1 teaspoon kosher salt

3/4 cup extra virgin olive oil

MUSSELS

1 poblano chile, halved, seeded, and thinly sliced

1 white onion, halved and thinly sliced

4 cloves garlic, chopped

1 Roma tomato, chopped

1 tablespoon chopped fresh flat-leaf parsley

1/3 cup extra virgin olive oil

1/4 cup Fumé Blanc or other dry white wine

4 pounds very fresh mussels, scrubbed and debearded
   if necessary

1 baguette, warmed, for serving

To make the pesto, combine all the ingredients in a food processor or blender and purée until smooth. Use right away or cover tightly and store in the refrigerator for up to 2 days.

To make the mussels, combine the poblano, onion, garlic, tomato, parsley, oil, and wine in a large pot or sauté pan with a lid. Cover and cook over medium-high heat for 2 minutes, or until the vegetables wilt. Increase the heat to high, add the mussels, cover, and cook until the mussels open, about 5 minutes. Discard any mussels that do not open.

To serve, ladle the mussels, along with the vegetables and juices, into bowls. Swirl some cilantro pesto over each bowl and serve right away, accompanied with the extra pesto, a warm baguette, and a spare bowl for the shells on the side.

SHELLFISH BOUILLABAISSE *with Aioli*

Serves 4

Rather than including whitefish fillets and saucing the dish with rouille, Annie transforms the classic bouillabaisse of Marseilles into a shellfish stew garnished with aioli-topped crostini. She takes innovation a step further by adding a good measure of Chardonnay to the broth, and thereby situates the dish squarely in the Napa Valley.

Serve with a CHARDONNAY

AIOLI

1 large egg yolk

4 cloves garlic, minced or pressed

1/2 cup extra virgin olive oil

1 tablespoon freshly squeezed lemon juice

1/4 teaspoon kosher salt

1 tablespoon warm water

BOUILLABAISSE

1/4 cup extra virgin olive oil

2 celery stalks, finely chopped

2 leeks, including light green parts, finely chopped

1 large clove garlic, minced

Large pinch of saffron threads, or 1/4 teaspoon powdered saffron

Pinch of cayenne pepper

1 tablespoon chopped fresh flat-leaf parsley

1 teaspoon chopped fresh thyme

2 bay leaves

1/2 teaspoon kosher salt

1/2 teaspoon freshly ground black pepper

11/2 cups Chardonnay

11/2 pounds tomatoes, peeled, seeded, and chopped into 1/2-inch chunks (page xx)

11/2 pounds mussels, scrubbed, debearded if necessary

3/4 pound medium shrimp, shelled, deveined if necessary, tails on

8 large sea scallops

16 crostini (page 14)

To make the aioli, combine the egg yolk and garlic in a food processor. With the machine running, gradually add the oil in a thin stream. Process in the lemon juice, salt, and warm water. Serve right away, or cover and refrigerate for up to 3 days.

To make the bouillabaisse, heat the oil in a large saucepan over medium heat. Add the celery and leeks and sauté, stirring frequently, until wilted but not browned, about 5 minutes. Stir in the garlic, saffron, cayenne, parsley, thyme, bay leaves, salt, and pepper. Sauté, stirring, for 2 minutes, or until the celery and leeks are soft. Increase the heat to high, stir in the wine and tomatoes, and bring to a boil. Add the mussels, cover the pot, and bring to a boil again, about 2 minutes. Add the shrimp and scallops, cover, and cook until the mussels are opened and the shrimp and scallops are just firm, 3 to 4 minutes. Discard any mussels that do not open.

To serve, remove the bay leaves and ladle the bouillabaisse into shallow bowls. Arrange the crostini around the perimeter of the bowls and place a dollop of aioli on each slice. Serve with the remaining aioli on the side for each to add as desired.

MAYONNAISE

Mayonnaise frequently plays a role in Annie's recipes, and there are several renditions of it in this book. Some use the whole egg (lemon mayonnaise for tuna, page 36), and some use only the egg yolk, as in this aioli. Margrit uses the whole egg, partly out of thrift and partly out of practicality—the white helps bind the mayonnaise without having to add another binder such as mustard. Annie often opts for the richer, more classic French version of mayonnaise that calls for the yolks only. It's a matter of the moment and the dish, she says; both are good.

PAELLA *with Shrimp, Sausage, and Green Beans*

Serves 4

Annie calls her paella "quick." And so it is, in comparison to recipes that call for twice as much preparation and cooking time. She accomplishes that boon by streamlining with fewer ingredients while retaining the spirit of the classic dish. Green beans are her colorful addition.

Serve with a RIOJA

2 tablespoons extra virgin olive oil

1 pound sweet Italian sausage, cut into 1/2-inch rounds

1/2 cup chopped yellow onion

2 cloves garlic, minced

1/2 cup chopped red or green bell pepper

2 cups Arborio rice

1/2 cup Chardonnay or other fruity white wine

3 cups chicken stock (page xix)

1/2 teaspoon hot paprika, preferably Hungarian

Large pinch of saffron threads

18 large or 10 jumbo shrimp, shells and tails on, deveined

2 fresh or 4 canned plum tomatoes, coarsely chopped, with juices

1 cup green beans, cut into 1/2-inch pieces

2 tablespoons chopped fresh flat-leaf parsley

1 lemon, quartered

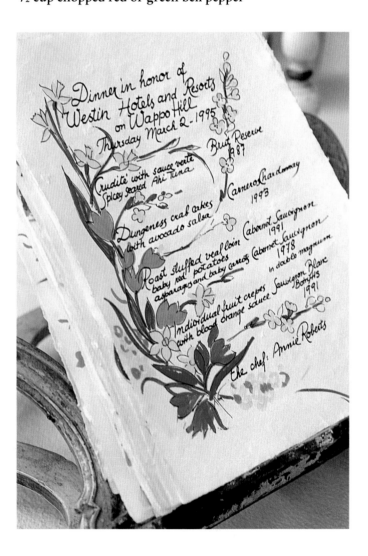

In a large, wide, and deep sauté or paella pan, heat the oil over medium heat. Add the sausage and sauté until lightly browned, about 2 minutes. Stir in the onion, garlic, and bell pepper and sauté until wilted, about 3 minutes.

Increase the heat to high and add the rice. Stir to coat the rice and cook until opaque, about 1 minute. Stir in the wine, stock, paprika, and saffron and bring to a boil. Decrease the heat to medium-low, cover the pan, and simmer for 15 minutes, or until most of the liquid is absorbed.

Add the shrimp, tomatoes with their juices, and green beans, making sure to push the shrimp tails down into the rice. Cover again and cook until the liquid has been completely absorbed and the shrimp are beginning to turn pink, 2 to 3 minutes.

Sprinkle with the parsley and serve right away, accompanied with the lemon wedges.

Sweet Finales

FRUIT REIGNS SUPREME as the after-dinner treat for Annie and Margrit. Apples in a tart or tender crêpes; plums, apricots, or cherries baked in a galette. The list goes on to include California's own Meyer lemons, and of course, grapes in the form of wine turned into a sweet wine gelée. Pears are a personal favorite of both mother and daughter. Margrit remembers their fragrant blossoms signaling spring in the meadows and hills around her childhood home. Annie shares the same sense as she drives to work along a road lined with pear trees, enjoying the thought of pears poached in one of the winery's rich reds. Sometimes, there's a chocolate indulgence with a fruit sauce or a bowl of berries to accompany, or Annie's cookies fanning a fruit sorbet. But it's not only for the love of seasonal fruit that Annie and Margrit rely on it as a primary player in desserts. It's also because fruit pairs so well with after-dinner wines, and in this chapter you will find a full cast of sweet creations to satisfy that style.

PEARS POACHED IN MERLOT
with Black Peppercorns, Cinnamon, and Clove

Serves 4

In an unusual take on poached pears, Annie includes black peppercorns, a spice not often found in desserts, and poaches in a syrup of Margrit's beloved Merlot wine. Annie chooses Merlot because "of all the reds, it has the most fruit and sits soft in the mouth, so the spices give it character and make it more interesting." In addition to serving the pears on their own, she suggests that they would also be good with pound cake.

Serve with a MERLOT

2 cups Merlot

¹/₂ cup sugar

¹/₂ cup water

4 firm, slightly underripe Anjou, Bartlett, Bosc,
  or Comice pears

6 black peppercorns

1-inch piece cinnamon stick

1 whole clove

Zest of ¹/₂ lemon, in strips

¹/₂ cup heavy cream

1 tablespoon finely shredded fresh mint, for garnish

In a nonreactive saucepan, combine the wine, sugar, and water. Bring to a boil over high heat, decrease the heat to medium, and simmer, stirring, until the sugar dissolves, about 1 minute. Remove from the heat.

Peel the pears and core them from the bottom, leaving the stem intact and adding them to the wine syrup as you go. Add the peppercorns, cinnamon, clove, and zest to the syrup and turn to mix and coat the pears. Drape a length of cheesecloth over the pears so they will stay moist during cooking. Return the pan to the stove top and bring to a simmer over medium-high heat. Partially cover and cook until the pears are barely tender but not soft all the way through when pierced with a fork, 12 to 15 minutes, depending on the size and ripeness. Remove from the heat and let sit until cool.

Gently transfer the pears to a bowl. Strain the syrup through a fine mesh sieve over the pears. Cover and refrigerate for at least 2 hours or up to overnight.

To serve, lightly whip the cream until thickened. Place one pear in each of 4 bowls. Ladle the syrup over the pears, top with a dollop of the cream, and sprinkle shredded mint over all.

PEARS POACHED IN MOSCATO D'ORO
with Moscato d'Oro Sabayon

Serves 8

Poaching pears in Robert Mondavi Moscato d'Oro is admittedly an extravagance. Saucing the pears with a sabayon flavored with more of the Moscato makes for a truly deluxe dessert. Annie first served this for the 1994 Harvest Dinner, a press event that takes place every year in September, and now presents it in the Vineyard Room for extra-special occasions like Robert Mondavi Winery winter concerts. One bottle of Moscato will provide for both cooking the poached pears and the sabayon.

Serve with ROBERT MONDAVI MOSCATO D'ORO

PEARS

3 cups Robert Mondavi Moscato d'Oro

½ cup sugar

Zest of 1 lemon, in strips

3-inch length vanilla bean, halved lengthwise

2-inch piece cinnamon stick

4 ripe but firm Anjou, Bartlett, Bosc, or Comice pears, peeled, halved, and cored

MOSCATO D'ORO SABAYON

4 large egg yolks

¼ cup sugar

Pinch of kosher salt

½ cup Robert Mondavi Moscato d'Oro

⅔ cup heavy cream

To poach the pears, combine the wine, sugar, zest, vanilla bean, and cinnamon stick in a large saucepan and stir to mix. Bring to a boil over medium-high heat, add the pears, cut side down, and decrease the heat to medium. Cover and cook until the pears are barely tender but not soft all the way through when pierced with a fork, about 4 minutes. Remove the pan from the heat, uncover, and set aside until completely cool. Use right away, or refrigerate in the poaching liquid for up to 3 days.

To prepare the sabayon, combine the egg yolks, sugar, and salt in the top of a double boiler or a stainless-steel bowl. Whisk to mix, then whisk in the wine. Set over a saucepan with 2 inches of boiling water. Gently whisk until the egg mixture has tripled in volume, about 5 minutes. Transfer the bowl to a larger bowl of ice water and continue whisking until the mixture has cooled.

In a bowl, beat the cream until soft peaks form. Fold into the cooled egg mixture. Use right away, or cover and refrigerate for up to 4 hours.

To serve, spoon the sabayon sauce onto each of 8 plates. Lift the pear halves out of the poaching liquid and place 1 on each plate. Cut the lemon zest strips from the poaching liquid into very thin strips, strew them over the pears, and serve.

WINTER APPLE TART

Makes one 8-inch tart; serves 6

When fall breezes blow across the coastal mountains and valleys of northern California's Mendocino, Sonoma, and Napa Counties, it's hard to miss the scent of fresh apples. A bushel basket of the season's selections to transform into apple tarts is the stuff of chefs' dreams. Margrit serves her rendition of apple tart with a Robert Mondavi Johannisberg Riesling, whose crisp, fruity character enhances the apples.

Serve with a JOHANNISBERG RIESLING

PASTRY DOUGH

3/4 cup all-purpose flour

Pinch of kosher salt

5 tablespoons cold unsalted butter, cut into
   1/2-inch pieces

2 1/2 tablespoons cold water

APPLE FILLING

4 large apples, such as Gravensteins, Braeburns, or
   Golden Delicious

1 tablespoon water

1/8 teaspoon ground cardamom

1 tablespoon sugar

GLAZE

2 tablespoons apricot jam

1/4 teaspoon finely chopped lemon zest

2 tablespoons freshly squeezed lemon juice

1 tablespoon brandy

1 cup heavy cream, lightly whipped

To make the pastry dough, combine the flour, salt, and butter in a food processor or bowl. Pulse, rub in with your fingers, or cut in with a pastry cutter until crumbly. Briefly mix in the water and gather into a ball. Wrap in plastic wrap and press into a flat disk. Let rest for at least 30 minutes or up to 4 hours in the refrigerator, or 20 minutes in the freezer. When ready to use, bring to room temperature and proceed with the recipe.

To cook the pastry crust, preheat the oven to 400°F. On a lightly floured surface, roll out the dough into a 10-inch round. Line an 8-inch tart pan with the dough. Trim the edges. Prick the bottom with a fork and place in the oven. Bake until golden, about 20 minutes, pressing the edges up and the center down with a fork halfway through baking. Remove from the oven and allow to cool.

To make the filling, peel, core, and chop 2 of the apples. Put in a small saucepan and add the water, cardamom, and sugar. Cover and cook over medium heat until soft, about 5 minutes. Allow to cool, then mash with a fork or purée in a food processor.

To make the glaze, mix together the jam, zest, lemon juice, and brandy in a small bowl.

To assemble the tart, spread the apple purée evenly over the bottom of the baked tart shell. Core and very thinly slice the remaining 2 apples and arrange them in a circular design over the purée. Spread the apricot glaze over the apple slices and bake until the apples are tender, about 15 minutes.

Slice and serve warm or at room temperature, topped with the whipped cream.

FRESH PLUM GALETTE

Makes one 10-inch galette; serves 10

Santa Rosa plums grow almost in Annie's backyard. She takes advantage of their availability from late
June through September in a beautiful, irresistible galette laced with almond.

Serve with a MOSCATO D'ORO

SWEET GALETTE DOUGH

1 1/2 cups all-purpose flour

1 tablespoon sugar

Pinch of kosher salt

1/2 cup cold unsalted butter, cut into 1/2-inch pieces

1/4 cup cold water

1/4 cup slivered or sliced almonds, ground

2 teaspoons all-purpose flour

1 1/2 tablespoons granulated sugar

8 red plums (1 1/2 to 1 3/4 pounds), halved, pitted, and sliced 1/4 inch thick

2 tablespoons unsalted butter, melted

3 tablespoons raw sugar, for sprinkling

To make the dough, combine the flour, sugar, and salt in a food processor and pulse once to mix. Add the butter and pulse until the mixture resembles coarse meal. Add the water quickly and mix just until the dough comes together. Gather into a ball, wrap in plastic wrap, and press into a flat disk. Refrigerate for at least 30 minutes or up to overnight. Remove from the refrigerator 30 minutes before rolling out.

In a small bowl, mix together the almonds, flour, and granulated sugar. Set aside.

To make the galette, preheat the oven to 400°F. Lightly grease a large baking sheet with butter or line it with parchment paper. On a lightly floured surface, roll the dough out into a 14-inch round and place it on the baking sheet. Sprinkle the almond mixture over the dough, leaving a 2-inch border. Arrange the plums overlapping in a circle over the almond mixture. Fold the border of the dough over to enclose the fruit by about 2 inches, pleating as you go, leaving the center exposed. Brush the melted butter over the fruit and dough and sprinkle the raw sugar over the dough.

Place in the oven and bake for 40 to 45 minutes, or until the crust is golden and cooked through and the plum juices are bubbly. Remove and allow to cool. Slice and serve.

RHUBARB TART

Makes one 8- to 9-inch tart; serves 6

This dessert is so established in Margrit's repertoire that she doesn't even have to look up her recipe when she makes it, as proved when she quickly jotted it down on the back of a card during an editorial meeting for this book. If the rhubarb stalks are older, thick, and not supple, peel them with a vegetable peeler to remove the tough outer strings.

Serve with a MOSCATO D'ORO

PASTRY DOUGH

1¼ cups all-purpose flour

Pinch of kosher salt

½ cup cold unsalted butter, cut into large cubes

3 tablespoons ice water

FILLING

1 pound rhubarb stalks, cut into ½-inch dice

½ cup granulated sugar

3 large eggs

1 cup heavy cream

Pinch of kosher salt

½ cup firmly packed dark brown sugar

To make the pastry dough, combine the flour, salt, and butter in a food processor and pulse until barely mixed. Pulse in the water, 1 tablespoon at a time, to make a crumbly mixture. Gather into a ball, wrap in plastic wrap, and press into a flat disk. Refrigerate for 30 minutes. Bring to room temperature before rolling out.

On a lightly floured surface, roll the dough out into a 9- to 10-inch round and line an 8- or 9-inch pie dish or tart pan with it. Crimp the edges. Place in the freezer until frozen, at least 20 minutes.

To make the filling, toss together the rhubarb and ¼ cup of the granulated sugar in a colander. Set aside to drain for 40 minutes or so, then shake off the excess liquid. In a food processor, combine the eggs, cream, salt, brown sugar, and the remaining ¼ cup granulated sugar. Pulse to mix.

Preheat the oven to 400°F. Spread the rhubarb on the bottom of the frozen crust. Pour the egg mixture over the rhubarb and bake for 30 minutes. Decrease the heat to 375°F and continue baking for 20 to 25 minutes, or until a knife inserted in the center comes out clean. Remove from the oven and allow to cool completely. Slice and serve.

HAZELNUT TART *with Chocolate Glaze*

Makes one 9- to 10-inch tart; serves 8

Though Annie usually eschews serving a chocolate dessert with a dessert wine, with this tart that she describes as "not real chocolaty," she offers a Sauvignon Blanc Botrytis because its honeyed overtones play well with nuts.

Serve with a SAUVIGNON BLANC BOTRYTIS

2 cups hazelnuts

DOUGH

1¼ cups all-purpose flour

Pinch of kosher salt

1 tablespoon sugar

7 tablespoons cold unsalted butter, cut into small pieces

3 to 4 tablespoons ice water

¼ cup unsalted butter

5 tablespoons sugar

1 cup heavy cream

1 tablespoon honey

2 ounces bittersweet chocolate, chopped

1 tablespoon water

To prepare the hazelnuts, preheat the oven to 425°F or place a cast-iron skillet over high heat. Place the nuts on a baking sheet or in the skillet and toast, stirring or shaking the pan frequently, until the skins blister, 10 to 12 minutes. Transfer the nuts to a kitchen towel and cover with another towel. When cool enough to handle, rub the nuts between the 2 towels to loosen the skins. With your fingers, peel away the skins, as many as you can, but don't worry if they don't all come off. Coarsely chop the nuts and set aside.

To make the dough, combine the flour, salt, and sugar in a food processor and pulse to mix. Add the butter and pulse 3 times. Add 3 tablespoons of the ice water and pulse a few more times until the mixture is moist and holds together when squeezed but still hasn't formed a ball. Add up to 1 more tablespoon water if necessary. Gather into a ball, wrap in plastic wrap, and press into a flat disk. Refrigerate for at least 1 hour or up to 3 days. Bring to room temperature before rolling out.

Preheat the oven to 425°F. On a lightly floured surface, roll the dough out into a 10- to 11-inch round and line a 9- to 10-inch removable-bottom tart pan with it. Trim the edges. Place in the freezer until frozen, at least 20 minutes. Remove from the freezer, prick the bottom with a fork, and place in the oven. Bake for 10 minutes, decrease the heat to 350°F, and press the edges up and the center down with a fork. Continue baking until golden and dry, about 15 minutes. Remove from the oven and allow to cool. Maintain the oven heat at 350°F.

To make the filling, melt the butter in a saucepan over medium-high heat. Add the sugar, cream, and honey and bring to a boil. Whisk to mix, decrease the heat to low, and continue cooking for 2 minutes, or until the sugar dissolves and the mixture is thickened. Stir in the hazelnuts. Pour the mixture into the tart shell. Place a length of aluminum foil on the bottom rack of the oven to catch spills and bake the tart for 30 minutes, or until bubbling up. Transfer to a wire rack and allow to cool completely.

When the tart is cool, melt the chocolate with the water in a double boiler over barely simmering water. Or, put the chocolate in a microwave bowl, sprinkle with the water, and microwave on high for 2 minutes, or until soft but not bubbling. Whisk to mix and smooth. Dip a fork or the tip of a teaspoon into the chocolate and drizzle freeform designs across the top of the tart. Slice and serve.

APRICOT AND CHERRY GALETTE

Makes one 10-inch galette; serves 10

One of Annie's favorite taste combinations is stone fruit, almonds, and dessert wine. For this galette, she sprinkles raw sugar over the fruit because it absorbs the fruit juices as it cooks without melting down completely, leaving a bit of sugar crystal shine across the top. Most grocery stores stock almond paste in tubes in the baked goods section.

Serve with a MOSCATO D'ORO

1 recipe sweet galette dough (page 176)

ALMOND FILLING
1/2 cup almond paste
1/4 cup unsalted butter, at room temperature
1 tablespoon granulated sugar
2 tablespoons all-purpose flour
1 large egg, beaten

2 pounds ripe apricots, halved and pitted
1/2 pound cherries, pitted
2 tablespoons unsalted butter, melted
1 tablespoon raw sugar

Lightly grease a large baking sheet with butter or line it with parchment paper. On a lightly floured surface, roll the dough out into a 14-inch round about 1/4 inch thick. Place on the prepared baking sheet and refrigerate for 30 minutes.

To make the filling, combine the almond paste and butter together in a bowl. Using an electric mixer on high speed, beat until light and fluffy, about 5 minutes. Add the granulated sugar and flour and beat until well blended. Add the egg and beat until incorporated.

Preheat the oven to 400°F. Spread the almond filling on the crust, leaving a 2-inch border. Arrange the apricot halves, cut side down, over the filling. Place the cherries over the apricots. Fold the border of the dough over to enclose the fruit by about 2 inches, pleating as you go, leaving the center exposed. Brush the folded-over edge of the crust with the melted butter and sprinkle the raw sugar over the fruit. Bake for 40 to 45 minutes, until the crust is golden, the fruit is cooked through, and the juices are bubbly. Remove from the oven and allow to cool. Slice and serve.

PHOEBE'S PUMPKIN PIE

Makes one 9-inch pie; serves 6 to 8

Annie's sister, Phoebe, makes a pumpkin pie that is legendary in the family and de rigueur at Thanksgiving. Her secrets: she uses a pie dough she learned from Margrit, and she always takes the time to bake a fresh sugar pumpkin or butternut squash for the filling.

Serve with a MOSCATO D'ORO

FILLING

1 (1-pound) sugar pumpkin or butternut squash

2 large eggs, lightly beaten

3/4 cup sugar

1/2 teaspoon kosher salt

1 teaspoon ground cinnamon

1/2 teaspoon ground ginger

1/4 teaspoon ground cloves

1 1/2 cups half-and-half

1 recipe pastry dough (page 178), at room temperature

1 cup heavy cream, lightly whipped

To prepare the filling, preheat the oven to 375°F. Cut the pumpkin in half, scoop out the seeds, and place the halves, cut side down, on a baking sheet. Bake until tender, 45 to 50 minutes, depending on the size. Remove and allow to cool enough to handle, then scoop out the pulp. Use right away, set aside at room temperature for up to several hours, or refrigerate overnight.

In a food processor or blender, combine the pumpkin pulp with the eggs, sugar, salt, cinnamon, ginger, cloves, and half-and-half. Blend until smooth, 15 to 30 seconds.

Preheat the oven to 425°F. On a lightly floured surface, roll the pie dough out into a 10-inch round and line a 9-inch pie pan with it. Crimp the edges. Refrigerate for 30 minutes. Pour the filling into the pie shell and bake for 15 minutes. Decrease the heat to 350°F and bake for 40 minutes more, or until a knife inserted in the center comes out clean. Remove from the oven and allow to cool on a wire rack.

To serve, slice the pie into portions and garnish each with a dollop of whipped cream.

APPLE NAPOLEONS
with Vanilla Pastry Cream and Strawberry Sauce

Serves 6

Annie renders Napoleons, one of the grand French pâtisserie delights, easy enough to do at home. For starters, she calls for ready-made phyllo dough sheets, available in the freezer section of most supermarkets. Then, she deconstructs the making of the layers into several steps that can be done in advance. Once all that's done, voilà! you're ready to present Napoleons for dessert. Annie advises not to worry if the stacks look a little wobbly and ragged around the edges the first time you make them—so was Napoleon at first, but successive forays will result in more svelte accomplishments.

Serve with a MOSCATO D'ORO

PASTRY

10 (14 by 17-inch) sheets phyllo dough, at room temperature

6 tablespoons unsalted butter, melted

1/2 cup sugar

PASTRY CREAM

4 large egg yolks

3/4 cup sugar

2 tablespoons cornstarch

2 cups milk

1/2 vanilla bean, split lengthwise

1/4 cup heavy cream, whipped to soft peaks

APPLE FILLING

2 tablespoons unsalted butter

4 Golden Delicious apples, peeled, quartered, cored, and sliced 1/4 inch thick

1/2 cup sugar

2 tablespoons freshly squeezed lemon juice

STRAWBERRY SAUCE

2 cups fresh strawberries, hulled, or frozen unsweetened strawberries, thawed

1/4 cup sugar

1/2 tablespoon freshly squeezed lemon juice

Preheat the oven to 325°F. Lightly grease 2 baking sheets.

Spread 1 sheet of phyllo on a work surface, keeping the other sheets covered with a damp towel. Brush with butter and sprinkle with sugar. Repeat with 4 more layers until you have a stack 5 layers high. Cut the stack into nine 4-inch rounds or rectangles and place them on the prepared baking sheets without crowding. Repeat the process with the remaining 5 sheets of phyllo to make a total of 18 rounds or rectangles. Bake until golden on the bottom and around the edges, 10 to 15 minutes. Remove from the oven and allow to cool completely. Use right away, or set aside for up to several hours.

To make the pastry cream, whisk together the egg yolks, 1/2 cup of the sugar, and the cornstarch in a bowl. In a saucepan, combine the milk, the remaining 1/4 cup sugar, and the vanilla bean and bring just to a boil over medium heat. Remove the vanilla bean. Whisk the milk mixture into the egg yolk mixture, then return to the saucepan. Cook over medium heat, stirring constantly, until the mixture is thickened like a soft custard, 7 to 10 minutes. Remove from the heat and allow to cool.

Fold the whipped cream into the cooled custard and set aside at room temperature. Allow to cool completely and use right away, or cover and refrigerate up to overnight.

To make the filling, melt the butter over medium-high heat in a sauté pan. Add the apples, sugar, and lemon juice and stir to mix. Cover and cook until the apples release their juices, 1 to 2 minutes. Continue cooking,

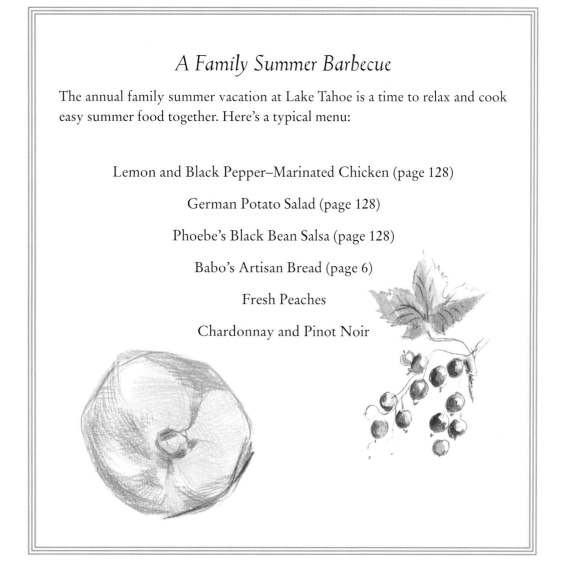

A Family Summer Barbecue

The annual family summer vacation at Lake Tahoe is a time to relax and cook easy summer food together. Here's a typical menu:

Lemon and Black Pepper–Marinated Chicken (page 128)

German Potato Salad (page 128)

Phoebe's Black Bean Salsa (page 128)

Babo's Artisan Bread (page 6)

Fresh Peaches

Chardonnay and Pinot Noir

uncovered, until the juices have evaporated, 5 to 7 minutes. Set aside at room temperature.

To make the strawberry sauce, combine the strawberries, sugar, and lemon juice in a food processor and purée as finely as possible. If desired, strain through a fine mesh sieve to extract the seeds. Use right away or refrigerate up to overnight.

To assemble the Napoleons, place a phyllo round or rectangle on each of 6 dessert plates. Spread some pastry cream over the phyllo and spoon some apple filling over the pastry cream. Repeat 2 times until you have 3 layers on each plate. Spoon the strawberry sauce over the top of each and serve.

CHRISTMAS STEAMED BREAD PUDDING

Serves 16

Margrit learned to make *torta di natale* from her friend Maria Bernasconi, "an old Ticinese" whom Margrit met in the Napa Valley. She personified a way of life Margrit grew up with, raising chickens and rabbits, growing her own vegetables, and cooking every day. At Christmas, Maria would turn out this nostalgic delight, whose texture is a cross between persimmon pudding, fruit cake, and bread pudding. It can also be baked in loaf pans for gift giving or in small ramekins for individual desserts.

Serve with the red wine accompanying the entrée

4 cups whole milk

1/2 vanilla bean, halved lengthwise

1 (3/4-pound) day-old baguette, cut into 3/4-inch cubes

24 amaretti cookies (about 31/2 ounces), crushed

1/8 teaspoon almond extract

3 large eggs

1 cup sugar

Pinch of kosher salt

1/4 cup unsalted butter, at room temperature

Zest of 1 lemon, finely chopped

11/2 tablespoons freshly squeezed lemon juice

1/2 cup mixed candied lemon and orange rind, cut into 1/4-inch dice

1/2 cup dark raisins

1/2 cup blanched almonds

2 tablespoons pine nuts

1/2 teaspoon ground cinnamon

Pinch of freshly grated nutmeg

1 cup heavy cream, lightly whipped

In a large saucepan, combine the milk and vanilla bean. Cook over medium heat until bubbles form around the edges of the pan. Remove from the heat, add the bread cubes, and stir to submerge them. Cover and let stand for 3 hours.

Preheat the oven to 350°F. Grease the bottom and sides of an 8 by 10-inch baking dish.

Add the cookies and almond extract to the milk and bread mixture and let soften for 5 minutes. Purée the mixture in a food processor or press through a food mill.

In a large bowl, combine the eggs, sugar, and salt and beat with an electric mixer on high speed to a creamy consistency. Beat in the butter. Add the zest, lemon juice, candied citrus, raisins, almonds, pine nuts, cinnamon, nutmeg, and the milk mixture. Stir to mix. Turn into the prepared dish and cover with aluminum foil. Set the dish in a larger dish and place in the oven. Pour in water to come about 11/2 inches up the sides of the pudding dish. Bake for 1 hour, then uncover and continue baking for 1 hour more, or until barely firm in the center. Remove from the oven and allow to cool slightly.

To serve, divide among dessert plates and spoon whipped cream over the top.

PEACH AND BLACKBERRY CRISP

Serves 6 to 8

Annie's fruit crisp is one for all seasons. In the spring and summer, the same topping may also be used for cherries, apricots, or blackberries. In the fall and winter, she uses pears or apples.

Serve with a MOSCATO D'ORO *or* MOSCATO BIANCO

TOPPING

1 cup slivered almonds

2 cups all-purpose flour

2 tablespoons granulated sugar

1 cup packed light brown sugar

1/2 teaspoon ground cinnamon

12 tablespoons unsalted butter, cut into bits, at room
   temperature

8 large ripe peaches, peeled, pitted, and cut into
   1/2-inch slices

4 cups fresh blackberries

1/4 cup granulated sugar

Preheat the oven to 375°F. To make the topping, put the almonds in a dry sauté pan over medium-high heat and stir until toasted, about 4 minutes. Remove and allow to cool slightly, then finely chop in a food processor. Transfer to a bowl. Add the flour, granulated sugar, brown sugar, and cinnamon and stir to mix. Add the butter and mix with your fingers until evenly distributed and the mixture is crumbly.

Put the peaches and berries in a 9 by 11-inch baking dish. Add the sugar and toss to mix. Spread the topping evenly over the fruit. Bake until the topping is browned and the fruit juices are bubbling, about 35 minutes. Remove from the oven, allow to cool slightly, then serve.

PRUNE CAKE

Makes one 10-inch cake or 8-inch, 2-layer cake; serves 16

European home cooks rely on their excellent neighborhood pâstisseries for sweet treats, so Margrit's mother didn't bake much. But on holidays, when all the shops were closed, a dense, moist homemade prune cake would often be the dessert. It freezes well, so Margrit often doubles the recipe, bakes the batter in four 8-inch cake pans, makes a three-layer cake, and freezes the fourth. For wine, she might serve a Moscato d'Oro or another glass of the red that accompanied the entrée.

Serve with a MEDIUM-BODIED RED WINE *or a* DESSERT WINE

2 cups all-purpose flour

1 teaspoon baking soda

1 teaspoon baking powder

1/2 teaspoon ground cinnamon

1/4 teaspoon ground cloves

1/4 teaspoon ground allspice

1 1/2 cups sugar

1 cup vegetable oil

2 large eggs

1 cup sour milk (see Note)

1 teaspoon pure vanilla extract

1 cup pitted prunes, chopped

1 cup walnuts, chopped

1 cup heavy cream, lightly whipped

Preheat the oven to 350°F. Lightly grease and flour a 10-inch springform pan or two 8-inch round cake pans. Sift together the flour, baking soda, baking powder, cinnamon, cloves, and allspice into a bowl.

In a large bowl, combine the sugar and oil and beat with an electric mixer until well mixed. Add the eggs and continue beating until blended. Beat in the sour milk in batches, alternating with the flour mixture. Stir in the vanilla, prunes, and nuts. Turn into the prepared pan(s) and bake until a knife inserted in the center comes out clean, about 1 hour. Remove from the oven and place the pan(s) on a wire rack to cool completely.

To serve, unmold the 10-inch cake and place on a platter. Spread the cream over the top. Or, unmold the 8-inch layers and place one layer on a platter. Spread half the cream over the cake. Set the second layer atop the first and spread the remaining cream over the top. Slice and serve.

MARGRIT'S TIP

Following her mother's tradition, Margrit always makes sour milk for the prune cake recipe. It adds a welcome tart note, and it also works for waffles, biscuits, and many other baked foods. To make sour milk, add 1 tablespoon distilled white vinegar to 1 cup of milk and let stand for 10 minutes. Buttermilk makes a good substitute.

CHOCOLATE SOUR CREAM CAKE
with Raspberry Sauce

Makes one 9 by 13-inch cake; serves 10 to 12

When Annie's boys, Quinn and Nathan, were young, chocolate sour cream cake was always the birthday cake of choice. In those days, she iced the cake with chocolate frosting and decorated it with chocolate sprinkles. In the more grown-up version here, raspberry sauce is the only embellishment.

Serve with the red wine accompanying the entrée

1³/₄ cups all-purpose flour

1³/₄ cups sugar

³/₄ cup unsweetened cocoa powder

1¹/₂ teaspoons baking soda

1 teaspoon kosher salt

²/₃ cup unsalted butter, at room temperature

2 cups sour cream

2 large eggs

1 teaspoon pure vanilla extract

RASPBERRY SAUCE

2 cups fresh or frozen raspberries

Sugar

Squeeze of lemon juice (optional)

Confectioners' sugar, for dusting

Preheat the oven to 350°F. Lightly grease and flour a 9 by 13-inch baking dish. In a large bowl, combine the flour, sugar, cocoa, baking soda, and salt. Using an electric mixer on low speed, blend in the butter, sour cream, eggs, and vanilla. Increase the speed to medium and beat for 3 minutes. Pour the batter into the prepared dish and bake until a knife inserted in the center comes out clean, 40 to 45 minutes. Remove from the oven and allow to cool.

To make the raspberry sauce, purée the raspberries in a food processor. Sweeten with sugar to taste and flavor with lemon juice. Serve as is or strain through a fine mesh sieve for a smooth sauce. Use right away, or cover and refrigerate for up to 3 days.

To serve, lightly dust the cake with sieved confectioners' sugar. Spoon a pool of raspberry sauce onto each plate. Cut the cake into portions and place atop the sauce.

WALNUT CRÊPES
with Caramelized Apple Filling and Vanilla Bean Ice Cream

Serves 6 to 8

Northern California is a nut-growing region: new-crop walnuts and almonds are available each year just about the time apples are being harvested. Annie brings her Swiss heritage of crêpe making, adds a bit of nut crunch with walnuts, and serves the crêpes with homemade vanilla ice cream. She likes the sensation of the warm crêpes and cold ice cream mixing in the mouth. The ice cream recipe makes a quart, but you'll probably only need a pint to accompany the crêpes, so there will be some for later.

Serve with a LATE HARVEST RIESLING

VANILLA BEAN ICE CREAM

1 vanilla bean, split lengthwise

2 cups heavy cream

2 cups whole milk

9 egg yolks

3/4 cup sugar

CRÊPE BATTER

1 cup all-purpose flour

Pinch of kosher salt

2 1/2 tablespoons sugar

2 large eggs, beaten

3/4 cup whole milk

2 tablespoons unsalted butter, melted

1/2 cup very finely chopped walnuts

FILLING

1 tablespoon unsalted butter

4 Granny Smith or Golden Delicious apples, peeled, cored, and cut into 1/4-inch-thick slices

1/4 cup sugar

1 tablespoon finely chopped lemon zest

1/2 cup Late Harvest Riesling or other dessert wine

1 teaspoon freshly squeezed lemon juice

1/4 cup unsalted butter, melted

Confectioners' sugar, for dusting

To make the ice cream, in a saucepan, combine the vanilla bean halves, cream, and milk. Bring to a simmer over medium heat, stirring occasionally. Remove from the heat and set aside to steep for 5 minutes. Remove the vanilla bean.

Using an electric mixer, beat the egg yolks and sugar together until pale in color and doubled in volume. Gradually beat in the hot cream mixture. Return to the saucepan and set over low heat. Stir constantly with a wooden spoon until thickened enough to coat the spoon (160°F), about 15 minutes. Be careful not to let the mixture boil or it will curdle. Remove from the heat and pour through a fine mesh sieve lined with 2 layers of cheesecloth set over a large bowl. Allow to cool completely, then freeze in an ice cream maker according to the manufacturer's directions.

To make the crêpe batter, sift together the flour, salt, and sugar into a small bowl. In a large bowl, combine the eggs, milk, and butter. Add the dry ingredients and walnuts and mix thoroughly. Cover and refrigerate for at least 30 minutes or up to overnight.

To make the filling, melt the butter in a large non-stick pan over medium heat. Add the apple slices and cook, stirring often, until they begin to soften, about 10 minutes. Add 2 tablespoons of the sugar and the zest and continue cooking until the apples soften and begin to turn golden. Transfer the apples to a bowl. Add the wine and remaining 2 tablespoons sugar to the pan and cook until reduced and syrupy, 4 to 5 minutes. Add to the apples in the bowl. Stir in the lemon juice and set aside.

To cook the crêpes, brush an 8-inch nonstick skillet with some of the melted butter and heat over medium-high heat. Pour in a scant 1/4 cup of the crêpe batter and tilt the pan all around to evenly spread the batter across the bottom of the pan. Cook until browned on the bottom, about 1 minute. Turn over and cook briefly on the other side, about 30 seconds. Transfer to a platter and continue with the remaining batter, greasing the pan with more butter as you go. Stack the crêpes between waxed paper as you go. At this point, the cooked crêpes may be set aside at room temperature for up to 4 hours.

To serve, preheat the oven to 375°F. Place a small amount of the apple filling in the center of each crêpe. Roll up the crêpes to enclose the filling. Place the crêpes on a baking sheet and heat in the oven until warm, about 12 minutes. Cut the rolls in half on a diagonal and place 2 halves on each dessert plate. Dust with confectioners' sugar, add a scoop of ice cream, and serve right away.

SUGARED SCONES *with Berries and Cream*

Makes 12 scones

Annie's scones come out tender on the inside and golden on the outside. The secrets are two: using a small amount of whole-wheat flour in the batter for texture, and quickly mixing the dough together so it is not overworked and stays light. Topping the scones with cream and sugar before baking ensures a golden, sweet crust. Instead of serving them with berries and cream, you can also spread the scones with jam for a breakfast treat.

Serve with a MOSCATO D'ORO

3 cups all-purpose flour

1/2 cup whole-wheat flour

2 teaspoons baking powder

1 teaspoon baking soda

2 tablespoons sugar, plus extra for sprinkling

1/2 teaspoon kosher salt

1/2 cup cold unsalted butter, cut into 1/2-inch pieces

1/3 cup dried currants

1 large egg

1 cup heavy cream, plus 2 tablespoons for brushing

Fresh berries and whipped cream, for serving

Preheat the oven to 350°F. In a food processor, combine the flours, baking powder, baking soda, sugar, and salt. Pulse once to mix. Add the butter and pulse 3 times, until the mixture is crumbly. Stir in the currants.

In a small bowl, mix together the egg and the 1 cup cream. Add to the flour and butter mixture in the food processor and pulse 3 times to mix. Be careful not to overmix. Turn the dough out onto a lightly floured board and gently gather into a ball. Roll out 3/4 inch thick. Cut into 3- to 31/2-inch rounds. Turn the scones over and brush the tops with the 2 tablespoons cream. Sprinkle generously with sugar and place on a baking sheet, sugared side up. Bake for 20 to 25 minutes, or until golden on the bottom. Allow to cool and serve with berries and whipped cream.

CRISP DOUGHNUT HOLES *with Rhubarb Sauce*

Makes about 36 doughnut holes

Margrit loves to dine at the French Laundry restaurant in Yountville, California, both for Thomas Keller's brilliant savory dishes and for his doughnut holes, called *schenkeli* in German. They remind her of her grandmother from Appenzell, who made them for the children. At home, as at the French Laundry, the little sweet treats should be accompanied with coffee, and kirsch in the dough is essential for the true taste. The rhubarb sauce is a fine spread for waffles or pancakes also.

Serve with COFFEE *or* CAPPUCCINO

DOUGHNUT DOUGH

1³/₄ to 2 cups all-purpose flour

Pinch of kosher salt

Pinch of freshly grated nutmeg

1 teaspoon finely chopped lemon zest

¹/₄ cup unsalted butter, at room temperature

³/₄ cup sugar

2 large eggs

1 tablespoon kirsch liqueur

2 tablespoons heavy cream

RHUBARB SAUCE

1 pound tender rhubarb stalks, cut into ¹/₂-inch pieces (about 3 cups)

³/₄ cup sugar

1 tablespoon freshly squeezed lemon juice

1 tablespoon water

Vegetable oil, for frying

Granulated or confectioners' sugar, for dusting (optional)

To make the doughnut dough, sift together the flour, salt, and nutmeg into a bowl. Stir in the zest. In a separate bowl, combine the butter, sugar, and eggs and beat with an electric mixer on medium speed until foamy. Gradually beat in the flour mixture, kirsch, and cream. You should have a medium-stiff dough. If it seems too soft to roll into balls without sticking to your hands, blend in more flour. Cover and refrigerate for at least 4 hours or up to overnight.

To make the rhubarb sauce, combine the rhubarb, sugar, lemon juice, and water in a saucepan. Bring to a boil over medium heat, decrease the heat to low, and cook, stirring frequently, until the rhubarb is completely soft, about 30 minutes. Remove from the heat and allow to cool. Use right away, or cover and refrigerate for up to 2 weeks.

To cook the doughnut holes, flour your hands and shape the dough into balls 1 inch in diameter. Set on a plate as you go.

Pour the oil into a heavy skillet or sauté pan to a depth of 1 inch. Heat over high heat until a pinch of the dough sizzles when dropped in. Gently, taking care to avoid splashes, slip 6 to 8 of the dough balls into the oil. Decrease the heat to medium-low and fry until golden brown on the outside and cooked through on the inside, about 5 minutes. (Don't cook them too fast, because the dough has to be cooked through.) To test, use tongs to lift one out of the oil and cut it open. Using a wire strainer, transfer the doughnuts to paper towels to drain. Continue with another batch until all are cooked. Sprinkle with granulated sugar or dust with confectioners' sugar.

Place on a platter or dessert plates, spoon rhubarb sauce over the top, and serve right away.

MEYER LEMON CORNMEAL CAKE
with Pineapple Sorbet and Kiwi

Makes one 8-inch cake; serves 8 to 10

Most of Annie's cakes are made with all-purpose flour, but cake flour is necessary in this recipe to lighten the coarseness of the cornmeal. The result is a cake with a delicate yet textured crumb.

The sorbet recipe is almost infinitely variable. Lemon, lime, grapefruit, tangerine, mango, raspberries, and strawberries can all be used in place of the pineapple. For the Blessing of the Grapes celebration, Annie adds banana to the pineapple. Any of the variations will make about 2$^{1}/_{2}$ cups of sorbet to stand on its own or brighten many desserts other than the lemon cake.

Serve with a MOSCATO D'ORO *or* MOSCATO BIANCO

PINEAPPLE SORBET

1$^{3}/_{4}$ cups sugar

2 cups water

1 (3$^{1}/_{2}$- to 4-pound) ripe pineapple, peeled, quartered, and cored

$^{1}/_{4}$ cup freshly squeezed lime juice

1$^{1}/_{2}$ cups cake flour

$^{1}/_{3}$ cup cornmeal

2 teaspoons baking powder

$^{1}/_{4}$ teaspoon kosher salt

$^{1}/_{4}$ cup buttermilk

$^{1}/_{4}$ cup freshly squeezed Meyer lemon juice

$^{1}/_{2}$ cup unsalted butter, at room temperature

1 cup sugar

3 large eggs

1 teaspoon grated Meyer lemon zest

5 kiwis, peeled and cut into $^{1}/_{4}$-inch rounds

Fresh berries, if available

To make the sorbet, in a small saucepan, stir together the sugar and water and bring to a boil over medium-high heat, until the sugar dissolves. Stir again, remove from the heat, and allow to cool to room temperature.

Chop the pineapple into 1-inch pieces and purée in a food processor. Press through a fine mesh sieve into a bowl (you should have about 2 cups of purée). Sweeten the purée with the sugar syrup, starting with half the amount and tasting the mixture before adding more. The amount of sugar syrup ultimately needed will depend on the ripeness and sweetness of the pineapple. Stir in the lime juice. Freeze in an ice cream maker according to the manufacturer's instructions.

Preheat the oven to 350°F. Lightly butter the bottom and sides of an 8-inch springform pan and dust with cornmeal. Sift together the flour, cornmeal, baking powder, and salt into a bowl. Combine the buttermilk and lemon juice in a separate bowl.

Using an electric mixer on high speed, beat the butter in a large bowl until creamy. Gradually beat in the sugar until creamy (this will take a few minutes). Add the eggs,

ANNIE'S TIP

You don't absolutely have to have an ice cream maker for sorbets. You can pour the mixture into a metal bowl or heavy plastic container (not glass because it's too fragile) and place in the freezer. Then, about every 30 minutes or so, use a fork or heavy whisk to break up the crystals that have formed around the edges and mix them into the center with the still-liquid part. This way you get a sorbet or granita texture rather than a solid frozen block. It will take about 2 hours. Remove from the freezer 20 minutes before serving.

The Blessing of the Grapes: A Harvest Lunch

In a tradition unique to the Robert Mondavi Winery, each year at harvest time a priest is invited to bless the grapes and ensure a good vintage. It's an occasion to celebrate not only the harvest, but also to honor all the workers who have brought the grapes in. After the blessing, there is a grand lunch banquet for all to enjoy. Annie particularly loves cooking for this event, while Margrit coordinates the activities.

Chiles Rellenos (page 34)

Roasted Tomato Salsa (page 34)

Achiote-Rubbed Pollitos (page 130)

Guacamole (page 130)

Tortillas

Pinot Noir

Pineapple Sorbet (page 192)

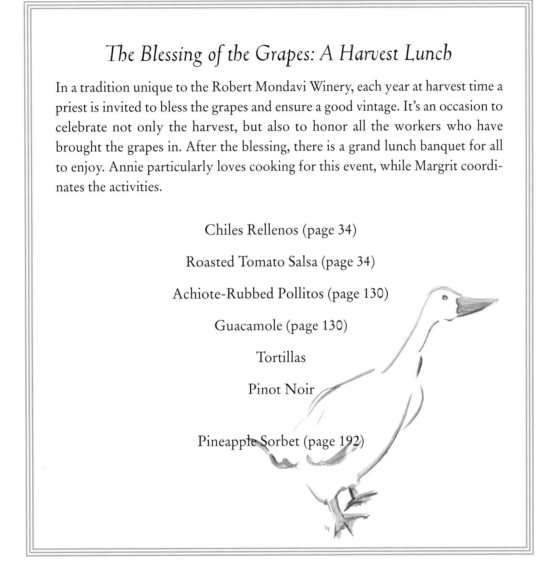

one at a time, beating well after each addition. Mix in the lemon zest. With the mixer on low speed, add the dry ingredients in 3 batches, alternating with the buttermilk mixture. Spread the batter into the prepared pan and bake until golden and firm to the touch in the center, 35 to 40 minutes. Remove from the oven and allow to cool in the pan for 20

minutes. Invert onto a wire rack and remove the sides and bottom of the pan. Allow to cool to room temperature.

To serve, cut the cake into wedges and place on dessert plates. Add a dollop of pineapple sorbet alongside each cake slice and garnish the plates with kiwi slices and fresh berries. Serve right away.

ANNIE'S COOKIES

From teatime ginger cookies for the Robert Mondavi company Christmas party with eight hundred invitees, to delicate tuiles to garnish house-made ice cream in the Vineyard Room, to four hundred miniature shortbreads for box lunches for the summer music festival, Annie makes cookies. She also likes to serve an array of them with a small scoop of her sorbet (page 192) for a summer luncheon.

GINGER COOKIES

Makes 12 cookies

Annie's ginger cookies are snappy, but they're not gingersnaps. Rather, they're a powerhouse of ginger in a small bite.

1/2 cup unsalted butter, at room temperature

1/2 cup firmly packed dark brown sugar

1 tablespoon ground ginger

1/2 teaspoon pure vanilla extract

1 cup all-purpose flour

1/4 teaspoon baking soda

Pinch of kosher salt

Raw sugar, for sprinkling

Preheat the oven to 350°F. Line a baking sheet with parchment paper. In a large bowl, cream together the butter and brown sugar until smooth, about 2 minutes. Add the ginger, vanilla, flour, baking soda, and salt and mix until the dough comes together.

Transfer the dough to a lightly floured work surface and roll out to 1/4 inch thick . Using a fluted 3 1/2-inch pastry cutter, cut out 12 rounds. Place them on the prepared baking sheet and sprinkle with the raw sugar. Bake until lightly browned, about 10 minutes. Allow to cool on the baking sheet. Serve right away, store in an airtight container for up to 2 days, or freeze for up to 1 month.

Margrit hand-painted these tiles for Annie's kitchen at the Vineyard Room.

TUILES

Makes 14 to 16 cookies

Tuiles are so-called because they are shaped like French clay roof tiles. It's not actually very hard to get them into that shape; just drape the cookies over a rolling pin while they're still warm and they'll naturally droop into a tile shape.

1 cup sliced almonds

3/4 cup sugar

3 tablespoons all-purpose flour

3 egg whites

2 1/2 tablespoons unsalted butter, melted

Preheat the oven to 350°F and place a rack in the middle position. Lightly grease 2 baking sheets.

In a large bowl, stir together the almonds, sugar, and flour. Beat the egg whites with a fork until foamy. Stir into the dry ingredients, along with the melted butter. Drop level tablespoonfuls of the batter 1 inch apart onto the prepared baking sheets. Using a fork, spread the batter out into thin 3-inch rounds. Place in the oven and bake until golden but still soft, about 10 minutes.

Remove from the oven and, while still warm, drape the cookies over a rolling pin or dowel so they dry in a U shape. Allow to cool this way until hardened enough to handle. If the cookies get too cool to shape, rewarm them briefly for 1 or 2 minutes until bendable again. Very gently transfer the tuiles back to the baking sheets and set aside until ready to serve. They may be loosely covered in plastic wrap and stored for up to 1 day.

SUGAR-COATED SHORTBREAD

Makes about 50 cookies

Annie often doubles this recipe to make plenty of cookies for large winter holiday parties or gift giving. Once chilled, the logs can be wrapped in plastic wrap and refrigerated for up to 2 days, or frozen for up to 1 week. The cookies can then be conveniently baked in several batches on different days.

1 1/2 cups unsalted butter, at room temperature

3/4 cup plus 1 tablespoon granulated sugar

3 cups plus 2 tablespoons all-purpose flour

1 egg white, beaten with a whisk until frothy

1 cup raw sugar

In a large bowl, cream the butter and sugar together with an electric mixer on medium speed until light and fluffy, about 5 minutes. Add the flour all at once and mix on low speed just until coming together; do not overmix. Gather the dough into a smooth ball. Divide the ball into 2 parts. Shape each part into a log about 1 1/4 inches in diameter. Put the logs on a baking sheet and refrigerate until hard and chilled all the way through, at least 2 hours or up to 4 hours.

To cook, preheat the oven to 350°F. Line baking sheets with parchment paper. Brush each log with beaten egg white and roll it in the raw sugar. Cut each log into 1/2-inch-thick rounds and place the rounds 1 inch apart on the prepared baking sheets. Bake, without turning over, until golden on the bottom and semi-firm on top, 12 to 15 minutes. Remove from the oven and allow to cool on the baking sheets. Serve right away or store in an airtight container for up to 1 week.

CHESTNUT AND KIRSCH SWEET VERMICELLI

Serves 6 to 8

"Vermicelli" is Margrit's name for her version of Mont Blanc, the classic French dessert whose cap of whipped cream mimics that always snow-capped Alpine mountain. She omits the traditional chocolate because her mother never included it. But, kirsch, the cherry-flavored Swiss liqueur, was always in her mother's pantry for adding to sweets, including this one, and Margrit emphasizes you must have kirsch for the vermicelli.

Fresh chestnuts you peel yourself are undoubtedly the tastiest kind; they are also the most work. Already peeled and cooked freeze-dried chestnuts in jars (from France) or vacu-wrapped in boxes (from Spain), available in gourmet food stores, are excellent second choices and an easier way to go. The canned chestnuts that are more widely available and on the shelf year-round lack flavor and are not a choice if you want the essence of chestnut.

Serve with a SAUVIGNON BLANC BOTRYTIS

1½ pounds chestnuts, or 1 pound freeze-dried, peeled, and cooked chestnuts

½ cup milk

1 vanilla bean

¼ cup sugar

¼ cup heavy cream

2 tablespoons kirsch liqueur

1 cup whipped cream, for garnish

If using fresh chestnuts, make an incision in each with a sharp paring knife. Boil them in lightly salted water for 10 minutes. Remove from the water a few at a time and, when just barely cool enough to handle, peel away the outer shell and inner skin. Or, roast them in a hot oven until the skin opens and proceed in the same way. The trick is to work quickly once the chestnuts are removed from the water or oven because the loosened skins re-adhere as they cool. If this happens, return them to the hot water or oven briefly. Once peeled, cook the chestnuts in a fresh pot of boiling water until tender, about 30 minutes. Drain and purée in a food processor.

Put the chestnut purée in a large bowl. Combine the milk and vanilla bean in a saucepan and bring to a boil. Remove the vanilla bean and add the milk to the chestnuts. Add the sugar, cream, and kirsch and mix well. Cover and refrigerate for 1 hour or up to overnight.

To serve, pass the chestnut mixture through a food mill fitted with the large-hole plate, or press through a metal colander or potato ricer into a serving bowl, making a mound. Top with the whipped cream and serve.

MIDSUMMER DELIGHT:
MOSCATO D'ORO GELÉE *with Fresh Berries*

Serves 6

Margrit "borrowed" this recipe for jelled dessert wine from Annie (Annie says "stole"), added lemon zest, and contributed it to a cookbook of recipes from Napa Valley winemakers and their spouses. Unlike most of the recipes in this book, there's not a serve-with wine recommendation because, as Margrit explains in her straightforward way, the wine is in the gelée.

1 envelope (2¹/₂ teaspoons) unflavored gelatin

1¹/₂ cups Moscato d'Oro

¹/₂ teaspoon finely chopped lemon zest

1 teaspoon freshly squeezed lemon juice

¹/₂ cup sugar

3 cups mixed fresh berries, such as raspberries, blackberries, blueberries, and sliced strawberries

6 small sprigs mint, for garnish (optional)

Sprinkle the gelatin over 1 cup of the wine in a small saucepan. Let stand until softened, about 5 minutes. Heat gently over low heat until the gelatin dissolves, about 1 minute. Do not boil. Remove from the heat, add the remaining ¹/₂ cup wine, the zest, juice, and sugar, and stir to mix well and dissolve the sugar. Pour into a 9 by 13-inch glass baking dish or 10-inch pie pan and refrigerate until jelled, at least 3 hours or up to overnight (if refrigerating overnight, cover with plastic wrap).

To serve, divide the berries among 6 large wine glasses or dessert plates. Cut the gelée into 1-inch squares. Using a metal spatula, place 4 or 5 squares on top of each serving of berries, garnish with the mint sprigs, and serve.

INDEX

═══